CW00552075

ASSESSING THE PROSPECTS FOR
GREAT POWER
COOPERATION
IN THE INDO-PACIFIC

SCOTT W. HAROLD, NATHAN BEAUCHAMP-MUSTAFAGA, SOO KIM

RAND PROJECT AIR FORCE

For more information on this publication, visit **www.rand.org/t/RRA597-2**.

About RAND

The RAND Corporation is a research organization that develops solutions to public policy challenges to help make communities throughout the world safer and more secure, healthier and more prosperous. RAND is nonprofit, nonpartisan, and committed to the public interest. To learn more about RAND, visit www.rand.org.

Research Integrity

Our mission to help improve policy and decisionmaking through research and analysis is enabled through our core values of quality and objectivity and our unwavering commitment to the highest level of integrity and ethical behavior. To help ensure our research and analysis are rigorous, objective, and nonpartisan, we subject our research publications to a robust and exacting quality-assurance process; avoid both the appearance and reality of financial and other conflicts of interest through staff training, project screening, and a policy of mandatory disclosure; and pursue transparency in our research engagements through our commitment to the open publication of our research findings and recommendations, disclosure of the source of funding of published research, and policies to ensure intellectual independence. For more information, visit www.rand.org/about/research-integrity.

RAND's publications do not necessarily reflect the opinions of its research clients and sponsors.

Published by the RAND Corporation, Santa Monica, Calif.
© 2023 RAND Corporation
RAND® is a registered trademark.

Library of Congress Cataloging-in-Publication Data is available for this publication.

ISBN: 978-1-9774-0764-1

Cover: Porcupen/Adobe Stock; Mass Communication Specialist 3rd Class Bobby J Siens/U.S. Navy.

Limited Print and Electronic Distribution Rights

About This Report

The 2018 *National Defense Strategy* (NDS) starts with the assertion that "Interstate strategic competition, not terrorism, is now the primary concern in U.S. national security." Even the NDS, however, acknowledges the need for cooperation with competitors, albeit "from a position of strength and based on our national interests." As part of a larger study of cooperation in an era of strategic competition, we assessed the potential for U.S. security cooperation with China and Russia in the Indo-Pacific. The other volumes in this series are

- *Vanishing Trade Space: Assessing the Prospects for Great Power Cooperation in an Era of Competition—A Project Overview*, RR-A597-1, by Raphael S. Cohen, Elina Treyger, Nathan Beauchamp-Mustafaga, Asha Clark, Kit Conn, Scott W. Harold, Michelle Grisé, Marta Kepe, Soo Kim, Ashley L. Rhoades, Roby Valiaveedu, and Nathan Vest
- *Assessing the Prospects for Great Power Cooperation in Europe and the Middle East*, RR-A597-3, by Elina Treyger, Ashley L. Rhoades, Nathan Vest, Nathan Beauchamp-Mustafaga, Raphael S. Cohen, and Asha Clark
- *Assessing the Prospects for Great Power Cooperation in the Global Commons*, RR-A597-4, by Raphael S. Cohen, Marta Kepe, Nathan Beauchamp-Mustafaga, Asha Clark, Kit Conn, Michelle Grisé, Roby Valiaveedu, and Nathan Vest.

The research reported here was commissioned by Headquarters Air Force A-5 Strategy Section and conducted within the Strategy and Doctrine Program of RAND Project AIR FORCE as part of a fiscal year 2020 project "China, Russia, and the United States: Intersecting Points of Cooperation and Competition." This research was completed in September 2020, before the February 2022 Russian invasion of Ukraine and before the U.S. military withdrawal from Afghanistan in August 2021. It has not been subsequently revised.

The views expressed in this article are those of the authors and do not reflect the official policy or position of the U.S. Department of Defense or the U.S. government.

RAND Project AIR FORCE

RAND Project AIR FORCE (PAF), a division of the RAND Corporation, is the Department of the Air Force's (DAF's) federally funded research and development center for studies and analyses, supporting both the United States Air Force and the United States Space Force. PAF provides the DAF with independent analyses of policy alternatives affecting the development, employment, combat readiness, and support of current and future air, space, and cyber forces. Research is conducted in four programs: Strategy and Doctrine; Force Modernization and Employment; Workforce, Development, and Health; and Resource Management. The research reported here was prepared under contract FA7014-16-D-1000.

Additional information about PAF is available on our website:
www.rand.org/paf/.

This report documents work originally shared with the DAF on September 30, 2020. The draft report, issued in September 2020, was reviewed by formal peer reviewers and DAF subject-matter experts.

Acknowledgments

This project would not have been possible without the support of many people. First, we would like to thank LeeAnn Borman, Scott Wheeler, Gerry Sohan, and Jim Welton of the Headquarters Air Force A-5 Strategy Section for sponsoring the project and guiding it through its many phases. RAND Project AIR FORCE Strategy and Doctrine Program Director Stacie Pettyjohn provided invaluable feedback and guidance on earlier briefings and draft of this report. We also would like to thank our internal reviewer, Jeffrey W. Hornung, and our external reviewer, Elizabeth Wishnick, for their insightful comments.

Contents

Tables

Summary[1]

Issue

Great power competition with China and Russia may be the defining characteristic of the next several decades of the 21st century. An understanding of whether it is possible to cooperate with either country (or both) on key U.S. policy goals and, if so, what implications such cooperation might carry for relations with the other power, is an important component of assessing the best pathway forward for U.S. foreign and defense policies. Cooperation with China and/or Russia might help tamp down intensifying strains in the Indo-Pacific region; help advance key shared interests; and/or prove useful in enhancing the ability of the United States to compete vis-à-vis the other power. Across seven key U.S. policy goals—maintaining a peaceful and open regional order; promoting and preserving regional alliances; expanding strategic cooperation with Indonesia, Malaysia, and Vietnam; managing cross-Strait differences between China and Taiwan; achieving the denuclearization of North Korea; countering terrorism and violent Islamist extremism in Afghanistan and Southeast Asia; and shaping India's regional role and strategic orientation—what is the trade space for cooperation? What are the obstacles to such cooperation? And how might cooperation with one power affect the other?

Approach

We began by looking at official U.S., People's Republic of China (PRC), and Russian policy documents, statements, and government press releases, as well as the record of the two countries' actual behavior. We also analyzed secondary sources on PRC and Russian foreign and defense policies to gain additional insight into how leaders in Beijing and Moscow assess the desirability of engaging with Washington across these seven issue areas.[2] We then gauged the extent of alignment, identified conflicting interests, estimated each country's perceived stakes, and looked for any evidence of past willingness to bargain. Assessing the obstacles to cooperation, we evaluated issues of trust, audience costs, differing definitions of key terms,

---

[1] This research was completed in September 2020, before the February 2022 Russian invasion of Ukraine and before the U.S. military withdrawal from Afghanistan in August 2021. It has not been subsequently revised.

[2] At the outset of the study, we had planned to travel to China and Russia to better understand the perspectives of officials and subject-matter experts in those nations on the questions at the heart of our study. Unfortunately, the rapid worsening of relations, combined with the COVID-19 pandemic, precluded this approach, forcing us to rely more heavily than we would have preferred on written sources. As a consequence, some behind-the-scenes nuances or developments occurring after the release of these official documents may not be captured in our analysis.

third-party problems, perceptions of an issue's immediacy (or lack thereof), issue linkages, legal constraints, and capacity/capabilities to act. Finally, we explored second-order effects of cooperation on U.S. relations with the other party.

Conclusions

Our review of Chinese and Russian views of the seven issues at the heart of U.S. policy in the Indo-Pacific reveals largely irreconcilable differences in policy goals. In particular:

- Both China and Russia regard a free and open Indo-Pacific as cover for U.S. interests that comes at their expense, though the region is far more important for China than for Russia.
- Both countries are hostile to the current U.S.-centric regional alliance architecture and seek to undermine it to enhance their own influence.
- Neither country is eager to see the United States deepen strategic cooperation with Indonesia, Malaysia, or Vietnam, with China worried about the impact on regional competition and Russia concerned that these countries might shift their defense purchases to the United States.
- China regards U.S. efforts to support and defend Taiwan as interference in its internal affairs; Russia is largely irrelevant to this issue.
- Although both China and Russia oppose North Korean acquisition of nuclear weapons, they regard U.S. efforts to compel North Korea to abandon them through sanctions as destabilizing and unlikely to succeed, and do not support the U.S. approach.
- Both powers criticize U.S. counterterrorism efforts in Afghanistan and Southeast Asia as a way to erode U.S. global influence and impose costs on Washington, with Russia hoping to tie the United States down in Afghanistan.
- Neither country is supportive of deepening U.S.-India strategic ties, with China seeing this as a form of containment and Russia regarding it as likely to come at the expense of New Delhi's traditionally warm relations with and reliance on Moscow.

Recommendations

In light of the stark divergence in Chinese and Russian interests and views and those of the United States across the priority issues in the Indo-Pacific region, our key recommendations are as follows:

- Do not assume that opportunities for cooperation or to divide China and Russia exist but have been overlooked.
- Prepare for long-term competition but avoid conveying an impression that this connotes a U.S. goal of regime change.

- Continue to leverage existing U.S.-China military risk reduction mechanisms; expand these to new domains if possible and encourage China to abide by them when engaging with U.S. allies and partners.
- Do not premise U.S. policy on North Korean denuclearization or withdrawal from Afghanistan on eliciting substantial Chinese or Russian cooperation, but maintain open lines of communication to deconflict in the event of a North Korean collapse.
- Minimize the impact of cooperation with China or competition with Russia on ties with India, Indonesia, Malaysia, and Vietnam and waive CAATSA (Countering America's Adversaries Through Sanctions Act) sanctions on them.
- Ensure that Taiwan has the ability to deter and resist PRC coercion.

CHAPTER ONE

Introduction[1]

As the United States responds to the challenge of a renewed era of great power competition with the People's Republic of China (PRC) and Russia, it is important for U.S. policymakers and defense officials to understand how these two key actors view the steps America takes to cooperate with the other country in key spaces and on important policy issues.[2] Where do Washington's policy goals overlap or come into conflict with the aims of Beijing and Moscow? To what extent can the United States reasonably seek to achieve meaningful cooperation on its key policy goals? And what would the implications of cooperating with China or Russia on each of these issues be for relations with the other nation? Does cooperation with one improve the prospects of cooperating or competing with the other? In this report, we explore these questions with relevance to the Indo-Pacific.[3] Specifically, we look at how China and Russia view the following seven key U.S. policy goals in the region as articu-

---

[1] This research was completed in September 2020, before the February 2022 Russian invasion of Ukraine and before the U.S. military withdrawal from Afghanistan in August 2021. It has not been subsequently revised.

[2] The nature of the China-Russia relationship is, in itself, an important question and one that has been treated extensively elsewhere. For our purposes, we treat China and Russia as distinct actors with similar (though not identical) interests that share a view of the United States and the U.S.-centric rules-based liberal international order as threatening to their policy preferences in a number of key arenas. On China-Russia relations, see Elizabeth Wishnick, "In Search of the 'Other' in Asia: Russia-China Relations Revisited," *Pacific Review*, Vol. 30, No. 1, 2017; Andrea Kendall-Taylor and Jeffrey Edmonds, "Addressing Deepening Russia-China Relations," Center for a New American Security, August 31, 2020; Alexander Korolev, "Russia's Reorientation to Asia: Causes and Strategic Implications," *Pacific Affairs*, Vol. 89, No. 1, March 2016; Artyom Lukin, "Russia and the United States in the Asia Pacific: A Perspective of the English School," *Asian Perspective*, Vol. 42, No. 3, 2018; and Bobo Lo, *Russia and the New World Disorder,* Washington, D.C.: Brookings Institution, 2015.

[3] In terms of geography, the term *Indo-Pacific* as used in this study refers to that area sitting to the west of the U.S. West Coast and running all the way to the westernmost shores of Pakistan, north from Alaska to Russia and the Japanese archipelago and south to the southernmost tips of Australia and New Zealand. It encompasses East Asia (China, Russia, the two Koreas, and Taiwan), Southeast Asia (primarily the Association of Southeast Asian Nations), and South or South-Central Asia (India, Pakistan, Bangladesh, and Afghanistan), as well as Oceania and the Pacific Islands, among other territories (we do not list every country in the region here). In terms of bodies of water, it most notably encompasses the Pacific and Indian oceans, the Sea of Japan, the East China Sea, and the South China Sea, as well as the Taiwan Strait.

lated in key U.S. policy documents, such as the 2017 *National Security Strategy* and the 2019 *Indo-Pacific Strategy Report*:

- the quest to build a free and open Indo-Pacific where global commons remain open to all and territorial disputes are resolved free from coercion
- the imperative to defend U.S. treaty allies Australia, Japan, the Philippines, the Republic of Korea, and the Kingdom of Thailand
- efforts to expand and deepen U.S. partnerships with emerging powers in the region, most notably Indonesia, Malaysia, and Vietnam
- continued efforts to deter China from seeking to absorb Taiwan through subversion, economic coercion, diplomatic pressure, or the use of force and striving to encourage both sides of the Taiwan Strait to resolve their differences through dialogue (as, indeed, Taipei has shown it seeks to do)
- seeking the complete, verifiable, and irreversible denuclearization of the Democratic People's Republic of Korea (DPRK, or North Korea)
- countering violent extremism by radical Islamist terror groups such as al Qaeda, the Islamic State of Syria and Iraq (ISIS), the Taliban, and other entities in Afghanistan and Southeast Asia
- deepening the U.S.-India Strategic Partnership into a comprehensive relationship between the world's oldest and the world's largest democracies.[4]

Our study of U.S. goals in the Indo-Pacific and how they mesh or conflict with Chinese and Russian aims and strategies indicates that the space for cooperation is vanishingly small and the imperative to compete in this vast geographic space is overwhelming. Across each of the seven issue areas we explored, Chinese and Russian views of the necessity of competition with the United States have driven them to adopt policy positions starkly at odds with U.S. goals and interests, even if sometimes they adopt language designed to obscure this. Even in areas such as pursuing North Korean denuclearization or counterterrorism, the views and goals of Beijing and Moscow put them sharply at odds with the United States, leading to activities such as support for the violation of UN sanctions and the payment of assassination bounties to the Taliban for the killing of American forces in Afghanistan.

As a consequence, the United States will need to prepare for a long-term geostrategic competition with both China and Russia. Doing so will require clear and consistent support for widely accepted norms of behavior, such as those that undergird the goal of a "free and open Indo-Pacific," and continued support for, and from, traditional allies such as Australia, Japan,

---

[4] U.S. policy goals in the Indo-Pacific are derived from several sources, including The White House, *The National Security Strategy of the United States*, Washington, D.C., 2017; U.S. Department of Defense (DoD), *Summary of the 2018 National Defense Strategy of the United States: Sharpening the American Military's Competitive Edge*, Washington, D.C., 2018b; U.S. Department of Defense, *Indo-Pacific Strategy Report: Preparedness, Partnerships, and Promotion of a Networked Region*, Washington, D.C., 2019; and U.S. Department of State, *A Free and Open Indo-Pacific—Advancing a Shared Vision*, Washington, D.C., 2019.

the Republic of Korea, the Philippines, and Thailand. This alone will likely not be sufficient, however, and so the United States must continue to seek out opportunities to expand cooperation with countries such as India, Indonesia, Malaysia, and Vietnam while also defending (and cooperating with) Taiwan against Chinese aggression. U.S. policies toward problems such as denuclearizing North Korea and countering terrorism and violent extremism will need to be designed apart from any expectation that they will be able to elicit any substantial Chinese or Russian support.

Where feasible, U.S. policy can seek to deconflict or reduce the risk of misperceptions and unintentional or accidental conflict with China and Russia through improved (or, in some cases, new) dialogue mechanisms and risk reduction agreements to facilitate operating in greater proximity and with greater frequency across a free and open Indo-Pacific.

The United States can also support its overall vision of the region and the alliance architecture it has built by encouraging China to extend such agreements on military-to-military contact, risk reduction, deconfliction, and de-escalation to U.S. allies and partners, at the same time advising these allies on how best to manage military contacts with the People's Liberation Army (PLA).

With Russia, the United States can consider waiving the application of the Countering America's Adversaries Through Sanctions (CAATSA) Act to Moscow's arms deals with India, Indonesia, Malaysia and Vietnam; such weapons would most likely be used in defense of these nations' territorial claims against Chinese encroachment, and imposing sanctions on their purchase would damage U.S. efforts to deepen ties with these strategically important actors.

While remaining cautious about the extent to which such steps will help change the substance or tenor of these difficult relationships, the United States can nevertheless seek incremental cooperation on issues such as deconfliction in a North Korean collapse scenario and attempt—perhaps informally at first—to communicate with China about how to render safe North Korean nuclear weapons lest they flow out into the international community in the wake of any implosion of the DPRK regime.

With respect to the counterterrorism mission in Afghanistan, both China and Russia see the United States as likely to depart and have been looking to either increase the magnitude of that defeat through strategic messaging or keep the United States tied down there for as long as possible so as to prolong the pain and increase the costs of that war. At the same time, once U.S. withdrawal occurs, both Beijing and Moscow could conceivably find themselves drawn in to defend their own equities, which means that the United States might have some leverage to negotiate with China and Russia on how the U.S. drawdown occurs and how their own investments might serve to stabilize Afghanistan in the post–U.S. withdrawal period.

Finally, desirable as it may be to imagine that U.S. policy could drive substantial wedges between Beijing and Moscow through clever trades and maneuvering, we find no evidence that this is either politically feasible nor realistically plausible, given the views of both the Chinese Communist Party (CCP) and the Putin regime that the greatest threat to their continued rule comes from the United States.

Data and Methodology

To explore this topic and the questions posed at the start of this chapter, we collected and analyzed information of several distinct types, including official policy documents; speeches and statements by senior government officials, agencies, bureaus, ministries, and departments; open source media reporting on the actions and explanations for these by the key actors in each government; and writings by subject-matter experts offering insights into some of the background thinking and reasons for the actions and perspectives of the various parties. We had hoped to conduct direct elicitation of perspectives from U.S., Chinese, and Russian officials, as well as academics, think-tank experts and other subject-matter experts in third countries, but our plans to do so were impeded by the outbreak of the COVID-19 pandemic, resulting in the somewhat more limited, document-based analysis in this report.

In our research design, we focused on the U.S. objectives listed above because these are outlined in authoritative U.S. policy documents and have been consistent, with minor adjustments in emphasis and description, across current and previous U.S. administrations, suggesting that they are central to U.S. policymakers' concerns with the region.[5] Some issues, such as cooperation on humanitarian assistance and disaster relief (HA/DR), did not make the cut because we see them as insufficiently central to overall U.S. national policy toward the region; others, such as countering nuclear proliferation, are dealt with in a companion volume that looks at great power cooperation on global commons issues.[6]

An important caveat is that we did not closely examine regional development as a possible focus for cooperation, because we did not assess it to hold much promise in closing the strategic differences between Washington and Beijing. The Belt and Road Initiative (BRI) is a key developmental initiative of Chinese President Xi Jinping's overarching foreign policy agenda, together with the Asian Infrastructure Investment Bank and the New Development Bank.[7] Originally stretching from China to Europe and focused on building infrastructure

---

[5]   We recognize, as one reviewer pointed out, that the selection of seven key U.S. policy goals can inherently appear to bias our results in the direction of greater competition by essentially asking China or Russia to support goals that stem from U.S. national interests and values. This is a fair critique. At the same time, the approach herein enables us to assess the prospects of cooperation with China and Russia on the issues of greatest importance to the United States. It also enables us to identify differences in emphasis or policy between China and Russia, and to explore how cooperation with either country might be seen by the other.

[6]   Raphael S. Cohen, Marta Kepe, Nathan Beauchamp-Mustafaga, Asha Clark, Kit Conn, Michelle Grisé, Roby Valiaveedu, and Nathan Vest, *Assessing the Prospects for Great Power Cooperation in the Global Commons*, Santa Monica, Calif.: RAND Corporation, RR-A597-4, 2023.

[7]   Jonathan Hillman, *The Emperor's New Road: China and the Project of the Century*, New Haven, Conn.: Yale University Press, 2020; Nadège Rolland, *China's Eurasian Century? Political and Strategic Implications of the Belt and Road Initiative*, Seattle, Wash.: National Bureau of Asian Research, May 23, 2017. For a recent Chinese overview, see State Council Information Office of the People's Republic of China, "China and the World in the New Era," September 28, 2019b.

The New Development Bank was previously known as the BRICS Development Bank, as it was established by the BRICS states: Brazil, Russia, India, China, and South Africa.

and connectivity, the BRI is now an all-encompassing framework that touches almost all parts of the globe (except North America), and China claims that it includes 138 countries.[8] At its core, the BRI is intended to address an estimated $1.7 trillion per year need for infrastructure to support development in Asia with as much as a rumored $1 trillion total, though actual reported investment as of 2017 was only $90 billion.[9] Beyond infrastructure in Asia, the BRI also now includes the "Digital Silk Road," "Health Silk Road," "Arctic Silk Road," and "Space Silk Road," among others. The accompanying strategic vision is Xi's notion of a "community of common destiny," which essentially a vision for a China-centric and China-led world order.[10]

The response of the United States to the BRI has largely been to acknowledge the need for greater investment in regional infrastructure while criticizing the specifics of BRI on the grounds of poor governance and a lack of transparency,[11] and to increase its engagement with the Indo-Pacific on issues related to infrastructure investment.[12] The United States has announced a $60 billion investment effort through the Better Utilization of International Lending for Development (BUILD) Act, along with a new foreign development agency (the International Finance Development Corporation), and also pushed for a greater focus on good governance and transparency under the Blue Dot Network and Clean Network Initiative.[13] Other U.S. allies have also increased their efforts, such as Japan's $116 billion commitment on Asian infrastructure in 2016 under the "Partnership for Quality Infrastructure."[14] Other countries in the Indo-Pacific have also expressed concerns over growing Chinese

---

[8]   State Information Center of China, "已同中国签订共建"一带一路"合作文件的国家一览 [List of Countries That Have Signed Cooperation Documents with China to Jointly Build the 'Belt and Road']," Belt and Road Portal, updated January 2020.

[9]   For the estimate of Asia's infrastructure investment needs, see Asian Development Bank, *Meeting Asia's Infrastructure Needs*, 2017. For the grander estimate of BRI's scale, see Jane Perlez and Yufan Huang, "Behind China's $1 Trillion Plan to Shake Up the Economic Order," *New York Times*, May 13, 2017. For actual BRI spending, see Jonathan Hillman, "How Big Is China's Belt and Road?" Center for Strategic International Studies, April 3, 2018.

[10] A more accurate translation is "community with a common destiny for mankind." For analysis, see Liza Tobin, "Xi's Vision for Transforming Global Governance: A Strategic Challenge for Washington and Its Allies," *Texas National Security Review*, Vol. 2, No. 1, November 2018.

[11] Sue-Lin Wang, "United States Says IT Supports China's Infrastructure Connectivity Plan," Reuters, May 14, 2017.

[12] U.S. Department of State, 2019. For a recent treatment, see David R. Stilwell, "Advancing U.S. Engagement and Countering China in the Indo-Pacific and Beyond," testimony before the Senate Committee on Foreign Affairs , September 17, 2020.

[13] U.S. Department of State, 2019.

[14] Tobias Harris, "'Quality Infrastructure': Japan's Robust Challenge to China's Belt and Road," *War on the Rocks*, April 9, 2019.

influence and the possibility that Beijing will use the BRI to gain leverage at their expense.[15] Overall, it appears unlikely that the challenge of regional economic development will provide a strong impetus for Washington and Beijing to cooperate. Instead, it appears more likely that they will put forward competing initiatives aimed at encouraging particular developmental approaches linked to their preferred visions of global order, a development that is more likely to spur competition than spark cooperation.

Measuring Cooperation in an Era of Great Power Competition

In this section, we define three key terms we use throughout the study—*stakes, policy alignment,* and *potential for cooperation*—and describe how we assessed them. Unfortunately, none of these concepts lent themselves to easy quantitative metrics that could be applied across the full range of foreign policy issues that make up great power relations. So, for this project, we adopted a simplified coding system for each variable.

To measure *stakes* involved, or how important the issue is to a county, we use a high-medium-low model. We coded the issue as "high" if the issue is vital to the state's or the regime's survival and/or mentioned in the country's white papers or senior leader speeches as a core national security concern. By contrast, "medium" issues are those that touch on the states' self-conceived sphere of influence or key allies, partners, or economic relationships but do not directly affect the state's and/or regime's survival. Finally, "low" issues are those that are peripheral issue to a state's interests. Generally, these issues receive less attention in leaders' public statements and official policy documents.

To measure *alignment,* we also looked at states' public statements—both in their white papers and in senior leader statements—and again used a three-part, high-medium-low coding structure. We code alignment as "high" if Russian or Chinese official documents and public statements support objectives/interests that are same as or harmonious with U.S. objectives, and "low" if they are not. We used "medium" if (1) Chinese and Russian statements on a subject are contradictory, (2) the messages coming from different parts of the government say different things (e.g., the Ministry of Defense takes a harder line than the Ministry of Foreign Affairs), or (3) statements appear to have substantive commonality with U.S. positions at first blush, but there is reason to believe that how China or Russia interpret their own public statements varies substantively from how the United States does (for example, all three great powers may be for combating terrorism, but how they define the latter may be very different).

Perhaps the ultimate measure of the *potential for cooperation* is whether countries have demonstrated willingness to commit resources to fulfill their commitments. As the adage goes, talk is cheap in geopolitics, and so the true measure of a country's willingness to cooperate is the sacrifices it is willing to make to attain its goals. We coded potential for coopera-

---

[15] Lucy Hornby, "Mahathir Mohamad Warns Against 'New Colonialism' During China Visit," *Financial Times,* August 20, 2018.

tion as "high" if there were concrete signs that a state will incur costs—both in terms of physical resources and in terms of more amorphous political capital—to achieve a shared goal; conversely, we coded a "low" if there such signs were absent. "Medium" was reserved for cases where China or Russia has given mixed signals about its commitment, made a commitment and then retracted it, or engaged in only half-hearted cooperation (e.g., passively allowing the United States to achieve a given policy outcome, but avoiding actively aiding its efforts).

Finally, we highlight one key factor we are *not* measuring in our assessment of cooperation: the motivations of states. The United States, China, and Russia often accuse each other of cooperating only out of self-interest, while casting themselves in a more benevolent light. For example, as former Russian army officer turned think-tank scholar Dmitri Trenin has written, "Herein lies an important lesson. . . . Washington never joins others. The United States can be relied upon, however, to reach out to Russia out of its own self-interest."[16] Rather than sifting through the mutual recriminations and trying to decipher motivations, we instead assessed cooperation by something more concrete, namely actions—what states do rather than why they do it.

Admittedly, the measurements for all three variables remain rather broad and do not capture the full nuances unique to each issue area.

Identifying Obstacles and Second-Order Effects

An assessment of alignment and willingness to cooperate produce the theoretically available trade space for cooperation. Of course, a theoretical opening for cooperation does not automatically mean that cooperation will occur, or even that a cooperative strategy on that issue would be an easy proposition. As we explain in the overarching companion report in this set,[17] cooperation in the international system is difficult, all the more so when it is between rival states engaged in multidimensional competition. Thus, we next seek to understand the more practical aspects of the potential for cooperation. In particular, we ask first, *what obstacles can be identified that make cooperation within the trade space difficult?* Our analysis of this question yielded a number of common obstacles across issues sets:

- a lack of mutual trust between parties with regard to a particular issue
- audience costs, or the domestic political costs that a leader is likely to incur were he to cooperate on a particular issue

---

[16] Dmitri Trenin, "What Does Russia Want from the United States?" Carnegie Moscow Center, April 15, 2020.

[17] Raphael S. Cohen, Elina Treyger, Nathan Beauchamp-Mustafaga, Asha Clark, Kit Conn, Scott W. Harold, Michelle Grisé, Marta Kepe, Soo Kim, Ashley L. Rhoades, Roby Valiaveedu, and Nathan Vest, *Vanishing Trade Space: Assessing the Prospects for Great Power Cooperation in an Era of Competition—A Project Overview*, Santa Monica, Calif.: RAND Corporation, RR-A597-1, 2023.

- the presence of third parties, whose participation or consent is important to the fate of cooperative ventures but whose interests diverge from the competitors' and/or each other
- issue linkages, or cases where issues on which cooperation is possible become tied to an issue on which it is not
- a lack of perceived immediacy or urgency to address an issue that may be approached cooperatively
- legal constraints that limit the shape that cooperation may take. (We note that on the last obstacle, we considered only legal constraints limiting the menu of actions for the United States and its allies where necessary and did not conduct an analysis of either the Russian or Chinese legal landscape).

The second component of our inquiry into the practicalities of potential cooperation opportunities asks *what second-order effects can be expected should the United States choose to pursue cooperation with respect to some issue?* While cooperation on any given issue should rightly be evaluated by reference to its direct effects—that is, to what extent it will advance the U.S. objective with respect to that issue—we think it necessary to consider second-order effects on other issues and considerations, as well as on the interests of third parties. Three broad categories of second-order effects should be considered in weighing cooperation possibilities. First, in view of the simultaneous competition with two rivals, we consider the effect of potential cooperation with one competitor on the other—whether these effects are to blunt or sharpen competition with the other, or to boost or undermine the Sino-Russian strategic partnership. Second, we consider the positive second-order effects, or "externalities," meaning the positive effects of cooperation on one issue on other issues or parties. And third, we examine negative externalities, or the cost to other U.S. goals or objectives of pursuing cooperation on a given issue. Second-order effects are particularly important for cooperative possibilities that in themselves appear of relatively minor value and can either increase or nullify the expected first-order gains from cooperation.

Thesis and Overview of the Report

The structure of the report is as follows.

In Chapter Two, we lay out the overarching American, Chinese, and Russian foreign policy objectives in the Indo-Pacific and describe how the trade space for cooperation with China and Russia appears to map across the seven key policy issue spaces identified above.

In Chapter Three, we turn to the first major U.S. goal, the promotion of a "free and open Indo-Pacific" where international air and maritime spaces are free for all to use and are not privatized into the sole preserve of a single great power.

In Chapter Four, we address the second major U.S. goal: the strengthening and defense of U.S. alliance and partnership relations with countries in the region, including Australia, Japan, the Philippines, the Republic of Korea, and the Kingdom of Thailand. These are, as the

Indo-Pacific strategy report of 2019 defines them, America's great "asymmetric advantage" in any great power competition.[18]

Because of the importance of such allies and partners, a third U.S. goal is the broadening and deepening of cooperation with nations that have not traditionally enjoyed close defense ties with Washington. Foremost among these are Indonesia, Malaysia, and Vietnam, and we consider great power cooperation on this issue in Chapter Five. Today, these countries represent "contested spaces," potentially serving as key indicators of the future direction of Southeast Asia's regional orientation.[19] (We view the goal of strengthening ties with India as so consequential that we analyze it separately, in Chapter Nine.)

In Chapter Six, we describe a fourth critical goal for the United States, that of ensuring that the resolution of the cross-Strait dispute between Beijing and Taipei is resolved peacefully, free from coercion, and with the genuine consent of the people of Taiwan.

In Chapter Seven, we discuss a fifth U.S. policy goal, the complete, verifiable, and irreversible denuclearization of North Korea and the cessation of its associated programs to develop ballistic missiles and other weapons of mass destruction.

In Chapter Eight, we examine the challenge of tracking, isolating, and defeating radical Islamist terrorism across the Indo-Pacific, primarily in South-Central Asia (Afghanistan and Pakistan) and Southeast Asia (primarily in Indonesia, Malaysia, the Philippines, Singapore, and Thailand).

In Chapter Nine, we explore the final U.S. goal for the region: the expansion of a strategic partnership between the United States and India.

Finally, in Chapter Ten we draw together the insights developed in the preceding chapters and identify implications and policy recommendations for U.S. policy, the Department of Defense (DoD)/Joint Force, and the U.S. Air Force specifically. We conclude that the best approach the United States can adopt is to prepare for a long-term period of geostrategic competition and not oversell the prospects of cooperation. The best-case scenario in the Indo-Pacific is relatively low-grade, nonstrategic cooperation that might best be characterized as risk mitigation.

---

[18] DoD, 2019.

[19] Patrick M. Cronin, Abigail Grace, Daniel Kliman, and Kristine Lee, *Contested Spaces: A Renewed Approach to Southeast Asia*, Washington, D.C.: Center for a New American Security, 2019.

CHAPTER TWO

American, Chinese, and Russian Objectives in the Indo-Pacific

The Indo-Pacific is an area of critical importance to the national security of the United States and China, as well as an arena of somewhat lesser priority for Russia. As recent scholarship on the deep roots of the U.S. role in the region, consequential choices about how to structure it at the outset of the Cold War, and America's enduring commitment to it going forward make clear, American foreign policy decisionmakers have seen the region as critical to U.S. interests, values, and national security for nearly a century and a half.[1] Likewise, research on U.S. overseas basing and force posture has examined some of the choices and value propositions that have informed U.S. strategy in the region over the past several decades, highlighting how U.S. forward basing in the region has been used, albeit certainly imperfectly and not without some downsides, to shape political outcomes favorable to American interests, advance American values, and keep security threats at a maximum distance from American shores while promoting development, democracy, and cost-sharing with U.S. allies and partners.[2] Leading voices from both the Democratic and Republican foreign and security policy circles regularly speak up in favor of the region's importance, noting in particular the U.S. alliances with Japan and South Korea. Even leading voices who have argued for a major shift in overarching U.S. national security strategy still tend to argue that, among the three main regions

---

[1]   Michael Green, *By More Than Providence: Grand Strategy and American Power in the Asia-Pacific Since 1783*, New York: Columbia University Press, 2017; Victor Cha, *Powerplay: The Origins of the American Alliance System in Asia*, Princeton, N.J.: Princeton University Press, 2016; Kurt Campbell, *The Pivot: The Future of American Statecraft in Asia*, New York: Twelve Books, 2016.

[2]   Stacie L. Pettyjohn, *U.S. Global Defense Posture, 1783–2011*, Santa Monica, Calif.: RAND Corporation, MG-1244-AF, 2012; Lynn E. Davis, Stacie L. Pettyjohn, Melanie W. Sisson, Stephen M. Worman, and Michael J. McNerney, *U.S. Overseas Military Presence: What Are the Strategic Choices?* Santa Monica, Calif.: RAND Corporation, MG-1211-AF, 2012; Michael J. Lostumbo, Michael J. McNerney, Eric Peltz, Derek Eaton, David R. Frelinger, Victoria A. Greenfield, John Halliday, Patrick Mills, Bruce R. Nardulli, Stacie L. Pettyjohn, Jerry M. Solinger, and Stephen M. Worman, *Overseas Basing of U.S. Military Forces: An Assessment of Relative Costs and Strategic Benefits*, Santa Monica, Calif.: RAND Corporation, RR-201-OSD, 2013.

in the world where the United States is committed, Asia is where Washington should double down, not withdraw.[3]

Analysts of Chinese foreign policy tend likewise to see the PRC as attentive first and foremost to the implications of security developments in the Indo-Pacific region.[4] For decades, China's leaders have debated how to prioritize China's foreign policy goals and what strategy would best achieve security, prestige, and power for the CCP and the PRC, and China's answers to these questions were revised in the late 2000s and early 2010s, when China adopted a more assertive posture focused on reshaping the region to better suit its interests.[5] In particular, since the convening of a major foreign policy work conference in October 2013, Xi's administration has highlighted the importance of "neighborhood diplomacy" (邻国外交), and since then it has consistently prioritized China's relations with countries in its immediate vicinity.[6] As one scholarly analysis has argued, Chinese leaders appear to have concluded that China's national security interests require it to play a more active role in reordering the Asia-Pacific along lines suitable to Beijing.[7] This serves to secure Chinese interests, especially territorial claims and developmental interests; increase Chinese influence and; thus decrease the U.S. ability to undermine Chinese control of the region. This regional dominance is necessary for Beijing's increasingly global ambitions under Xi, and it is also reinforced as a key area of competition as China's global expansion increases U.S. resistance to Chinese power in Asia.[8]

---

[3] For recent examples, see Richard Armitage and Joseph Nye, *More Important Than Ever: Renewing the U.S.-Japan Alliance for the 21st Century*, Washington, D.C.: Center for Strategic and International Studies, 2018; and Patrick M. Cronin, *The Cornerstone and the Linchpin: Securing America's Northeast Asian Alliances*, Washington, D.C.: Hudson Institute, 2019. For the retrench-everywhere-except-Asia argument, see John J. Mearsheimer and Stephen M. Walt, "The Case for Off-Shore Balancing," *Foreign Affairs*, July/August 2016.

[4] Andrew J. Nathan and Andrew Scobell, *China's Search for Security*, New York: Columbia University Press, 2012.

[5] David Shambaugh, "Coping with a Conflicted China," *Washington Quarterly*, Vol. 34, No. 1, 2010; Andrew Scobell and Scott W. Harold, "An 'Assertive' China? Insights from Interviews," *Asian Security*, Vol. 9, No. 2, July 3, 2013; Oriana Skylar Mastro, "Why Chinese Assertiveness Is Here to Stay," *Washington Quarterly*, Vol. 37, No. 4, 2015; Yan Xuetong, "From 'Keeping a Low Profile' to 'Striving for Achievement,'" *Chinese Journal of International Politics*, Vol. 7, No. 2, 2014; Ryan Hass, "The Trajectory of Chinese Foreign Policy: From Reactive Assertiveness to Opportunistic Activism," Brookings Institution, November 4, 2017.

[6] Ministry of Foreign Affairs of the People's Republic of China, "Xi Jinping: Let the Sense of Community of Common Destiny Take Deep Root in Neighbouring Countries," October 25, 2013; Ministry of Foreign Affairs of the People's Republic of China, "Wang Yi on Neighborhood Diplomacy: Making Friends with Heart, and Resolving Differences with Sincerity and Promoting Cooperation with Persistence," July 18, 2019b.

[7] Stephen N. Smith, "Harmonizing the Periphery: China's Neighborhood Strategy Under Xi Jinping," *Pacific Review*, 2019.

[8] For one authoritative statement of Chinese diplomacy in recent years, see "Xi Urges Breaking New Ground in Major Country Diplomacy with Chinese Characteristics," Xinhua, June 23, 2018.

For Russia, the region represents a more distant and less consequential source of security, economic, and diplomatic partners. For Moscow, Russia's relationships with India, Japan, the Philippines, and Vietnam are certainly important, but they pale in comparison to the importance of ties with the United States, Europe, and China (and even many countries in Central Asia). At the same time, Russia's relations with countries in the Indo-Pacific may serve as a gateway for Moscow to gradually recover its relevance in the region after losing much of its political and economic capital in the years following the dissolution of the Soviet Union.[9] Instrumental to Russia's reassertion of its geopolitical importance are its relations with China, which arguably is more influential than Russia and is a viable competitor to U.S. interests. Although Russia benefits from its affiliation with and support for Chinese policies in the region, excessive dependence on China only undermines Russia's aspirations to become an important member of the Indo-Pacific community by perpetuating an image of the country as little more than "China's Number Two." For countries that view China as a potential threat, perceptions of a Russian alignment with Beijing may only breed greater distrust toward Moscow. In addition, Russia's freedom of action becomes more limited with greater dependence on China and increased policy coordination with Beijing. Thus, for Russia, a more extensive engagement with Indo-Pacific states serves to balance Russia more equitably against China, create opportunities for Moscow to gradually distance itself from Beijing's orbit, and pursue a more independent foreign policy to support Russia's goals to establish itself as a global power.[10]

In this chapter, we explore the overarching equities that each country has at stake in the region, identify where these overlap and where they clash, and describe the "trade space" where cooperation might be used to tamp down competitive pressures and achieve outcomes favorable to U.S. interests, values, and national security.

American Objectives in the Indo-Pacific

U.S. interests in the Indo-Pacific region are fundamentally related to preserving access to the global air and maritime commons in the region; shaping the evolution of regional norms and practices as expressed through multilateral organizations; and using these to support the open, liberal trading and investment order, peace and stability, and the free flow of people. The United States also seeks to assist those forces in each country that aim to promote, preserve, and protect free, democratic, rule-of-law societies. The United States aims to defend U.S. allies and partners from threats against them; counter the proliferation of weapons of

---

[9]   Julia Gurganus and Eugene Rumer, "Russia's Global Ambitions in Perspective," Carnegie Endowment for International Peace, February 20, 2019.

[10] For discussions of Russia's interests and policies toward Asia, see Bobo Lo and Fiona Hill, "Putin's Pivot: Why Russia Is Looking East," Brookings Institution, July 31, 2013; and Jeffrey Mankoff, "Russia's Asia Pivot: Confrontation or Cooperation?" *Asia Policy*, No. 19, January 2015.

mass destruction; staunch the growth of radical terrorist groups and their hate-filled ideologies; and deepen U.S. cooperative relations with new partners. Finally, the United States seeks to manage competitive and conflictual relationships with revisionist powers such as China, Russia, and North Korea.

The United States has sought to accomplish these goals through a combination of political support, economic engagement, informational or values-based competition, and large-scale permanent and rotational military deployments. By deploying large numbers of advanced military forces to garrison U.S. allies Japan and South Korea, the United States has deterred large-scale conflict with North Korea or China. Further back in time, the United States also stationed forces (including nuclear weapons) in Taiwan, as well as in the Philippines, Thailand, and South Vietnam. The U.S. alliance with Australia has been updated to facilitate regular rotations of U.S. forces through Darwin, and an agreement with Singapore in the past decade has provided rotational access for U.S. naval forces to that country.

Chinese Objectives in the Indo-Pacific

China seeks to assert dominance in the Indo-Pacific region and supplant the United States as the leading power in what it perceives as its own rightful area of preeminence. In Xi's telling, Beijing is restoring its "rightful place" as the historical power in Asia. Under Xi, China has taken a much more active approach to identifying its interests and achieving its policy objectives in the Indo-Pacific region. Of note, because China defines many of its interests and objectives as directly opposed to U.S. presence and involvement in the region, there is often little tangible cooperation on the matters of greatest importance to Washington.

Xi has set an ambitious set of goals, derived from an expanding assessment of China's interests. In his speech to the 19th Party Congress in November 2017, Xi said that the CCP's goal was the "Chinese Dream of national rejuvenation," defined as "build[ing] China into a great modern socialist country that is prosperous, strong, democratic, culturally advanced, harmonious, and beautiful" by 2050.[11] This comes with a set of specific, if loosely defined, goals across domestic and international issues reflecting China's broad policy objectives. For example, economically, by 2035 the Party expects that "China's economic and technological strength [will have] increased significantly. China [will have] become a global leader in innovation."[12] Extending out to 2050, internationally, the Party expects that "China [will have] become a global leader in terms of composite national strength and international influence," as "a proud and active member of the community of nations."[13] In the military domain,

---

[11] Xi Jinping, "Secure a Decisive Victory in Building a Moderately Prosperous Society in All Respects and Strive for the Great Success of Socialism with Chinese Characteristics for a New Era," speech at 19th Party Congress, October 18, 2017.

[12] Xi, 2017.

[13] Xi, 2017.

Xi has called for the PLA's modernization to be "basically completed" by 2035 and for it to become a "world-class force" by 2050.[14] These reflect Beijing's planned transition from its current regional focus to a more active global role by 2050, which clearly but implicitly assumes greater dominance of Asia—and weaker U.S. power—over the coming decades.[15]

To understand China's key interests and policy priorities, it is necessary to understand its authoritarian ruling party, the CCP. According to the Defense Intelligence Agency, the Party's "strategic objectives" are first to perpetuate CCP rule, followed by maintaining domestic stability, sustaining economic growth and development, defending national sovereignty and territorial integrity, and securing China's status as a great power.[16] In practice, the Party's goal is to remain in power, which is accomplished by suppressing domestic opposition (maintaining domestic stability), sustaining economic growth to maintain a veneer of public support, defending the Party's interpretation of China's territorial borders to garner patriotic support through nationalism, and projecting the image of a powerful and influential China to make the case that the Party is improving the lives of the Chinese people and China's place in the world.[17]

The CCP's main focus is its domestic rule, clearly evident in the above identification of the CCP's strategic objectives, and thus its foreign policy is often an extension of its domestic agenda. This has long been understood as an important determinant in Chinese foreign policy. As Andrew J. Nathan and Andrew Scobell wrote in 2012, commenting on core areas of continuity in Chinese foreign policy across the previous decades, "The main tasks of Chinese foreign policy are still defensive: to blunt destabilizing influences from abroad, to avoid territorial losses, to moderate surrounding states' suspicions, and to create international conditions that will sustain economic growth."[18] However, they also noted that "What has changed is that these internal and regional priorities are now embedded in a larger quest: to define a global role that serves Chinese interests but also wins acceptance from other powers."[19] Domestic interest groups, power struggles, and nationalism inevitably factor into China's external behavior in some ways and at some times, but there is a broad elite consensus in

---

[14] Xi, 2017.

[15] Daniel Tobin, *How Xi Jinping's "New Era" Should Have Ended U.S. Debate on Beijing's Ambitions*, Washington, D.C.: Center for Strategic International Studies, May 2020.

[16] Defense Intelligence Agency, *China Military Power: Modernizing a Force to Fight and Win*, Washington, D.C., January 2019, p. 12.

[17] Defense Intelligence Agency, 2019, p. 12.

[18] Nathan and Scobell, 2012, p. xii. For similar arguments, see Lu Ning, *Dynamics of Foreign-Policy Decisionmaking in China*, New York: Routledge, 1997; Kenneth Lieberthal and Michel Oksenberg, *Policy Making in China: Leaders, Structures, and Processes*, Princeton, N.J.: Princeton University Press, 1988; Chen Jian, *Mao's China and the Cold War*, Chapel Hill, N.C.: University of North Carolina Press, 2001.

[19] Nathan and Scobell, 2012.

Beijing about the direction in which the Party should lead the nation.[20] Xi has charted China on a bolder pursuit of China's interests, but there is fundamentally substantial continuity in Beijing's objectives and approach to foreign policy.[21]

Russian Objectives in the Indo-Pacific

Russia categorically rejects the U.S. terminology of an *Indo-Pacific* on the grounds that the concept imposes U.S.-centric values and institutions that do not reflect the priorities and interests of the multipolar world Russia sees and wants to see. To articulate its resistance to the Indo-Pacific concept, Moscow insists upon the term *Asia-Pacific* as the terminology more fitting for the region. Moscow's rejection of the concept and supplanting of the expression, however, does not equate to its being indifferent to the region as a space in which Moscow has strategic goals. Indeed, because Russia seeks to firmly establish its identity as a Eurasian state, it places a high priority on its ability to garner a more expansive network of partners with Indo-Pacific states through economic and military exchanges. Underpinning but also constraining Russia's overall strategy in the Indo-Pacific is its relationship with China, the region's most influential state. Russia's affiliation with China may grant it a greater degree of acceptance as a Eurasian state, and to the extent that it does so Moscow's ties with Beijing enhance its integration in the Indo-Pacific and give it a wider network of partners. At the same time, with many of the Indo-Pacific states involved in territorial disputes with China or subject to some form of economic or political pressure from Beijing, Moscow's association with Beijing could also hamper prospects of deepening relations with these countries. Russia must therefore carefully balance the gains and potential costs in tilting too heavily toward China publicly—hence its policy of non-interference and "neutrality" when countries seek Russia's support in their disputes with China, or want Russia to play a mediating role.

Second, Russia resists pressures from the West for states in the region to support what it terms a "bloc-based mentality" and a biased "rules-based world order."[22] At the heart of Russian diplomacy is an effort to undermine U.S. and Western influence by strengthening the role of Russia and other authoritarian actors such as China, a policy Moscow euphemistically describes as supporting the "democratic principles of international communication based on

---

[20] Rush Doshi, *The Long Game: China's Grand Strategy to Displace American Order*, Oxford, UK: Oxford University Press, 2021; Rush Doshi, "Beijing Believes Trump Is Accelerating American Decline," *Foreign Policy*, October 12, 2020.

[21] Robert Blackwill and Kurt Campbell, *Xi Jinping on the Global Stage: Chinese Foreign Policy under A More Powerful but Exposed Leader*, Washington, D.C.: Council on Foreign Relations, 2016; Rush Doshi, "Hu's to Blame for China's Foreign Assertiveness?" Brookings Institution, January 22, 2019.

[22] Vladimir Putin, "Vladimir Putin on Foreign Policy: Russia and the Changing World," Valdai Club, February 27, 2012; Ministry of Foreign Affairs of the Russian Federation, "Acting Foreign Minister Sergey Lavrov's Remarks and Answers to Media Questions at a News Conference on Russia's Diplomatic Performance in 2019 Moscow, January 17, 2020," January 17, 2020a.

law."[23] This is not only Russia's response to the U.S.-led international order, but specifically, its suggestion of an alternative paradigm for countries in the region to consider. Russia's involvement in and advocacy of regional and multilateral dialogue and cooperation frameworks, including the Brazil-Russia-India-China–South Africa (BRICS) grouping, the Russia-India-China (RIC) trilateral grouping, the Eurasian Economic Union (EAEU), the Shanghai Cooperation Organization (SCO), and the Association of Southeast Asian Nations (ASEAN), reflect its underlying preference for what it describes as a "multipolar" world, in contrast to the U.S.-centric liberal international order.[24]

The extent to which Russia is willing to cooperate with other countries in the Indo-Pacific space is likely to be limited. Russia's relations with Japan, for instance, are hampered by mutual distrust stemming from their long-standing historical and territorial disagreements and Japan's status as a U.S. treaty ally. U.S.-Russia cooperation on counterterrorism, while existent, yields little in the way of substantive gains to U.S. interests in the counterterrorism space, perhaps costing more than it saves in terms of human lives, exposure of U.S. military and intelligence vulnerabilities, and, more broadly, the undermining of U.S. efforts to counter terrorism and violent extremism around the world.[25] And Russia's insistence on an independent, self-sufficient foreign policy that generally goes against the grain of international norms is likely to hamper its ability to make substantial progress toward it strategic goals through partnerships and cooperation with states in the Indo-Pacific.

Mapping the Trade Space in the Indo-Pacific

Starting with the concept of a "free and open Indo-Pacific" (FOIP) both China and Russia claim to already support the region's freedom and openness in principle and practice and therefore oppose this U.S. policy goal, regarding it as cover for U.S. efforts to enhance its regional force posture at their expense. In light of this, it is likely that competition over FOIP (or any renamed but similar goal a future U.S. administration might pursue) is unavoidable and cooperation unlikely.

Turning next to the goal of defending U.S. allies, this is an area where the United States has no room to compromise, whereas China and Russia regard the alliance network as a core American strength, a fundamental component of an "unfair" U.S.-centric international order that threatens their interests, and a major impediment to their own ability to expand their

---

[23] Ministry of Foreign Affairs of the Russian Federation, January 2020a.

[24] Andrew Radin and Clint Reach, *Russian Views of the International Order,* Santa Monica, Calif.: RAND Corporation, RR-1826-OSD, 2017; Elizabeth Buchanan, "What Russia Wants in a Multipolar World," *The Interpreter,* Lowy Institute, October 31, 2019b.

[25] Michael Carpenter, "Russia's Counterproductive Counter-Terrorism," testimony before the Commission on Security and Cooperation in Europe (Helsinki Commission), June 12, 2019; Tom Bowman, "Defense Secretary Expresses Concern over Russian Support for Taliban," NPR, March 31, 2017.

influence.[26] Because of this, little room for cooperation appears to exist on the U.S. goal of strengthening and defending American alliance commitments in the Indo-Pacific.

A third U.S. goal we identified for the Indo-Pacific is strengthening new security partnerships with Indonesia, Malaysia, and Vietnam. This goal is intended to bolster the region's status quo orientation so as to constrain actors such as China or Russia who might seek to revise the regional order in an illiberal direction, and is understood as such in Beijing and Moscow. Inasmuch as policies of seeking new ties with Jakarta, Kuala Lumpur, and Hanoi aim to improve the ability of Indonesia, Malaysia, and Vietnam to resist (primarily) Chinese coercion, constrain or compete for influence with China, and marginalize actors such as Russia who sell arms in the region, cooperation with Beijing and Moscow in this space is highly unlikely. One possible exception—explored further in Chapter Five—might be the prospect of waiving CAATSA sanctions on Indonesia, Malaysia, or Vietnam to enable these nations to better resist Chinese coercion or aggression.

Ensuring that any differences Beijing has with Taipei are resolved peacefully and free from coercion is yet another area where cooperation between the United States and China appears highly unlikely. The PRC continues to view the resolution of Taiwan's status as an internal affair and holds that foreign countries have no right to comment on or interfere in China's handling of cross-Strait ties. China is therefore unwilling to compromise in any way with the United States on Taiwan.[27] Though Russia's expressions of caution and concern over PRC behavior during the 1954 and 1958 Taiwan Strait crises heightened Mao Zedong's mistrust of the Soviet Union and helped precipitate the Sino-Soviet split, it seems unlikely that Russia would play a similar role in cautioning Chinese restraint today, given changes in the two countries' relative power and influence and Russia's tendency to regard developments that come at the expense of the United States as beneficial to its own interests.

One area where the three parties have, at least in principle, a shared interest and a past history of some policy coordination is in attempting to dissuade North Korea from developing, testing, and fielding a nuclear weapon capability and associated ballistic missile delivery systems. The U.S. approach differs substantially from the Chinese and Russian strategies for achieving complete, verifiable, and irreversible denuclearization in that the United States seeks to force North Korea to abandon its nuclear program through the use of sanctions, whereas China and Russia express a strong faith in the value of dialogue disconnected from consequences if the North persists in developing its weapons of mass destruction (WMD)

---

[26] Adam P. Liff, "China and the U.S. Alliance System," *China Quarterly*, Vol. 233, March 2018; Radin and Reach, 2017.

[27] This is not to say that, should a Taiwan government come to power that Beijing regards as pliable or focused on a conception of Taiwan's identity that emphasizes the historical connection to China, the PRC wouldn't work to tighten ties, though it would be doing so with an aim of further constraining Taiwan's room to maneuver. Against such a backdrop, China may be less exercised about certain types of U.S. contacts with Taiwan, though it is unlikely in the extreme to approve of anything that strengthens Taiwan's ability to exercise autonomy or resist PRC coercion. See Robert Sutter, *Taiwan's Future: Narrowing Straits*, Seattle, Wash.: National Bureau of Asian Research, 2011.

capabilities. Additionally, Beijing and Moscow gain in influence vis-a-vis Washington, Seoul, and Tokyo from the need of the democratic allies to elicit support from China and Russia if they wish to restrain North Korea. Furthermore, substantial evidence exists of Chinese assistance to the North Korean nuclear program in a variety of forms, including efforts to block, delay, and water down sanctions or condemn North Korean violations of UN Security Council resolutions over its nuclear program; failure to police sanctions violations and at-sea bunkering; and transfer of dual-use platforms and technology. Russia, likewise, has been found complicit in North Korea's sanctions-evasion activities through illicit trade, illegal ship-to-ship transfers, and hiring of North Korean labor. Collectively, these insights suggest that the appearance of a commonality of goals is belied by the reality of the three countries' actual approaches and interests.

Another area where the Chinese and Russian equities would appear, at least on the surface, to coincide with those of the United States is in the area of countering violent extremism. To be sure, the three countries have each experienced jarring terror attacks over the past two decades, with the September 11, 2001, and 2015 San Bernardino attacks in the United States; the 2014 Kunming Railway Station knife attack in China; and the 2002 Dubrovka Theater siege in Moscow and the 2004 school siege in Beslan in Russia among the most noteworthy. Yet in terms of responding to the threat of violent extremist groups in South-Central and Southeast Asia, the Chinese and Russian approaches have focused primarily on domestic repression and curtailing of civil liberties, with little effort to support or hunt down terrorist groups overseas. Indeed, Chinese and Russian connections to the Taliban suggest they are hedging against the possibility that the regime in Kabul may not survive while also recognizing that the war in Afghanistan represents a distraction and a drain on U.S. resources that they wouldn't mind seeing continue.[28] In Southeast Asia, Beijing and Moscow have been happy to sell arms to the Philippines, Thailand, and Indonesia but have provided little in the way of intelligence, training, or direct support against insurgents. Overall, both China and Russia tend to criticize the U.S. approach to counterterrorism as fueling conflict.

Finally, the United States also seeks to broaden and deepen its ties with India, a country with which it shares "common values, including the rule of law and democratic principles" and whose emergence it supports as a "leading global power and vital partner in efforts to ensure that the Indo-Pacific is a region of peace, stability, and growing prosperity."[29] Notably, in a Joint Statement issued in February 2020, Washington and New Delhi committed to build "Comprehensive Global Strategic Partnership" that would leverage India's status as a Major Defense Partner of the United States to focus on jointly contributing to "peace, stability, and

---

[28] Yun Sun, "China's Strategic Assessment of Afghanistan," *War on the Rocks*, April 8, 2020; Henry Meyer, "Russia Seeks 'Good Relations' with Taliban as US Troops Exit," Bloomberg, March 10, 2020.

[29] U.S. Department of State, Bureau of South and Central Asian Affairs, "U.S. Relations with India: Bilateral Relations Fact Sheet," June 21, 2019a.

a rules-based order in the Indo-Pacific."[30] Such a goal, and India's participation in the Quadrilateral Dialogue (between the United States, Japan, Australia, and India), as well as trilateral dialogues with the United States and Japan and separately Japan and Australia, all position New Delhi as a major player in counterbalancing the ability of a rising China to dominate the Indo-Pacific.[31] Consequently, Beijing regards deepening U.S.-India ties as a direct challenge and not one it is inclined to regard as something it can cooperate on. Similarly, the growth in U.S., Japanese, European, and Australian connections and cooperation with India competes with the influence Russia had with India as a result of cooperation during the Cold War; for this reason, Russia finds little to laud or cooperate with in the deepening relationship between the United States and India.

In short, across five of the seven areas examined here, U.S. policy goals and the strategies for reaching them are regarded with hostility by China and Russia. In a few cases—most notably on countering North Korean nuclear weapon proliferation and combating terrorism and violent extremism, there is a modicum of rhetorical alignment or claims that cooperation is possible. Unfortunately, in practice, there has been precious little in the way of substantive agreement or positive steps to move forward in tandem. Additionally, although Russia and China diverge in their perspectives on some topics—most notably in their own competition for influence in North Korea and over the issue of Russian arms sales to countries that might turn those weapons against Chinese forces, such as India, Indonesia, and Vietnam—to date such differences have proven completely manageable by the two sides, who are more united by their opposition to the U.S.-centric order than they are divided by such lower-level considerations.

In the following chapters, we delve more deeply into each individual policy goal and explore the dimensions of competitive pressures and cooperative opportunities, such as they are.

---

[30] Donald J. Trump and Narendra Modi, "Joint Statement: Vision and Principles for the United States–India Comprehensive Global Strategic Partnership," February 25, 2020.

[31] Scott W. Harold, Tanvi Madan, and Natalie Sambhi, *U.S.-Japan Alliance Conference: Regional Perspectives on the Quadrilateral Dialogue and the Free and Open Indo-Pacific*, Santa Monica, Calif.: RAND Corporation, CF-414-GOJ, 2020; U.S. Department of State, "Joint Statement on the U.S.-India-Japan Trilateral Meeting," April 5, 2018a; Ministry of Foreign Affairs of Japan, "Japan-Australia-India Trilateral Dialogue Senior Officials Meeting," December 8, 2017.

CHAPTER THREE

Maintaining a Peaceful and Open Regional Order

The overarching U.S. policy framework in the Indo-Pacific, as described by former President Donald Trump in his speech in Da Nang, Vietnam, in November 2017, has been to promote a "free and open Indo-Pacific."[1] As analysts have noted, the Trump administration's policy framework shared some important similarities to the preexisting "pivot" or "rebalance" to the Asia-Pacific of the Obama administration and to the approaches taken by the Bush and Clinton administrations, while also shifting focus to emphasize competing with China more explicitly.[2] The U.S. goal is to ensure a region where "sovereign and independent nations, with diverse cultures and many different dreams, can all prosper side-by-side, and thrive in freedom and in peace."[3] In practice, because of the large maritime dimension of the region's geography, this has tended to translate into three basic goals, as outlined in the 2015 *Asia-Pacific Maritime Security Strategy*: safeguarding freedom of the seas, which requires preserving access to the region and the ability to transit through its international air and maritime spaces; deterring conflict and coercion; and promoting adherence to international law and standards.[4] This has meant increased attention to U.S. ability to access and operate in the Western and Southern Pacific, the East China Sea, the South China Sea, and the Indian Ocean.

The perspectives of the United States, China, and Russia on the broad issue of a free and open Indo-Pacific and the more specific issues of access to the various air and maritime theaters described above are explored in the next sections.

---

[1] Donald J. Trump, "Remarks by President Trump at APEC CEO Summit, Da Nang, Vietnam," speech delivered at the Ariyana Da Nang Exhibition Center, Da Nang, Vietnam, November 10, 2017.

[2] Michael J. Green, "Trump and Asia: Continuity, Change and Disruption," Asan Forum, April 18, 2019; Scott W. Harold, "Transformational Leaders in Asia: The Case of Donald Trump," Asan Forum, January 20, 2020.

[3] Trump, 2017.

[4] U.S. Department of Defense, *Asia-Pacific Maritime Security Strategy*, Washington, D.C., 2015a.

Understanding the Equities

To unpack the concept of a free and open Indo-Pacific, identify where it requires competition with China and Russia, as assess the extent, if any, to which cooperation might be possible, in the next sections we lay out some specific American, Chinese, and Russian views on the subject.

U.S. Equities

As described in the 2019 Department of State report *A Free and Open Indo-Pacific: Advancing a Shared Vision*, U.S. policy is committed to "upholding a free and open Indo-Pacific in which all nations, large and small, are secure in their sovereignty and able to pursue economic growth consistent with international law and principles of fair competition. We will compete vigorously against attempts to limit the autonomy and freedom of choice of Indo-Pacific nations."[5] The U.S. Indo-Pacific strategy focuses on economics, security, and governance, with particular attention to how the United States can work with regional allies and partners to bolster these in each of the four main subregions of the Indo-Pacific: the Western and Southern Pacific, the East China Sea, the South China Sea, and the Indian Ocean.

In the Western and Southern Pacific, the U.S. focus has primarily centered on working with allies and partners to offer assistance, commensurate with good global governance standards and alternatives to dependence on Beijing, to countries faced with rising sea levels; offers of PRC infrastructure financing; illegal, unreported, and unregulated fishing by PRC poachers; and Chinese criminal activities, such as counterfeiting, bribery, and money laundering.[6] In tandem with Australia's "Pacific Step Up," Japan's "free, open and inclusive Indo-Pacific vision," New Zealand's "Pacific Reset," and Taiwan's "New Southbound Policy," the U.S. Indo-Pacific Strategy seeks to build partner capacity, provide diplomatic support and development resources, and offer assistance in assessing, renegotiating, or even declining PRC offers of BRI funding through the Blue Dot Network and the Better Utilization of International Lending for Development (BUILD) Act.[7] The United States has also exercised jointly with partners such as Australia, Japan, and South Korea in exercise Pacific Vanguard to demonstrate a broad-based support for maintaining the region's free and open status.[8]

In the East China Sea, along the Japanese archipelago running down through the Ryukyu Island chain, the issues at stake focus on ensuring that the U.S. Navy and Air Force, as well as

---

[5] U.S. Department of State, 2019.

[6] Derek S. Grossman, Michael S. Chase, Gerard Finin, Wallace Gregson, Jeffrey W. Hornung, Logan Ma, Jordan R. Reimer, and Alice Shih, *America's Pacific Island Allies: The Freely Associated States and Chinese Influence*, Santa Monica, Calif.: RAND Corporation, RR-2973-OSD, 2019.

[7] Daniel Runde and Romina Bandura, "The BUILD Act Has Passed: What's Next?" Center for Strategic and International Studies, October 12, 2018.

[8] "U.S., Japan, South Korea, Australia Hold First Naval Drills in Western Pacific," Reuters, May 23, 2019.

the vessels and planes of U.S. allies and partners, retain access to the waters and air spaces of the region, including the international waters of the Taiwan Strait. In sustaining access and deterring coercion, the United States has clarified and restated that Article Five of the Treaty of Mutual Security and Cooperation applies to the Japanese-administered Senkaku Islands, updated the U.S.-Japan Defense Guidelines in 2015 to ensure a seamless ability to plan for and respond to any potential gray zone coercion by China, helped Japan develop its amphibious capabilities, and sold Japan arms and equipment that would help preserve stability across this large region.[9] Similarly, the United States has sold arms to Taiwan intended to help maintain a balance of forces that will prevent the PRC from coercing Taiwan, absorbing the country, and transforming the island into a platform for power projection within the region.[10] And to signal its continuing commitment to fly, sail, and operate wherever international law allows, the U.S. Department of State regularly issues protests against any excessive claims or efforts to restrict international air and maritime spaces, while the U.S. Air Force and U.S. Navy have routinely flown through areas that China has sought to restrict access to in the East China Sea.[11] Similarly, U.S. vessels and aircraft routinely transit through the Taiwan Strait and air-space near Taiwan to make clear that the United States does not regard China as having any authority to restrict the use of the air and maritime spaces around Taiwan.[12]

In the South China Sea, the United States has condemned Chinese bullying of other nations and infringements on their economic activities and rights,[13] conducted regular freedom of navigation operations, conducted training and exercises (including bi-,[14] tri-, and multilateral[15] exercises with allies and partners), encouraged other nations to make diplomatic representations challenging activities by China that are not compliant with the United

---

[9] Obama, Barack, and Abe Shinzo, "Joint Press Conference with President Obama and Prime Minister Abe of Japan," April 24, 2014; U.S. Department of Defense, "Readout of Secretary of Defense Mattis' Meeting with Japanese Minister of Defense Onodera," October 23, 2017b; U.S. Department of Defense, "The Guidelines for U.S.-Japan Defense Cooperation," April 27, 2015b; Scott W. Harold, Koichiro Bansho, Jeffrey W. Hornung, Koichi Isobe, and Richard L. Simcock II, *The U.S.-Japan Alliance Conference: Meeting the Challenge of Amphibious Operations*, Santa Monica, Calif.: RAND Corporation, CF-387-GOJ, 2018.

[10] Shirley A. Kan, *Taiwan: Major U.S. Arms Sales Since 1990*, Washington, D.C.: Congressional Research Service, 2014; Scott W. Harold, "Making Sense of US Arms Sales to Taiwan," *Institut Montaigne Blog*, July 23, 2019b.

[11] U.S. Department of Defense, *Report to Congress—Annual Freedom of Navigation Report, Fiscal Year 2018*, Washington, D.C., 2018a.

[12] Joseph Ditzler, "Navy Sends Another Guided-Missile Destroyer Through Taiwan Strait," *Stars and Stripes*, June 8, 2020; Keoni Everington, "US Navy C-40 Reported Flying Directly over Taiwan," *Taiwan News*, June 9, 2020.

[13] Morgan Ortagus, "Chinese Coercion on Oil and Gas Activity in the South China Sea," U.S. Department of State, July 20, 2019.

[14] Nicholas V. Huynh, "U.S. Navy, Royal Australian Navy Team Up in South China Sea," U.S. Navy, April 29, 2020.

[15] "US, Japan, India and Philippines Challenge Beijing with Naval Drills in South China Sea," Reuters, May 9, 2019.

Nations Convention on the Law of the Sea (UNCLOS),[16] and supported the Philippines' successful filing at the International Tribunal on the Law of the Sea while also urging all countries to fly and sail through these international air and maritime spaces so as to make clear that the PRC cannot privatize them. Former Secretary of State Mike Pompeo stated that the United States will remain committed to ensuring that the South China Sea remains open to all types of navigation and that China cannot close sea lines of communication.[17] Additional U.S. efforts to ensure a free and open South China Sea have focused on building partner capacity through the Maritime Security Initiative (especially for maritime and air domain awareness and maritime law enforcement); countering piracy, drug smuggling, or human and arms trafficking; and developing shared norms and supporting regional HA/DR efforts.

In the Indian Ocean, U.S. efforts to promote a free and open Indo-Pacific have centered on seeking to accelerate India's naval development (especially its maritime domain awareness); expanding defense cooperation, training, and military exercises (both bilaterally and together with allies such as Japan and Australia); and encouraging India to operationalize a broader regional profile as envisioned in the Modi administration's Act East policy and its participation in the Quadrilateral Dialogue. In addition, as previously noted, in 2016 India was deemed a Major Defense Partner, and in 2019 it was deemed eligible for funding under the United States' Maritime Security Initiative, giving the United States additional authorities to help promote India's ability to partner on efforts to police regional maritime spaces and balance against revisionist actors.[18]

Chinese Equities

Beijing shares some rhetorical agreement with Washington on important principles of the Indo-Pacific regional order, including freedom of navigation, striving for peace and stability, regional development, sovereign self-determination, and adhering to international law. However, Beijing believes the FOIP concept is fundamentally contrary to its primary interests in Asia and a direct threat to Chinese power and influence in the region. Beijing has a high interest in the future of the Indo-Pacific but a substantially different—indeed, fundamentally opposed—vision for the region's future. Beyond mere bromides about stability and respect for sovereignty, China has little actual alignment with the United States on policy. However, we assess that Beijing has demonstrated mixed willingness to bargain with Washington because of its moderate engagement on issues of military-military deconfliction. It is important to note, however, that China has not demonstrated a willingness to bargain on issues of impor-

---

[16] Kelly Craft, U.S. Representative to the United Nations, "Protesting China's Unlawful Maritime Claims at the UN," letter to António Guterres, Secretary-General of the United Nations, June 1, 2020.

[17] Jim Gomez, "Pompeo: US to Make Sure That China Can't Blockade South China Sea," Associated Press, March 1, 2019.

[18] U.S. Department of State, Bureau of Political-Military Affairs, "Fact Sheet: U.S. Security Cooperation with India," June 4, 2019.

tance to the regional order—freedom of navigation, peaceful resolution of disputes, following international law—and we do not foresee that happening in the future.

China, as a nation in the Indo-Pacific, has high stakes in the future regional order. This is most pronounced from the perspective of China's global ambitions, since East Asia and the broader Indo-Pacific region are the stepping-stones for Beijing's path toward global influence. Most important, however, is the CCP's fundamental interest in regime security—the Chinese leadership views securing its immediate periphery as an important requirement for ensuring its political security goes unchallenged at home. This informs the PRC's stance on Taiwan: As discussed more in Chapter Six, the island's democratic political system presents a direct challenge to the CCP's claim of one-party dictatorship as the acceptable norm for Chinese "civilization." And the CCP's focus on regime stability extends to domestic stability, since many countries in the region, especially Southeast Asia, have large ethnic Chinese communities that Beijing fears can transmit information about, and spread anti-CCP sentiment to, the broader Chinese public that threatens CCP control.

Economically, China's trade with Indo-Pacific nations accounts for roughly half of all its global trade volume, making it an important engine for Chinese economic growth.[19]

Beijing nominally agrees with the United States on several important issues under FOIP, but in practice its interpretations are unacceptable to Washington. As Xi said at 19th Party Congress,

> China remains firm in pursuing an independent foreign policy of peace. We respect the right of the people of all countries to choose their own development path. We endeavor to uphold international fairness and justice, and oppose acts that impose one's will on others or interfere in the internal affairs of others as well as the practice of the strong bullying the weak.[20]

Xi similarly explained in 2014 that China supports the "basic norms governing international relations such as respecting sovereignty, independence and territorial integrity and non-interference in internal affairs, respect the social systems and development paths chosen by countries on their own, and fully respect and accommodate the legitimate security concerns of all parties."[21] On the issue of freedom of navigation, Beijing's 2017 white paper on its security policies in Asia stated that

> China has always been committed to resolving disputes peacefully through negotiation and consultation, managing disputes by setting rules and establishing mechanisms, realizing mutually beneficial outcomes through cooperation for mutual benefit, and uphold-

---

[19] Authors' calculations using data from the World Integrated Trade Solution (WITS) database.

[20] Xi, 2017.

[21] Xi Jinping, "New Asian Security Concept for New Progress in Security Cooperation," speech at the Fourth Summit of the Conference on Interaction and Confidence Building Measures in Asia, May 21, 2014.

ing peace and stability as well as freedom of navigation and overflight in the South China Sea.[22]

Chinese Foreign Minister Wang Yi similarly stated in August 2015 that "China always maintains that countries enjoy freedom of navigation and overflight in the South China Sea in accordance with the international law. Up to now, there has not been a single case in which freedom of navigation in the South China Sea is impeded," and in 2016 added, "China is the largest country bordering the South China Sea, so we hope, more than any other country, to uphold the freedom of navigation in the South China Sea."[23] On the surface, these statements would seem to suggest that China's policy and preferred norms in the Indo-Pacific align very well with the United States' FOIP strategy, including on the specific issues of freedom of navigation, avoiding conflict and promoting international law.

Closer observation of Chinese policy and action, as well as the broader strategies that China has put forward, however, reveal that Beijing's rhetorical support is conditional, and based on assumptions that are unlikely to be acceptable to Washington. In practice, Beijing seeks to control the transit of air and maritime traffic within its South China Sea claims— about 90 percent of the total area. Chinese diplomats often attempt to legitimize their position by muddying the U.S. claim. For example, Wang's assertion on respecting the freedom of navigation in the South China Sea also came with clear conditions. In 2016, he said, "I want to remind some people that the freedom of navigation does not give them a license to do whatever they want."[24] Another senior Chinese diplomat similarly commented that "freedom of navigation is not an absolute freedom to sail at will. The US Freedom of Navigation Programme should not be confused with freedom of navigation that is universally recognized under international law. The former is an excuse to throw America's weight about wherever it wants."[25] He added, "Although naval ships are not subject to UNCLOS provisions of innocent passage, they are required by many countries to obtain prior permission or provide advance notice to enter foreign territorial waters. Such is the provision of China's Law on the Territorial Sea and the Contiguous Zone."[26]

---

[22] State Council Information Office of the People's Republic of China, "China's Policies on Asia-Pacific Security Cooperation," January 2017.

[23] Ministry of Foreign Affairs of the People's Republic of China, "Foreign Minister Wang Yi Meets the Press," March 9, 2016b; Ministry of Foreign Affairs of the People's Republic of China, "Wang Yi on the South China Sea Issue at the ASEAN Regional Forum," August 6, 2015.

[24] Ministry of Foreign Affairs of the People's Republic of China, 2015, 2016b.

[25] Liu Xiaoming, "China Will Not Tolerate US Military Muscle-Flexing off Our Shores," *The Guardian*, June 27, 2018.

[26] Liu, 2018.

Another clear example has been China's response to the Philippines' attempts to question Chinese territorial claims in the South China Sea through international law.[27] In 2013, after China seized control of Scarborough Shoal, a feature both countries claimed but that the Philippines had been in control of, the Philippines filed an arbitration case at The Hague under the 1982 UNCLOS, to which both Manila and Beijing are ratified parties and which allows any signatory to appeal to an international tribunal to settle conflicting interpretations of the international treaty. The case turned on whether the features in the South China Sea claimed by China were actually islands, reefs, or features, all of which generate different amounts of territorial rights for their legally recognized owner.[28] Beijing refused to participate and waged a public opinion campaign to dispute the applicability of UNCLOS to this situation.[29] In the end, the tribunal ruled in 2016 that the features provided to no legal basis for any country to claim resources—indirectly but clearly rejecting China's claims there.[30] Nevertheless, despite being obligated under UNCLOS to accept the ruling, Beijing has rejected it as "nothing more than a piece of waste paper" and still claims much of the South China Sea, now clearly in defiance of international law.[31] In 2017, Xi reportedly threatened Philippines President Duterte over Manila's continuing claim, with Duterte later claiming Xi told him, "We're friends, we don't want to quarrel with you, we want to maintain the presence of warm relationship, but if you force the issue, we'll go to war."[32] This conditionality reveals why China's rhetorical positions betray a conflict with U.S. policy positions.

---

[27] For a critical history of Beijing's claims in the South China Sea, see Bill Hayton, "The Modern Origins of China's South China Sea Claims: Maps, Misunderstandings, and the Maritime Geobody," *Modern China*, Vol. 45, No. 2, May 4, 2018. For a broader history of the South China Sea, see Bill Hayton, *The South China Sea: The Struggle for Power in Asia*, New Haven, Conn.: Yale University Press, 2014.

[28] For a simple review of the case, see Greg Torode and Thomas Escritt, "Factbox: Why the Philippines' South China Sea Legal Case Matters," Reuters, July 11, 2016.

[29] Ministry of Foreign Affairs of the People's Republic of China, "Position Paper of the Government of the People's Republic of China on the Matter of Jurisdiction in the South China Sea Arbitration Initiated by the Republic of the Philippines," December 7, 2014c.

[30] Jane Perlez, "Tribunal Rejects Beijing's Claims in South China Sea," *New York Times*, July 12, 2016. For the actual ruling, see Permanent Court of Arbitration, "The South China Sea Arbitration: The Republic of the Philippines vs The People's Republic of China," The Hague, Netherlands, July 12, 2016. For one analysis, see Robert D, Williams, "Tribunal Issues Landmark Ruling in South China Sea Arbitration," *Lawfare*, July 12, 2016.

[31] Ministry of Foreign Affairs of the People's Republic of China, "Statement of the Ministry of Foreign Affairs of the People's Republic of China on the Award of 12 July 2016 of the Arbitral Tribunal in the South China Sea Arbitration Established at the Request of the Republic of the Philippines," July 12, 2016c. For an analysis of Chinese views on the issue, see Michael Swaine, "Chinese Views on the South China Sea Arbitration Case Between the People's Republic of China and the Philippines," *China Leadership Monitor*, August 24, 2016. For an analysis three years later of China's compliance with the ruling, see Center for Strategic and International Studies, Asia Maritime Transparency Initiative, "Failing or Incomplete? Grading the South China Sea Arbitration," July 11, 2019.

[32] Manual Mogato, "Duterte Says China's Xi Threatened War if Philippines Drills for Oil," Reuters, May 19, 2017.

Beijing's specific reaction to the Trump administration's FOIP strategy is based on a combination of long-standing fears of U.S.-led encirclement plus a suspicion that Washington will struggle to find willing partners in the region. According to a June 2020 study by Joel Wuthnow of National Defense University, "At the official level, Beijing has already developed a counternarrative . . . raising questions about the motives, sustainability, and implications of the U.S. strategy, while positioning China as more in tune with the region's sensibilities."[33] This counternarrative comes instead of direct Chinese criticism and rebuttals to the general FOIP strategy, since "Chinese officials are seeking to avoid a rhetorical confrontation with the United States that would not be well received in the region, where appetite for an escalating U.S.-China rivalry is low."[34] However, Chinese analysts

> have focused greatly on the quadrilateral dialogue and U.S. relations with India, Japan, and Australia, confirming prior Chinese concerns about strategic encirclement; expressed deep concerns about the motives and ramifications of the strategy for Chinese interests; and identified regional ambivalence toward U.S. objectives as the main constraint that may be exploited to minimize risks. . . . Although Beijing will still oppose aspects of the U.S. approach that it disagrees with, such as freedom of navigation operations and U.S. arms sales to Taiwan, [it] might be willing to reach a consensus on other issues, [such as] military crisis communications.[35]

Washington has sought to engage Beijing on the future of the region for a long time. In one sense, Nixon's rapprochement with Mao was centered on the topic of the regional balance of power and rules of the road—at that time, both Washington and Beijing agreed that it was in their common interest to deny, and indeed actively oppose, Soviet influence in Asia. In more recent decades, Washington has engaged Beijing on the topic consistently since the Bush administration. Early on in that administration, the mid-air collision of a Chinese fighter jet and a U.S. EP-3 surveillance aircraft in the international airspace over the South China Sea brought to the fore the key issue of freedom of navigation and overflight. A more structured framework was described in Robert Zoellick's call for China to become a "responsible stakeholder" in 2005.[36]

The Obama administration increased the emphasis on dialogue about the rules of the road in Asia, routinely highlighting disagreements about China's approach to the freedom of navigation and countries' sovereign autonomy. At the last U.S.-China Strategic and Economic Dialogue under the Obama administration in June 2016, the two countries proclaimed:

---

[33] Joel Wuthnow, *Just Another Paper Tiger? Chinese Perspectives on the U.S. Indo-Pacific Strategy*, Washington, D.C.: National Defense University, June 2020, pp. 1–2, 5.

[34] Wuthnow, 2020, p. 4.

[35] Wuthnow, 2020, pp. 2 and 12.

[36] Robert Zoellick, "Whither China? From Membership to Responsibility," remarks to the National Committee on U.S.-China Relations, September 21, 2005.

The two sides respect and support ASEAN Centrality and ASEAN-led mechanisms in the evolving regional architecture of the Asia-Pacific and decided to continue to make concerted efforts with countries in the region to build an open economy in the Asia-Pacific; promote respect for international law, including the UN Charter; and address various non-traditional security challenges such as fighting piracy, disaster prevention and mitigation, and disease prevention and control, including continuing to facilitate practical cooperation in earthquake emergency response and maritime search and rescue. The two sides reaffirmed their commitment to uphold the principle of peaceful resolution of disputes, and work with other countries in the region to promote peace, stability, and prosperity in the Asia-Pacific.[37]

The Trump administration continued some engagement on these issues with China but largely described past policy as a failure and sought a clearer policy of asserting U.S. interests instead of finding common ground. In the last Track 1 U.S.-China Diplomatic and Security Dialogue in November 2018, "The two sides committed to support peace and stability in the South China Sea, the peaceful resolution of disputes, and freedom of navigation and overflight and other lawful uses of the sea in accordance with international law. Both sides committed to ensure air and maritime safety, and manage risks in a constructive manner."[38]

In the unofficial Track 1.5 and Track 2 space, there have long been conversations between U.S. and Chinese interlocutors on regional norms and rules of the road. One recent example is the U.S.-China Track 2 Dialogue on Maritime Issues and International Law, hosted on the U.S. side by the National Committee on U.S.-China Relations (NCUSCR) and on the Chinese side by the National Institute for South China Sea Studies (under the PRC government).[39] Occurring over 2012–2018, the dialogue series was intended to "explore the issues surrounding China's recent maritime disputes and escalated tensions in both the South China Sea and the East China Sea in order to better understand their impact on China's relationships with its neighbors and U.S.-China relations, while at the same time provide suggestions for improving the management and settlement of current maritime disputes." Summarizing the last meeting, in 2018, the NCUSCR wrote that,

> Both sides felt the dialogue was productive in advancing mutual understandings of the issues regarding maritime disputes, the U.S.-China relationship, and regional relations of current importance to both China and the United States. More importantly, our par-

---

[37] U.S. Department of State, "U.S.-China Strategic & Economic Dialogue Outcomes of the Strategic Track," July 7, 2016b.

[38] U.S. Department of State, "U.S.-China Diplomatic and Security Dialogue," November 9, 2018b.

[39] National Committee on U.S.-China Relations, "2018 U.S.-China Track II Dialogue on Maritime Issues & International Law (United States)," undated. For an earlier dialogue on related issues in 2009, see Peter Dutton, ed., *Military Activities in the EEZ: A U.S.-China Dialogue on Security and International Law in the Maritime Commons*, Providence, R.I.: Naval War College China Maritime Studies Institute, Red Book Series No. 7, 2010.

ticipants again are in the process of drafting a list of ideas for managing tensions in this complex relationship that will be recommended to decisionmakers on both sides.[40]

It is unclear whether the list was ever drafted and presented to officials on either side. This reflects China's superficial rhetorical alignment but also the challenges of moving toward a deeper reckoning on the issues.

Beijing has demonstrated a strong willingness to commit resources to this issue, but specifically to oppose U.S. interests and policies supporting FOIP principles. Foreign Minister Wang extended an offer of cooperation in 2015, saying, "China stands ready to work with other parties to continue to ensure freedom of navigation and overflight in the South China Sea."[41] However, in practice, China has routinely challenged countries' rights to freedom of navigation through the South China Sea, claiming to "expel" at least five U.S. warships in the first half of 2020.[42] Criticizing a U.S. transit in April 2020, the PLA Southern Theater Command said, "The provocative actions of the United States seriously violated relevant international law norms, seriously violated China's sovereignty and security interests, artificially increased regional security risks, and were prone to cause unexpected incidents."[43] Beyond direct financial expenditures, Beijing has also committed military and paramilitary resources with the purpose of denying the freedom of navigation to the United States and regional countries. This most notably includes its continued harassment of U.S. and other vessels and aircraft in the South China Sea, taxing the PLA's manpower and readiness. This willingness to commit resources specifically against U.S. stated interests highlights the importance to China and dims the prospects of finding meaningful cooperation on the issue.

This contrast between a debate over abstract but fundamental international norms versus intangible but consequential raw power politics has long been at the core of U.S.-China engagement on issues of regional order. Already in 2009, summarizing a U.S.-China dialogue on military operations in exclusive economic zones (EEZs), Peter Dutton of the U.S. Naval War College wrote,

---

[40] National Committee on U.S.-China Relations, undated.

[41] Ministry of Foreign Affairs of the People's Republic of China, 2015.

[42] Liu Xuanzun, "PLA expels US warship illegally trespassing into S. China Sea," *Global Times*, May 28, 2020.

[43] Adela Suliman, "China Says It 'Expelled' U.S. Navy Vessel from South China Sea," *NBC News*, April 30, 2020. For the relevant Chinese statement, see Ministry of Defense of the People's Republic of China, "南部战区新闻发言人就美舰非法闯我西沙领海发表谈话 [The Spokesperson of the Southern Theater Command Issued a Remarks on the Illegal Intrusion of US Ships into Our Territorial Waters in Xisha]," April 28, 2020; Liu Xuanzun and Guo Yuandan, "PLA Expels Trespassing US Warship from Xisha Islands, Urges It to Fight COVID-19 at Home," *Global Times*, April 28, 2020.

For one nuanced reading of Chinese opposition on FONOPs, see Graham Webster, "How China Maintains Strategic Ambiguity in the South China Sea," *The Diplomat*, October 29, 2015.

Although the conflict is generally expressed by both Americans and Chinese in terms of international law, the friction is not fundamentally about correct legal interpretation of international law or of the provisions of the United Nations Convention on the Law of the Sea (UNCLOS). Rather, the legal conflict reflects a larger clash between China's objective of increasing its control over its near seas and the American interest in maintaining the freedoms of navigation on which the stability and security of the global maritime commons rely. The language of international law is nonetheless important, because it is the primary field of battle chosen by the parties to contest their claims.[44]

Russian Equities

The United States free and open Indo-Pacific strategy and its objectives are of medium importance to Russian interests. To clarify, Moscow is keenly aware of Washington's prioritization of the Indo-Pacific strategy, and how the successful implementation of this concept may be at odds with Russia's own strategic interests. Russia remains conscious of the U.S. vision of a free and open Indo-Pacific and has clearly expressed opposition to this construct, but it does not appear to have concentrated its policies and engagement efforts with countries in the region to effectively and resolutely challenge the U.S. position. Rhetorically, Russia rejects the concept outright and proposes an alternative model to counter U.S. and allied efforts in the Indo-Pacific. Russia has not articulated any interest in negotiating with the United States over the issue, nor has it expressed willingness to expend resources on meeting the United States' military, security, and economic challenges in the Indo-Pacific region.

Russia rejects the United States' Indo-Pacific concept as an imposition of the U.S.-led order upon the interests of the region's stakeholders and, critically, to Russia's strategic objectives in the region. The omission of the term *Indo-Pacific* in Russian official documents and use of *Asia-Pacific* or *Eastern* as substitutes suggest that Moscow's strategic interests in the region are at odds with Washington's objectives in the Indo-Pacific. Russia's most recent Foreign Policy Concept, published in 2016, provides a detailed description of its aims in engaging with the Indo-Pacific states through bilateral, regional, and multilateral constructs. The document underscores the strategic importance of the "Asia-Pacific Region" to Russia's foreign policy, and it notes explicitly that the region's significance is attributable to Russia's contributions and belonging to the region.[45] This appears to be aimed toward challenging the widely held perception that Russia, despite being geographically situated in Asia, is not readily identified as an integral player in the region compared with other states, such as China or Japan.

Further reinforcing this intent is Russia's articulation of its interest in participating proactively in the region's integration processes through the implementation of Russia's socio-

---

[44] Dutton, 2010.

[45] Ministry of Foreign Affairs of the Russian Federation, "Foreign Policy Concept of the Russian Federation (Approved by President of the Russian Federation Vladimir Putin on November 30, 2016)," December 1, 2016b.

economic development programs. The document also makes references to Moscow's involvement in and support for multilateral organizations, including ASEAN and Asia-Pacific Economic Cooperation (APEC), and takes care to link Russia's affiliation with these more broadly accepted multilateral cooperative associations with its involvement in other frameworks that are categorically considered to run counter to U.S. interests—for instance, the SCO and the EAEU. In doing so, Moscow attempts to not only illustrate the complementarity of these programs but also elevate its own "nondiscriminatory" role and importance in promoting the goals and objectives of both Indo-Pacific and Eurasian states.[46]

Consistent with Russia's refusal to use the term *Indo-Pacific* in statements, Russian officials have also challenged the concept as being designed to serve U.S. hegemonic interests and relatedly, to contain or exclude China and by extension Russia.[47] President Vladimir Putin described the Indo-Pacific concept as a bloc-based, "un-Asian" structure unlikely to be feasible given the lack of enthusiasm among Asian states to join the Indo-Pacific construct, and proposed instead a large Eurasian partnership to bridge the interests of European and Asian countries.[48] Moscow's Foreign Minister Sergey Lavrov, speaking at a global conference in January 2020, criticized the Indo-Pacific concept as a divisive attempt by the United States, Japan, South Korea, Australia, and other countries to reconfigure the existing geopolitical structure and shift from the ASEAN-centered consensus, and asked, "Why do you need to call Asia-Pacific as Indo-Pacific? The answer is evident—to exclude China."[49] Russia's Foreign Ministry also dismissed the Indo-Pacific strategy as a part of U.S. "geopolitical engineering" harmful to regional security.[50]

Scholars point out that Russia's challenge to the U.S. Indo-Pacific concept and assertions that the strategy is designed to contain China are guided by Russia's own geopolitical ambitions in the region, which are closely linked to the rise of China's influence. Since the fall of the Soviet Union, Russia's foreign policy and identity have been circumscribed to Eastern Europe and the Near East. To shed this image and expand its scale of geographic reach, Russia has identified China as the cornerstone of its own engagement with the region, as well as the most viable counterbalance to what it perceives as the United States' geopolitical predomi-

---

[46] Alexey Muraviev, "Understanding Russia's Strategic Engagement with the Indo-Asia-Pacific," *Asia-Pacific Bulletin,* No. 475, May 6, 2019; Anton Tsvetov, "What Does Trump's Indo-Pacific Strategy Mean for Russia?" *The Diplomat,* April 17, 2018a.

[47] Ekaterina Koldunova, "Russia's Ambivalence About An Indo-Pacific Strategy," *Asia-Pacific Bulletin,* No. 476, May 6, 2019.

[48] Vladimir Putin, "Valdai Discussion Club Session," October 3, 2019.

[49] Ashok Sharma, "Russia Says US Indo-Pacific Strategy Is to Contain China," *The Diplomat,* January 15, 2020; Raisina Dialogue, "Russian Foreign Minister on 'Myopic Definition of the Indo-Pacific,'" video, January 15, 2020.

[50] Anton Tsvetov, "What Stands Between Russia and Close Ties with Indonesia?" *East Asia Forum,* June 3, 2018b.

nance.[51] That Russia and China share common authoritarian foundations, similar threat perceptions, and economic complementarities facilitates robust Russia-China relations.[52] This, however, does not equate to an unconditional Russian endorsement of China's policies toward the region. Rather, Russia calibrates its positions on policies relevant to China—for instance, by assuming neutral positions in China's territorial contentions or military skirmishes with Indo-Pacific nations—because this helps Russia maintain its foreign policy of strategic flexibility. Russia's position of neutrality on certain contentious issues reflects less of a true strategic or policy dissonance with China than Russia's tacit approval of China's policies. Given Russia's own interests toward countries in the Indo-Pacific—for instance, its lucrative military equipment and hardware sales to India and Vietnam, Moscow's explicit support for Beijing's policies would only diminish prospects for expanding cooperation with the region and establishing Russia's relevance and importance to the region. Neutrality thus helps Russia maintain healthy ties to China without jeopardizing the development of its interests in the Indo-Pacific. In previous years, U.S. Pacific Command (which became U.S. Indo-Pacific Command [INDOPACOM] in 2018) and the Russian military have held exchanges in both bilateral and regional settings, which suggests that U.S.-Russia military-to-military cooperation may not be impossible, and the United States may wish to signal an openness to cooperation and a willingness to explore such, provided Moscow reciprocates in ways that are advantageous to U.S. interests and values. At the same time, should the U.S. military consider exploring cooperative contacts with the Russian military, it should carefully assess the alignment and divergence between U.S. and Russian strategic and tactical objectives to ensure cooperation is in the best interests of the United States and its Indo-Pacific allies and partners.

Still, Russia's outright rejection of the United States' Indo-Pacific strategy, assertions that the concept is a plan to contain China—and by extension, Russia—and references to other regional and multilateral constructs as comparable substitutes to the Indo-Pacific concept more apposite to the region's interests suggest that the opportunity for U.S.-Russian cooperation on this front is limited. Having made its position on the Indo-Pacific concept quite clear, Moscow may find few justifications for engaging with the United States in this space, especially if its interactions with Washington risk estrangement from Beijing. Furthermore, given Russian perceptions toward the United States as an adversary, any willingness on Russia's part to engage or cooperate with the United States in the Indo-Pacific space would likely be insincere and yield few benefits to U.S. interests.[53]

---

[51] Gilbert Rozman, "Russia in Northeast Asia: In Search of a Strategy," in Robert Levgold, ed., *Russian Foreign Policy in the Twenty-First Century and the Shadow of the Past*, New York: Columbia University Press, 2007.

[52] Bobo Lo, "Going Legit? The Foreign Policy of Vladimir Putin," Lowy Institute, September 17, 2018.

[53] For a discussion on U.S. competition with Russia and China and Russia's strategic interests, see James Dobbins, Howard J. Shatz, and Ali Wyne, *Russia Is a Rogue, Not a Peer; China Is a Peer, Not a Rogue: Different Challenges, Different Responses*, Santa Monica, Calif.: RAND Corporation, PE-310-A, 2019.

Space for Cooperation

In light of the foregoing descriptions of the three countries' equities, it is clear that the fundamental goals and interests of the United States and China are sharply conflicting with respect to the goal of ensuring a free and open Indo-Pacific. U.S. and Russian views are also essentially set in opposition, though for Russia the Indo-Pacific is a lower priority than Europe, the Middle East, or Central Asia. The greatest commonality among the three countries lies in relatively low priority issues trumped by strategic competition, such as counterpiracy and HA/DR, though it may also be possible to at least minimize the risks of competition through the expansion of existing risk reduction and crisis communications mechanisms (more on this below). The three countries' views on cooperation on promoting a "free and open" regional order are captured in Table 3.1.

Unfortunately, while Chinese and Russian views of the Indo-Pacific differ in some respects—most notably in Russia's aspirations for greater influence in regional affairs, including through energy and arms sales, which sometimes conflict with China's own regional ambitions—they are largely united in opposition to the positions of the United States and its allies. There are no obvious wedges between China and Russia on this issue that the United States could conceivably exploit in the near future. Were China to achieve a position of regional hegemony and seek to close the air and maritime spaces of the region to Russian access, it is possible that Moscow might take a less favorable view of Beijing, but at that point it would likely be due to broader threats China might pose to Russian interests than those stemming from its dominance of the Indo-Pacific air and maritime spaces, which ultimately are not the main trading spaces that Russian trade or security forces require access to.

China, despite rhetorical alignment, is in practice opposed to U.S. FOIP principles across categories of freedom of the seas, freedom from coercion, and peaceful resolution under international law. At the tactical level, Beijing's clear determination to exercise control of sea lanes and airspace in and around territory it claims—most prominently the major international passage of the South China Sea—make it unlikely to be interested in any form of substantive cooperation. So far in peacetime, this control has been limited to foreign military assets, but it is unclear whether civilian traffic to other countries would be restricted in a kinetic contingency (for example, U.S. allies supporting U.S. operations against China). Any cooperation that includes U.S. activity within or near Chinese claims—for example, joint

TABLE 3.1

Interest in Cooperation on Promoting a Free and Open Indo-Pacific

Space for Cooperation	China	Russia
Stakes	High	Medium
Rhetorical alignment	Medium	Medium
Demonstrated willingness to commit resources	Low	Low

counterpiracy activities in Southeast Asia—are unlikely to be welcome.[54] As one 2013 article on U.S.-China military-military relations found, via interviews with Chinese interlocutors, although the United States would prefer to find ways to engage in counterpiracy in the South China Sea, "This location is more problematic for the Chinese side, as it could serve to legitimize the U.S. presence in waters where Beijing hopes to eventually exercise a veto over foreign military operations."[55]

Moreover, for the United States, such cooperation would suggest the acceptance of Chinese military or law enforcement presence in these waters, which is infeasible. One practical tactical-level positive outcome on this front would be U.S.-China military deconfliction for freedom of navigation operations, discussed below, but this appears a challenging proposition for winning Beijing's support. On the latter two principles of freedom from coercion and peaceful resolution of disputes under international law, Beijing's desire to revise the regional order against the wishes of its neighbors thus necessitates precisely the use of coercion and threatening of force.

China's opposition to the core principles undergirding the U.S. goal of FOIP—and active military pushback on U.S. actions to uphold those principles (including U.S.-only, bilateral, and multilateral exercises; transits; and freedom of navigation operations)—have not actually stopped U.S. military operations in the Indo-Pacific, though at times they have complicated them. Rather, the two sides' parallel determinations to use military force to uphold their competing visions for the region mean that U.S. and Chinese forces will likely increasingly come into contact with each other in international maritime and air spaces throughout the Indo-Pacific (and, recently, close to the U.S. homeland). In this case, one possible basic level of cooperation between Washington and Beijing would be for the two militaries to agree to mutual military deconfliction arrangements (such as the Code for Unplanned Encounters at Sea [CUES]) and, in the case of an accidental incident leading to an unintended crisis, crisis management and communication mechanisms. This would allow both sides to "agree to disagree" while hopefully avoiding leading their countries into a conflict both sides seek to avoid.

To this end, the United States and China have a long, though somewhat uneven, history of military-to-military relations that have led to many agreements establishing communications channels and rules of the road to improve crisis management and avoid accidental escalation.[56] The need for these agreements was generally spurred by major U.S.-China mili-

---

[54] Ameya Karve and Ann Koh, "Piracy Incidents Rise with Navies Stretched in South China Sea," Bloomberg, July 16, 2020.

[55] Scott W. Harold, "Expanding Contacts to Enhance Durability: A Strategy for Improving US-China Military-to-Military Relations," *Asia Policy*, No. 16, July 2013, p. 115.

[56] For recent reviews of U.S.-China military-military relations, see Roy D. Kamphausen and Jessica Drun, "What Are Mil-Mil Ties Between the U.S. and China Good for?" *War on the Rocks*, April 22, 2016; Joel Wuthnow, Oriana Skylar Mastro, Scott W. Harold, and Li Chen, "The Future of China-U.S. Military Relations," ChinaFile, March 1, 2019; Andrew Erickson, "U.S.-China Military-to-Military Relations: Policy

tary incidents, especially the 1995–1996 Taiwan Strait Crisis and the 2001 mid-air collision of a Chinese J-8 fighter with a U.S. EP-3 surveillance plane in international airspace over the South China Sea.[57] A brief summary of existing U.S.-PRC military-to-military agreements is as follows:

- communications channels
  - 1998 U.S.-China presidential "nuclear" hotline
  - 1998 U.S.-China Military Maritime Consultative Agreement[58]
  - 2008 Defense Telephone Link[59]
  - 2014 Notification of Major Military Activities Confidence-Building Measures Mechanism[60]
  - 2015 Military Crisis Notification Mechanism[61]
  - 2015 Space hotline[62]

Considerations in a Changing Environment," *Asia Policy*, Vol. 14, No. 3, July 2019; Scott W. Harold, "Optimizing the U.S.-China Military-to-Military Relationship," *Asia Policy*, Vol. 14, No. 3, July 2019c.

[57] For an early review of U.S.-China crisis management, see Michael Swaine, Zhang Tuosheng, and Danielle Cohen, *Managing Sino-American Crises: Case Studies and Analysis*, Washington, D.C.: Carnegie Endowment for International Peace, 2006. For an appraisal in the early 2010s, see Avery Goldstein, "First Things First: The Pressing Danger of Crisis Instability in U.S.-China Relations," *International Security*, Vol. 37, No. 4, Spring 2013.

[58] U.S. Department of State, "Agreement Between the Department of Defense of the United States Of America and the Ministry of National Defense of the People's Republic of China on Establishing a Consultation Mechanism to Strengthen Military Maritime Safety," January 19, 1998. For one review, see David Griffiths, *U.S.-China Maritime Confidence Building: Paradigms, Precedents and Prospects*, Newport, R.I.: Naval War College, Maritime Studies Institute No. 6, 2010.

[59] "Agreement on the Establishment of a Secure Defense Telephone Link Between the Department of Defense, the United States of America and the Ministry of National Defense, the People's Republic of China," February 2008.

[60] "Memorandum of Understanding Between the United States of America Department of Defense and the People's Republic of China Ministry Of National Defense on Notification of Major Military Activities Confidence-Building Measures Mechanism," November 4, 2014. For DoD planning for future expansion of this mechanism, see U.S. Department of Defense, *Annual Report to Congress: Military and Security Developments: Involving the People's Republic of China 2017*, Washington, D.C., May 2017a, pp. 85–92.

[61] "Memorandum of Understanding Between the United States of America Department of Defense and the People's Republic of China Ministry of National Defense on Notification of Major Military Activities Confidence-Building Measures Mechanism—Annex III: Military Crisis Notification Mechanism for Use of the Defense Telephone Link," September 2015.

[62] Reflecting how long some of these agreements take to come to fruition, the U.S. government pursued this agreement since at least 2012. See Barbara Opall-Rome, "U.S. Wants a Space Debris Hotline with China Patterned on the One with Russia," *Space News*, February 13, 2012. For U.S. confirmation of agreement, see Sam Jones, "US and China Set Up 'Space Hotline,'" *Financial Times*, November 20, 2015.

- agreed standards of behavior
  - 2014 memorandum of understanding (MOU) on "Rules of Behavior for Safety" of Maritime Encounters[63]
  - 2015 MOU on "Rules of Behavior for Safety" of Air Encounters.[64]

There may still be room to grow these agreements, norms, and shared common understandings and expectations. In 2018, the two sides pledged to develop a "Crisis Deconfliction and Communication Framework."[65] Moreover, analysts have called for a hotline between the U.S. and Chinese national security councils and for a broadening the 2014 rules of behavior for maritime encounters to include the U.S. and Chinese coast guards.[66] However, progress on these types of agreements has always been halting, with many taking two or three years to negotiate. So far, the Chinese side has rejected a U.S. proposal for an annex to the 2014 Notification of Major Military Activities to include ballistic missile launches.[67]

Further improvement of these channels—while strongly desired by Washington—is unlikely to be undertaken with any zeal by Beijing, short of a true crisis that shakes the Chinese leadership's current belief that military tensions and uncertainty do more to advance China's interests than hurt it.

There are at least four major interrelated challenges to fuller implementation of these existing U.S.-China military agreements on the Chinese side.

First, Beijing has often be reluctant to actually use these agreements for their intended purposes during moments of crisis between the two militaries. As one report summarized about the 2001 EP-3 incident, despite the existence of both the presidential hotline and 1998 Military Maritime Consultative Agreement,

> China preferred not to communicate with the United States and instead, turned inward to develop a consensus on a preferred way forward. Only once that internal consensus had been established did Chinese interlocutors engage their U.S. counterparts. This approach

---

[63] "Memorandum of Understanding Between the Department of Defense of the United States of America and the Ministry of National Defense of the People's Republic of China Regarding the Rules of Behavior for Safety of Air and Maritime Encounters," November 10, 2014.

[64] "Supplement to the Memorandum of Understanding on the Rules of Behavior for Safety of Air and Maritime Encounters Between the Department of Defense of the United States of America and the Ministry of National Defense of the People's Republic of China," September 15, 2015.

[65] U.S. Department of State, 2018b. For more background, see Jim Garamone, "U.S., Chinese Military Leaders Sign Agreement to Increase Communication," *DOD News*, August 15, 2017.

[66] For the NSC hotline proposal, see Robert Pape, "A Hotline to Cool Asian Crises," *Washington Post*, April 29, 2014. For the coastguard proposal, see Wuthnow et al., 2019.

[67] Erickson, 2019, p. 130.

completely undermines the purpose of crisis management mechanisms and could poten-tially prevent China from acting quickly to de-escalate a developing crisis.[68]

This similar Chinese refusal to quickly engage also occurred after Tiananmen in 1989 and the U.S. bombing of the Chinese embassy in Kosovo in 1999. In a review of U.S.-China mili-tary ties, PLA expert Andrew Erickson found that

> Beijing declines many opportunities to communicate during a crisis and reduce risk that Washington suggests. For example, the United States will immediately accept a call from anyone in China's chain of command at any time; Chinese defense officials will not take an immediate call. Even though China is given 48 hours to take a call, there is no public evidence that the DTL [Defense Telephone Link] has actually ever been used during a crisis.[69]

Moreover, Erickson notes, "When China is willing to communicate, it shuns the hotline that the two sides labored to establish in favor of going through the Defense Attaché Office at the U.S. Embassy in Beijing."[70] Former DoD officials do report some issues with immediate com-munication on the U.S. side as well and have expressed optimism that the speed of connec-tion would improve over time.[71]

One reason for this lack of Chinese interest in crisis management can be attributed to the fact that, according to many foreign experts, Beijing generally believes it can control escala-tion and thus does not have to worry about accidental war.[72] This confidence—misplaced in the view of American observers with a memory of the Cuban Missile Crisis and other near misses from the Cold War—may embolden PLA leaders to take greater risks under the assumption that they can either predict how the United States will respond or control the evolution of an evolving crisis that may stem from the U.S. responses to PRC actions.

Second, another important part about this internal consensus-building within China is that the PLA has historically not readily or fully informed the CCP civilian leadership about the details of the crisis.[73] This was the case during the 2001 EP-3 incident, and, relatedly,

---

[68] Elbridge Colby and Abraham Denmark with John Warden, *Nuclear Weapons and U.S.-China Relations: A Way Forward*, Washington, D.C.: Center for Strategic and International Studies, PONI Working Group on U.S.-China Nuclear Dynamics, March 2013, p. 5.

[69] Erickson, 2019, p. 131.

[70] Erickson, 2019, p. 131.

[71] RAND interview with former DoD official, Washington, D.C., July 14, 2020.

[72] Burgess Laird, *War Control: Chinese Writings on the Control of Escalation in Crisis and Conflict*, Wash-ington, D.C.: Center for a New American Security, March 2017.

[73] For analysis of Chinese civilian-military relations and problems this causes for U.S.-China crisis man-agement, see James Mulvenon, "Civil-Military Relations and the EP-3 Crisis: A Content Analysis," *China Leadership Monitor*, January 30, 2002; James Mulvenon, "Rogue Warriors? A Puzzled Look at the Chinese ASAT Test," *China Leadership Monitor*, February 28, 2007; Andrew Scobell, "The J-20 Episode and Civil-

following the 2009 *Impeccable* incident, the Chinese Ministry of Foreign Affairs learned of the near collision from the U.S. embassy.[74] As Erickson notes, "Chinese officials must first await central policy edicts from Beijing before engaging their foreign counterparts, including accepting phone calls during times of tension or uncertainty."[75]

Third, these hotlines are not always connected, as China has "cut off the [2008 DoD–PRC Ministry of National Defense] hotline twice [through 2013], for extensive periods, in protest against US actions."[76] However, overall, the U.S. and Chinese militaries are working to institutionalize their relationship and communication channels, and the success of these efforts will be tested during the next major U.S.-China crisis. Beyond these strategic-level communication mechanisms, there is less detail available for mechanisms at the operational and tactical levels. There are no public reports of a direct link between INDOPACOM and any of the PLA's theater commands, perhaps because INDOPACOM is responsible for all of the Indo-Pacific, whereas each Chinese theater command only covers approximately one-third of China's coastline. At the tactical level, it is unclear what kinds of communication channels exist between military units on the two sides, but communication is possible and does occur. According to U.S. and Chinese press accounts, Chinese military personnel frequently notify U.S. (and other country) military aircraft and vessels that they are "intruding into Chinese territory waters," or some variation of the admonition for entering territory that China claims foreign militaries do not have a right to operate in.[77]

Finally, one frequent cause of these incidents is the risky behavior of Chinese military personnel. This is a feature, not a bug, of Chinese strategy, because the PLA believes that there are benefits to the lack of crisis management engagement with adversaries. As one scholar has written, "China engages in risky behavior intentionally to signal its resolve on maritime disputes."[78] This risky behavior was widely viewed as the cause of the 2001 EP-3 incident, and Chinese intercepts were frequently unprofessional over the 2010s in both the air and mari-

---

Military Relations in China," written testimony submitted to the U.S. China Economic and Security Review Commission, March 10, 2011. This may have changed in the Xi era with more centralized power, but we will not know for sure until another serious U.S.-China crisis occurs.

Erickson also notes that "These CBMs are voluntary, which makes it more difficult to achieve reciprocity. Although the U.S. Department of Defense published the English versions of the MOUs on its website, the PLA has never released the Chinese text, making it harder for outsiders to observe their level of functionality" (Erickson, 2019, p. 130).

[74] Erickson, 2019, p. 131; Mulvenon, 2002; Mulvenon, 2007; Gregory Kulacki and Jeffrey G. Lewis, "Understanding China's Antisatellite Test," *Nonproliferation Review*, Vol. 15, No. 2, June 12, 2008.

[75] Erickson, July 2019, p. 130.

[76] John Garnaut, "We Value Your Call: US and China Test Hotline," *Sydney Morning Herald*, April 4, 2013.

[77] Minnie Chan, "Chinese Military Lashes Out at American Warship's 'Intrusion' in South China Sea," *South China Morning Post*, April 28, 2020. For a similar response to an Australian transit, see Daniel Hurst, "South China Sea: Australian Warships Encounter Chinese Navy in Disputed Waters," *The Guardian*, July 23, 2020.

[78] Oriana Skylar Mastro, "The Future of China-U.S. Military Relations," ChinaFile, March 1, 2019.

time domains.[79] More recently, however, U.S. encounters with Chinese pilots in the air have become more professional, though the maritime domain is still fraught with risk; some U.S. observers believe that the military-to-military risk reduction agreements the two sides have signed may have contributed to the drop in unsafe intercepts over the past several years.[80] Although it is not possible to say definitively why such unsafe intercepts have decreased, previous U.S. administrations signed bilateral agreements to manage the military-to-military relationship with China over the past twenty or so years to put a floor under the relationship and possibly even shape China's emergence.[81] In particular, the 1998 Military Maritime Consultative Agreement (governing both naval and air forces)[82] and the 2014 agreement on a Code for Unplanned Encounters at Sea (CUES) plus associated air and coast guard annexes have been used to try to lock in agreements that would encourage the PRC to bring its military forces into greater alignment with international norms.[83]

Clearly, even if such arrangements have helped, they have not completely solved the problem of Chinese risk manipulation via military intercepts. Chinese fighter jets have continued to engage in unsafe behavior near U.S. aircraft, and PLA Navy (PLAN) vessels have routinely shadowed and harassed U.S. Navy vessels and seized unmanned U.S. platforms operating in the region's waters. PLAN ships are also alleged to have targeted U.S. naval patrol craft with lasers.[84] Moreover, despite China's promise not to militarize the artificial islands it has created in the South China Sea, the PLA has emplaced substantial heavy weaponry, power projection capabilities, radar systems, and air defenses on these islands and has sought to warn U.S. military aircraft away from what it terms a "military alert zone."[85] And of course China regularly complains when U.S. military aircraft and naval vessels transit through the South

---

[79] Elias Groll, "Did China Just Re-Enact the Famous 'Birdie' Scene from 'Top Gun' with U.S. Plane?" *Foreign Policy*, August 22, 2014; Matthew Brown, "U.S. Slams 'Unprofessional' Intercept by Chinese Fighter Jets," Associated Press, May 19, 2017.

[80] RAND interview with former DoD official, Washington, D.C., July 14, 2020.

[81] Harold, 2019c; Scott W. Harold, "The Future of China-U.S. Military Relations: A ChinaFile Conversation," ChinaFile, March 1, 2019a; Harold, 2013.

[82] "Agreement Between the Department of Defense of the United States of America and the Ministry of National Defense of the People's Republic of China on Establishing a Consultation Mechanism to Strengthen Military Maritime Safety," 1998.

[83] "Memorandum of Understanding Between the Department of Defense of the United States of America and the Ministry of National Defense of the People's Republic of China Regarding the Rules of Behavior for Safety of Air and Maritime Encounters," 2014.

[84] Ryan Browne and Barbara Starr, "Chinese Fighter Jet Performed 'Unsafe' Intercept of U.S. Navy Plane," CNN, July 24, 2017; Ben Blanchard and Andrea Shalal, "Angry China Shadows U.S. Warship Near Man-Made Islands," Reuters, October 26, 2015; Terri Moon Cronk, "Chinese Seize U.S. Navy Underwater Drone in South China Sea," *DoD News*, December 16, 2016; Kathrin Hille, "Chinese Navy Accused of Using Laser on U.S. Military Aircraft," *Financial Times*, February 28, 2020.

[85] Brad Lendon, Ivan Watson, and Ben Westcott, "'Leave Immediately': U.S. Navy Plane Warned over South China Sea," CNN, August 23, 2018.

China Sea in particular, arguing that the United States should "stop flexing [its] muscles . . . and . . . not provoke and escalate tensions in the South China Sea."[86]

For its part, Russia's categorical rejection of the Indo-Pacific strategy and efforts to advance alternative terminology—and by extension, spur rejection of the FOIP concept altogether—suggest little desire for cooperation with the United States in the Indo-Pacific space.[87] Mutual distrust, incompatible ideologies and strategic priorities, and Russian political, military, and cyber interferences in U.S. policymaking limit the space, if any, to lay the foundations of any sustainable U.S.-Russia cooperation in support of Washington's interests. Russian official documents interpret geopolitical trends in a different light to discredit Western influence. Moscow's most recent Foreign Policy Concept, from 2016, underscores the emergence of a multipolar international system and new centers of economic and political power—rather than acknowledging the prevalent U.S.-China strategic competition—and its support for an international system based on mutual respect and "non-interference" in domestic affairs.[88] China will remain the United States' prime competitor in the space for influence, but Russia will continue to present obstacles to U.S. foreign policy objectives by pushing for a multipolar world and challenging the Western norms of democracy and the rule of law.

The differences between the United States, China, and Russia on the goal of a free and open Indo-Pacific essentially relate to the differing views the three parties have on the nature of the international order, with the United States favoring the post–Cold War liberal international order and China and Russia regarding this as embodying a set of interests and values that pose a threat to the hold on power of the CCP and the Putin regime, and a constraint on the ability of these governments to exercise their preferred level of influence in areas they prioritize (primarily the Indo-Pacific for China, with Russia more focused on Europe, the Middle East, and Central Asia but certainly also interested in the Indo-Pacific). Therefore, the primary obstacle to cooperation on a free and open Indo-Pacific is the differing view the three parties hold on the nature of the international order they wish to live in, supplemented by an absence of strategic trust among the parties.[89]

The obstacles the three sides face to cooperation on maintaining a peaceful and open regional order can be broken down as distrust, audience costs, definitional issues, issue linkages, and immediacy. These are each examined in turn. (Third-party problems, legal con-

---

[86] Phil Stewart, "China Calls on U.S. to 'Stop Flexing Muscles' in South China Sea," Reuters, November 17, 2019.

[87] Richard Sokolsky and Eugene Rumer, "U.S.-Russia Relations in 2030," Carnegie Endowment for International Peace, June 15, 2020.

[88] Ministry of Foreign Affairs of the Russian Federation, 2016b.

[89] Kenneth N. Lieberthal and Wang Jisi, *Addressing U.S.-China Strategic Distrust*, Washington, D.C.: Brookings Institution, 2012; The White House, *United States Strategic Approach to the People's Republic of China*, May 26, 2020; U.S. Department of State Bureau of European and Eurasian Affairs, "Bilateral Relations Fact Sheet: U.S. Relations with Russia," June 25, 2019.

straints, and capacity or capability were not seen to be constraints on cooperation on regional order, and so these issues or obstacles are not discussed here.)

Distrust. For China, the biggest challenge to genuine U.S.-China cooperation on issues of the regional order is the lack of mutual trust between the two governments. Writing in 2012, Kenneth Lieberthal, a former senior director for Asia-Pacific Affairs at the National Security Council during the Clinton administration, and Wang Jisi, a longtime advisor to the Chinese leadership on U.S.-China relations at Peking University, concluded that despite three decades of engagement and frequent leadership meetings, "This history and these extensive activities have not, however, produced trust regarding long-term intentions on either side, and arguably the problem of lack of such trust is becoming more serious."[90] Specifically on the core principles embodied in FOIP—freedom of navigation (including for military operations in coastal states' EEZ waters) and open international passages, deterring conflict and coercion, and following international law and standards—matters have only worsened over the period since that study came out. Beijing built artificial islands in the South China Sea over 2015–2017 with the clear intention of creating veto power over transits through the South China Sea by fiat of military force, and Xi broke a public commitment to Obama during his 2015 visit to the White House that China would not militarize those islands. More recently, Beijing also refused to accept the 2016 International Tribune for the Law of the Sea ruling on its South China Sea territorial claims, and violated its treaty commitment to the United Kingdom over Hong Kong's autonomy.

For Russia, one challenge to productive U.S.-Russia cooperation in the maintenance of the regional order is the lack of trust between the two countries. This lack of trust between Washington and Moscow stems primarily from their divergent interests and strategic goals in the region. Russia registers U.S. efforts in the Indo-Pacific as an imposition of the U.S.-led order to the region; such suspicions prevent substantive progress in the cooperation between the two countries.

Audience costs. Although the PRC is a one-party dictatorship led by the CCP, and Xi has centralized a level of decisionmaking authority that comes close to equaling earlier CCP titans Mao Zedong and Deng Xiaoping, Xi is not able to make unilateral decisions without considering the opinions of other CCP elites.[91] These elites exist across the political (CCP) and military (PLA) sectors, among others, and have many ways to express their opinions on policy issues. While few details are known about CCP decisionmaking under Xi, there is occasional reporting that suggests he has faced elite criticism on certain issues (the U.S.-China trade war being one recent example).[92] On the issue of the regional order, elites across all three sectors could protest. CCP elites could criticize Xi for giving into the United States

---

[90] Lieberthal and Wang, 2012.

[91] For one recent examination of CCP elite pushback on Xi, see Richard McGregor, *Xi Jinping: The Backlash*, Penguin Books, 2019.

[92] Chris Buckley, "As China's Woes Mount, Xi Jinping Faces Rare Rebuke at Home," *New York Times*, July 31, 2018.

on core issues of Chinese sovereignty—Beijing's East or South China Sea claims being the most likely examples. PLA elites could claim that not pushing back on U.S. freedom of navigation operations legitimizes a U.S. military presence in China's EEZ waters and negates the intended operational value of its South China Sea bases.

Definitional issues. Although China does rhetorically embrace many of the principles of FOIP (though not the concept by name), what China actually means by these principles is something quite different. The simple but profound differences between U.S. and PRC views of what "freedom of navigation" entails make it possible that any U.S.-China engagement about cooperation on regional order issues will go in circles and never get off the ground. For Russia, Moscow's rejection of the Indo-Pacific concept suggests that there are gaps between Washington's delineation of the term and its goals and those of Moscow. Russia not only rejects the notion of an *Indo-Pacific* but it has chosen to replace this term with the more generic *Asia-Pacific* to indicate its opposition.

Issue linkage. For China, unsurprisingly, principled issues of the regional order are linked with other PRC priority issues. These include the interrelated issues of enforcing China's territorial claims and undermining U.S. alliances. As one study has noted in regard to Senkaku/Diaoyu Islands,

> As Chinese paramilitary forces increasingly challenged Japan's administration of the contested islands operationally, Beijing attempted to drive a diplomatic wedge between Washington and Tokyo over history issues," but "post-2010 efforts to drive wedges between allies have typically failed, if not backfired, with allies tightening their links with Washington and one another.[93]

Likewise, Russia's opposition to the U.S. objective of maintaining a peaceful regional order in the Indo-Pacific is linked to its geopolitical and strategic ambitions beyond the region. Moscow may look to the solidification of its stature and influence in the region as a stepping-stone to revitalizing its relevance in the region following the decline of its influence in the post–Cold War years. The reclamation of its footing in Asia, by extension, strengthens Russia's strategic position. Therefore, Russia may view U.S. efforts and engagement with the Indo-Pacific region as obstacles to its expansionary ambitions; thus, cooperation between the United States and Russia on this front would likely be difficult or short-lived at best.

Immediacy. Maintaining peace and order in the Indo-Pacific region is not an issue of immediate concern to Russia, as the region is not of high priority in Moscow's strategic interests. An issue of greater immediacy to Russian interests would likely be reflected in both Moscow's rhetoric and policy choices. In the case of Russia's position on the free and open Indo-Pacific, Moscow's alternative concept of the Asia-Pacific and its unequivocal rejection of the U.S. construct suggest opposition—perhaps even an unwillingness to cooperate with Washington on matters pertaining to this region. In addition, Russia appears to lack

---

[93] Liff, 2018, pp. 147, 158.

a cohesive, articulate strategy and policy implementation on the Indo-Pacific. Finally, the absence of any major or impending regional tensions, crisis, or conflict requiring Russia's involvement—or Moscow's inclination to get involved—also suggests that the Indo-Pacific region is not of immediate concern for Russia.

Second-Order Effects of Cooperation

Competition with China on a free and open Indo-Pacific could drive China to a greater degree of cooperation with Russia. Similarly, Russia may regard U.S. efforts to sustain the liberal international order in the Indo-Pacific as providing insight into the United States' overall reluctance to adjust the international order to suit Russia's preferences, giving it additional reason to make common cause with China. For China, the Indo-Pacific is and will remain the primary focus of its foreign policy, whereas for Russia, a U.S. prioritization on the Indo-Pacific region could conceivably be something Moscow sees as providing it with opportunities to advance its interests in other theaters such as Europe, Central Asia, or the Middle East. In the case of both Russia and China, the two actors are likely to continue to interpret U.S. policy and the interests it is in support of as threats to their regime security and interests. U.S. efforts to tighten alliance cooperation in the Indo-Pacific, especially if paired with U.S. efforts to rehabilitate and strengthen strained trans-Atlantic relations, may spur additional efforts by Beijing and Moscow to coordinate their positions and deepen their partnership.

Conclusion

As the foregoing analysis suggests, apart from some possible expansion of extant military-to-military risk reduction and crisis communications agreements and some relatively low-level, nonstrategic cooperation on counterpiracy and HA/DR, the goal of promoting a free and open Indo-Pacific is not one that presents much in the way of promising opportunities for cooperation between the United States, China, and Russia. Instead, FOIP likely requires a substantial commitment of U.S. policy attention, resources, diplomatic coordination with allies, and persistence and willingness to endure friction in the U.S. relationships with China and Russia in order to ensure these revisionist powers do not "privatize" or close off parts of the region.

CHAPTER FOUR

Promoting and Preserving Regional Alliances

The second objective the United States seeks in the Indo-Pacific centers on strengthening and defending the U.S. alliances with Australia, Japan, the Republic of Korea, the Republic of the Philippines, and the Kingdom of Thailand. The U.S.-centric regional alliance architecture is something both China and Russia object to and see as an obstacle to their ambitions or a threat to their security, for which reason the space for cooperation on regional architecture is highly constrained. Perhaps the best the United States can strive for in this arena is to seek to extend crisis communication and risk reduction mechanisms developed for managing U.S.-China and U.S.-Russia military-to-military contacts to include U.S. allies and partners. The goal of such an extension of U.S. agreements with China and Russia to include these other nations would be to reduce the prospect that misperception or accidental/unintentional contacts between allied/partner military forces and those of China or Russia could set off a conflict that might drag in the United States.

Understanding the Equities

To ground the discussion in the perspectives of the three countries, in this section we describe the perspectives of the United States, China, and Russia on the issues at stake in the U.S. alliance system in the Indo-Pacific.

U.S. Equities

As laid out in the *2017 National Security Strategy*, one of the key U.S. goals in the Indo-Pacific involves maintaining "a forward military presence capable of deterring and, if necessary, defeating any adversary. We will strengthen our long-standing military relationships and encourage the development of a strong defense network with our allies and partners."[1] As described in the 2019 *Indo-Pacific Strategy Report* issued by the U.S. Department of Defense, U.S. allies and partners constitute "a force multiplier for peace and interop-

---

[1]   The White House, 2017.

erability, representing a durable, asymmetric, and unparalleled advantage that no competitor or rival can match."[2]

A challenge for many observers has been in discerning the extent to which the more traditional elements of U.S. foreign policy under Trump actually reflected his own views and the depth of his commitment to U.S. allies and partners, many of which he harshly criticized over what he claimed was their refusal to spend sufficient amounts on defense, including on helping to offset the costs of U.S. forces stationed on their soil in the form of "host-nation support."

Generally speaking, however, U.S. goals with respect to U.S. allies and partners in the Indo-Pacific include

- deterring and defeating any direct kinetic threats or nonkinetic coercion
- encouraging allies and partners to increase their defense spending, jointness, interoperability with the United States armed forces, and host-nation support
- preserving and expanding U.S. facilities access, often on a rotational basis
- regularized training and exercises
- routine arms sales designed to help these allies and partners gain or maintain interoperability with the United States, offset the costs of developing next-generation hardware, and/or ensure continued military effectiveness
- intelligence-sharing
- enhancing cooperation on ballistic missile sensing, tracking, and defense
- increasing cooperation on nontraditional security issues, such as countering piracy, terrorism, smuggling, and responding to HA/DR needs.

The U.S. assumption of its allies and partners is that they will be in the lead on defending their own territories (especially where disputes arise over ownership), with the armed forces of the United States serving as the supporting element that will come in only should a threat exceed the ability of an ally or partner to respond on its own.[3] For this reason, U.S. arms sales and training and exercises are seen as ways to help improve local first responders so as to reduce strain on U.S. forces.

Chinese Equities

China has a fundamentally different vision for the regional security order and is opposed to U.S. alliances both in principle and in practice. China is most concerned by the alliances' military value to the United States, but in general China believes that the alliances represent a geostrategic orientation toward the United States that challenges China's ability to assert

---

[2] DoD, 2019, p. 16.

[3] For a general review of U.S. alliances in the late Obama administration timeframe, see Ashley J. Tellis, Abraham M. Denmark, and Greg Chaffin, eds., *Strategic Asia 2014–15: U.S. Alliances and Partnerships at the Center of Global Power*, Seattle, Wash: National Bureau of Asian Research, 2014.

power in the region. Overall, China has a high stake in opposing the U.S. alliance system and no rhetorical alignment with the United States on the issue, has not undertaken or indicated a willingness to bargain, and has demonstrated no intent to cooperate with the United States or dedicate resources to this issue.

China has immense interests in the regional security order and the fate of U.S. alliances in the region. From the perspective of regime security, the United States' criticism of the CCP means that any U.S. presence in the region poses a risk to the regime, and any U.S. relationship can be weaponized to undermine the CCP. From a security perspective, "Beijing interprets what Washington and its allies consider to be defensive measures as offensive provocations threatening China's own security."[4] Moreover, U.S. alliances bring the risk of U.S. military involvement in any number of regional contingencies—both for the U.S. security commitment and U.S. operational basing and access rights to prosecute the fight—that the Chinese military might otherwise win, whereas any PLA loss threatens to undermine CCP nationalist legitimacy and thus domestic support. Economically, China's reliance on energy imports on sea lines of communication that are controlled not by Beijing but instead by the U.S. military—especially the Malacca Strait, through which roughly 80 percent of Chinese oil and 20 percent of its gas pass—make China dependent on U.S. goodwill, and the alliances extend that risk by putting China in a position of having to avoid conflicts with its neighbors, too.[5]

China rarely comments on specific U.S. alliances in the region but from time to time makes clear its opposition to them both in principle and in practice.[6] In the late 1970s and early 1980s Chinese officials sometimes expressed an understanding of and support for the U.S.-Japan alliance insofar as it was believed to be serving as the "cork in the bottle of revived Japanese militarism," but by the 1990s and onward this position gradually faded out as the United States from the early 1980s onward began urging Japan ever more forcefully to step up its own contributions to regional security, to invest more in military modernization, to liberalize the rules constraining its use of the Self-Defense Forces as an instrument of policy, and to transform the alliance into a more dynamic, flexible, and interoperable, seamlessly integrated relationship. Similarly, the 2009 U.S.–Republic of Korea (ROK) Joint Vision Statement reoriented the alliance toward the provision of peace, security and prosperity for the Korean Peninsula, the Asia-Pacific region, and the world, thereby expanding the application of its relevance far beyond simply deterring North Korea.[7]

---

[4] Liff, 2018, p. 139; Adam P. Liff and G. John Ikenberry, "Racing Toward Tragedy? China's Rise, Military Competition in the Asia Pacific, and the Security Dilemma," *International Security*, Vol. 39, No. 2, Fall 2014.

[5] Office of the Secretary of Defense, *Annual Report to Congress: Military and Security Developments Involving the People's Republic of China 2019*, Washington, D.C.: U.S. Department of Defense, May 2019, p. 12.

[6] Liff, 2018, pp. 137–165.

[7] The White House, "Joint Vision for the Alliance of the United States of America and the Republic of Korea," June 16, 2009.

Perhaps as a consequence of the growing application and relevance of U.S. alliances with regional partners for U.S. global preeminence and regional strategy, in his 2017 speech, Xi's call for building a community of common destiny is explicitly juxtaposed against "resolutely reject[ing] the Cold War mentality and power politics, and take a new approach to developing state-to-state relations with communication, not confrontation, and with partnership, not alliance."[8] In practice, one expert has noted, Beijing has expressed "deepening frustration, if not outright opposition, vis-à-vis the US alliance system, as well as pessimism concerning its contribution to regional stability."[9]

China does not see all U.S. alliances in the region equally.[10] It is most concerned by the U.S.-Japan alliance, because of a combination of its strong ties, the capabilities of the Japanese military, Japan's opposition to Chinese ambitions, the risks of a clash over the disputed Senkaku/Diaoyu Islands, and the alliance's apparent relevance for military competition with China. The U.S.-ROK alliance's force presence near China is also unwelcome, especially advanced capabilities such as the Terminal High-Altitude Area Defense's (THAAD's) TPY-2 radar, but Seoul's better relations with (and greater dependence on) Beijing and shared antagonism against Tokyo mitigate these concerns somewhat. Australia's deepening security cooperation with the United States—and bilaterally with Japan—presents a relatively new and growing challenge to China. Chinese analysts are generally more sanguine about the U.S.-Philippines alliance, though the Philippines' UNCLOS case over the South China Sea raised criticism in Beijing of Manila being emboldened—or even controlled—by its U.S. allies. Duterte's general favorability toward Beijing has mitigated some of these concerns. Thailand, on the other hand, is usually not included in China's criticisms of U.S. alliances in the region.[11]

In the place of the U.S. alliance network, China has proposed a "new Asian security concept" based on the four principles of "common, comprehensive, cooperative and sustainable security."[12] *Common security*, according to this view, means considering others' needs for a universal, equal and inclusive security framework—namely, rejecting the "zero-sum" nature of U.S. alliances. By *comprehensive security*, China means addressing all types of security threats, including China's top nontraditional concerns of "terrorism, separatism and extremism." This stands in contrast with U.S. alliances that focus on hard-power military concerns of Chinese missiles, bomber patrols, and maritime militia, thereby allowing Beijing to frame its political threats as security concerns. *Cooperative security* means allowing

---

[8] Xi, 2017.

[9] Liff, 2018, p. 138.

[10] Liff, 2018, pp. 142–153.

[11] Liff (2018) notes that then–Secretary of Defense Carter left Thailand out of his Shangri-La Dialogue speech in 2015, which focused on U.S. alliances (Ash Carter, "A Regional Security Architecture Where Everyone Rises," speech at Shangri-La Dialogue, International Institute for Strategic Studies, May 30, 2015).

[12] Xi, 2014.

China a seat at the table for any consequential regional security decision, since its own security will be at stake—instead of U.S. alliances that exclude China and its security concerns. Finally, *sustainable security* is Beijing's reframing of economic development—which China provides—as security, instead of U.S. alliances' focus on hard military security concerns.[13] China claims that it seeks "partnership, not alliance," though Nadège Rolland of the National Bureau of Asian Research explains that the "community of common destiny for all humanity" (人类命运共同体) is a "network of strong strategic partnerships that resemble an alliance system while denying being one."[14] In the end, as Xi explained, the goal is to "innovate our security concept, establish a new regional security cooperation architecture, and jointly build a road for security of Asia that is shared by and win-win to all," because, "in the final analysis it is for the people of Asia to run the affairs of Asia, solve the problems of Asia and uphold the security of Asia."[15]

The United States and China have not engaged in much direct bargaining over the region's future security landscape. This is because the United States does not believe its alliance system should be the subject of compromise, and because it believes that existing official and unofficial forums, such as the East Asia Summit and the Shangri-La Dialogue, are sufficiently developed to facilitate necessary regional dialogue. According to a review of senior Track 1 official dialogues under the Obama and Trump administrations, the specific issue of the U.S. alliance system has never been on the table.[16] At the Track 1.5 and Track 2 dialogue level, there is still no substantive back-and-forth about what an acceptable U.S. alliance system would be for Beijing.

With China's intense opposition to U.S. alliances and a very different vision of its preferred regional security architecture, it is difficult to imagine substantive cooperation on this topic. Rhetorically, at least, China has not completely ruled out engaging with the United States on the issue of Indo-Pacific security issues. In 2014, Xi said, "We welcome all parties to play a positive and constructive role in promoting Asia's security and cooperation and work together to achieve win-win outcomes for all."[17] The crux of Beijing's argument about the region's future, however, is that the United States is not a regional power, but an "outside power" that is intervening in the local affairs of Asia. This important condition means that Washington should follow Beijing's rules, if it plays a role at all.

---

[13] David Cohen, "'A Clash of Security Concepts': China's Effort to Redefine Security," *China Brief*, Vol. 14, No. 11, June 4, 2014.

[14] Xi, 2017; Nadège Rolland, "Beijing's Vision for a Reshaped International Order," *China Brief*, Vol. 18, No. 3, February 26, 2018.

[15] Xi, 2014.

[16] For some examples of exhaustive lists of topics discussed at U.S.-China dialogues that exclude regional security and alliances, see U.S. Department of State, 2016b, 2018b; U.S. Department of State, "Briefing with Assistant Secretary for East Asian and Pacific Affairs David Stilwell on Readout of Secretary Pompeo's Meeting with Politburo Member Yang Jiechi," June 18, 2020.

[17] Xi, 2014.

In sum, there is little indication that China is interested in or willing to compromise on the issue of regional security architecture, and specifically U.S. alliances, in the Indo-Pacific.

Russian Equities

Russia places moderate importance on enhancing its relations with U.S. allies to strengthen its own network of partners to counter the United States' influence in the region. Moscow is not aligned rhetorically with Washington on the topic, nor has it expressed a willingness to negotiate or expend resources on addressing the issue. The Russian government has identified strengthening its position in the Indo-Pacific and enhancing relations with the states in the region as an area of strategic importance.[18] Russia's diplomatic efforts with U.S. treaty allies, including Japan, South Korea, Australia, and the Philippines, are cast in the light of its contributions to promoting regional stability and security. It should be noted, however, that Russia's relations with these states are largely circumscribed by their status as U.S. treaty allies.[19] Thus, the potential for any deepening of relations between Russia and a U.S. treaty ally and, relatedly, prospects for Russia-U.S. cooperation in this space seem quite low. To further the point, Russia's own equities and points of bilateral friction with these states also pose limitations on the potential for it to deepen and expand upon these relations.

In the case of Japan, Russia's Foreign Policy Concept vows to continue efforts to build good-neighborly relations and promote mutually beneficial cooperation with Japan with a view toward ensuring stability and security in the region.[20] To an extent, Moscow and Tokyo have made concerted efforts toward improving relations through political dialogue and confidence-building measures and economic relations. The two sides, however, have not been able to reach a settlement over signing a peace treaty to resolve their historical territorial dispute over the Kuril Islands/Northern Territories, which may be considered the most tender spot in their bilateral relations. Whereas Tokyo's official position explicitly states that the four islands of the Northern Territories are inherent territories of Japan illegally occupied by Russia, Moscow has made no direct mentions of the islands dispute in its official documents. This not only creates ambiguity in Russia's position over the islands, but, by not officially acknowledging the disagreement, Moscow may also wish to perpetuate the assumption that the islands belong to Russia and that this position is at no point up for negotiation. Such was the stance recently expressed by a Russian lawmaker, who restated that the Kuril Islands/Northern Territories issue is not even considered for discussion as a condition to the Russia-Japan peace treaty.[21] As a compromise, Moscow at one point in time suggested turning two of

---

[18] Ministry of Foreign Affairs of the Russian Federation, 2016b.

[19] Dmitri Trenin, "US Obsession with Containment Driving China and Russia Closer Together," Carnegie Endowment for International Peace, July 31, 2019.

[20] Ministry of Foreign Affairs of the Russian Federation, 2016b.

[21] Ministry of Foreign Affairs of Japan, "Northern Territories Issue," March 1, 2011; "Россия не ведет переговоров с Японией о принадлежности Курил [Russia Does Not Negotiate with Japan About the

the four islands over to Japan.[22] To date, Japan has been reluctant to embrace this suggested compromise.

Furthermore, Russia's two other conditions for the peace treaty—(1) Japan's recognition of Russia's de jure sovereignty over the South Kuril Islands and (2) security guarantees from Japan and the United States that the territory would be exempt from the U.S.-Japan Security Treaty allowing U.S. access to Japanese military bases and facilities on a permanent basis—have not yet been met to Moscow's satisfaction.[23] Japan has confirmed to Russia that the United States would need Tokyo's consent prior to establishing a military base. This, however, appears to have been insufficient in palliating Russian sensitivities toward the U.S.-Japan security alliance and the potential for the United States to develop a missile defense system in Tokyo "with a view to militarizing that part of the world."[24] More broadly, Russia is cognizant that the U.S.-Japan treaty alliance is the most important relationship for Japan and believes firmly that the alliance is aimed at the containment of Russia.[25] Thus, so long as Japan remains unwilling to pursue a foreign policy independent of its relations with the United States, Russia-Japan relations are unlikely to make significant improvements.[26]

Although Russia maintains political and economic ties with South Korea, Moscow's relations with Seoul appear to be relevant to the former's interests primarily in the context of inter-Korean tensions and the North Korean nuclear issue. Russia's Foreign Policy Concept makes no distinct mention of any strategic issues related exclusively to South Korea, but, rather, elaborates on its desires to maintain traditionally friendly relations with both Koreas through dialogue and tension-reducing measures and economic cooperation.[27] Under the administration of Moon Jae-in, South Korea's New Northern Policy emphasizes greater economic integration, cooperation, and investment between the two countries. The "9-Bridge Strategy" under this policy aims to increase South Korea–Russia cooperation in key sectors,

---

Kuril Islands]," *RIA Novosti*, June 30, 2020.

[22] Ministry of Foreign Affairs of the Russian Federation, "Выступление и ответы на вопросы СМИ Министра иностранных дел России С.В.Лаврова в ходе пресс-конференции по итогам переговоров с Министром иностранных дел Японии Т.Коно, Москва, 14 января 2019 года [Foreign Minister Sergey Lavrov's Remarks and Answers to Media Questions at a News Conference Following Talks with Japanese Foreign Minister T. Kono, Moscow, January 14, 2019]," January 14, 2019a.

[23] Vitaly Kozyrev, "Demystifying Russo-Japanese Peace Treaty Talks Before the June 2019 G20 Osaka Summit," *Asia Pacific Bulletin*, No. 479, May 6, 2019; Simran Walia, "Japan-Russia Dilemma over the Territorial Dispute," Observer Research Foundation, May 20, 2019; Yoko Hirose, "Japan-Russia Relations: Can the Northern Territories Issue be Overcome?"*cogitAsia* (blog), Center for Strategic and International Studies, April 3, 2018.

[24] Ministry of Foreign Affairs of the Russian Federation, 2019a.

[25] Ministry of Foreign Affairs of the Russian Federation, 2020a.

[26] For a discussion on Russia's perspectives on the U.S.-Japan alliance, see Gilbert Rozman, ed., *Japan-Russia Relations: Implications for the U.S.-Japan Alliance*, Sasakawa Peace Foundation, May 6, 2016.

[27] Ministry of Foreign Affairs of the Russian Federation, 2016b.

including railways, shipbuilding, agriculture, marine products, and gas.[28] Opportunities for Russia to export its liquid natural gas technology, the construction of a gas pipeline, and the building of a Northeast Asian Super Grid connecting South Korea, Russia, China, Mongolia, and Japan may, without a doubt, be profitable to Russia and help Moscow's strategic ambitions in the region. The New Northern Policy's design, however, has been paved with South Korea's aspirations to use expanded cooperation with Russia and China to promote peace and cooperation with North Korea.[29] Furthermore, the success of certain projects in the program—for instance, the transnational gas pipeline construction and the railway project—hinges upon North Korea's participation.[30]

Intermittent military tensions between Russia and South Korea may also pose challenges to building a more substantial and sustainable cooperative relationship between the two states. Russian planes occasionally fly in or around South Korea's air defense identification zone (ADIZ)—sometimes in coordination with their Chinese counterparts—which has become a point of friction between Moscow and Seoul.[31] That these incursions are often a joint Russia-China effort to intimidate South Korea as well as to pressure U.S.-Japan–South Korea trilateral interests suggests that Russia clearly sees South Korea as a U.S. ally that, much like Japan, is unlikely to make foreign policy decisions independent of strategic relations with Washington.[32]

Russia's relations with the Philippines are also limited by the Philippines' status as a U.S. treaty ally. Under the Duterte administration, the Philippines has pursued a more independent foreign policy and expressed a greater interest in defense cooperation with Russia. In October 2017, Manila and Moscow signed a defense cooperation agreement to designate areas for military technical cooperation, including research, training, and the procurement of Russian defense articles.[33] As a step toward diversifying its military equipment and balancing against China's influence in the region, the Philippines in recent years has sought Russian military assistance to upgrade the Philippines' outdated defense capabilities, including through Russia's delivery of assault rifles, warships, Kilo-class submarines, and Mi-17

[28] Liudmila Zakharova, "Economic Relations Between Russia and South Korea In the New Northern Policy," Korea Economic Institute of America, December 10, 2019.

[29] For an overview of South Korea's New Northern Policy, see Valentin Voloshchak, "A Closer Look At South Korea's Plan for Cooperation with Russia," *The Diplomat*, January 9, 2019.

[30] "New Northern Policy Seeks to Contribute to Peace on Korean Peninsula," *Yonhap News*, March 19, 2018.

[31] "Russia and South Korea Spar over Airspace 'Intrusion,'" BBC, July 24, 2019; "Six Russian Military Aircraft Break into South Korea's Air Defense Zone," *Korea Times*, October 22, 2019; Franz-Stefan Gady, "2 Russian Nuclear-Capable Bombers Enter South Korea's Air Defense Identification Zone," *The Diplomat*, June 17, 2018.

[32] "Russia and South Korea Spar over Airspace 'Intrusion,'" 2019; "South Korea Scrambled Jets to Warn Russian Warplanes in Air Defense Zone," Reuters, October 22, 2019.

[33] Anna Patricia L. Saberon, "Philippine Defense Cooperation with Russia: A Wake-Up Call for the United States?" *Asia-Pacific Bulletin*, East-West Center, No. 444, October 24, 2018.

medium-lift helicopters—which, though primarily symbolic, could pave the way for larger-scale acquisitions and serve as the basis for the two sides to explore diversifying the areas of cooperation.[34] Russia has responded with enthusiasm, even offering to assist the Philippines in acquiring the knowledge and capabilities needed to develop and produce its own arms for both domestic use and export "with no political conditions."[35] The Philippines' defense minister, however, expressed caution in responding to this offer, citing compatibility and interoperability issues between Filipino and Russian military technologies.[36] The true sticking point, however, may stem from Manila's concerns about the implications a closer military relationship with Moscow will have on its alliance with Washington.[37]

Russia's relations with Australia are also constrained by the latter's alliance status with the United States. Out of all of America's allies, Australia probably bears the most resemblance to the United States ideologically and has been willing to support some of Washington's more controversial policies, especially those bearing on Russian interests. This, naturally, breeds friction in Russia-Australia relations. Since Russia's annexation of Crimea, the Australian government has supported the U.S. sanctions regime and imposed an expansive range of its own sanctions against Russian businesses and entities, including travel bans on designated persons and restrictions on arms supply, oil production, and banking institutions.[38] Sanctions have targeted large Russian corporations, including Gazprom, Rosneft, VTB Bank, and Sberbank. Russia retaliated with its own sanctions against Australia, including suspensions on bilateral trade.[39] Russian critics have challenged Australia's policy preferences, arguing that its "deep embeddedness" in the U.S. security structures, high responsiveness to Washington's interests, and "lack of independence" in foreign policy decisions pose barriers to cooperation with Russia and complicate the political environment in their bilateral relations.[40]

---

[34] Richard Javad Heydarian, "Duterte's Pivot to Russia," Center for Strategic and International Studies, Asia Maritime Transparency Initiative, October 17, 2019.

[35] Raissa Robles, "Russia Offers Arms Technology to the Philippines with 'No Conditions' as US Ties Falter," *South China Morning Post*, October 24, 2019.

[36] Robles, 2019.

[37] Willard Cheng, "US Defense Official Warns PH on Buying Russian Military Equipment," *ABS-CBN News*, August 16, 2018.

[38] Alexander Korolev, "Australia's Approach to Cooperation with Russia," Russia in Global Affairs, December 17, 2019; Elizabeth Buchanan, "What a New Russian Ambassador Might Mean for Relations with Australia," *The Interpreter*, Lowy Institute, May 27, 2019; Department of Foreign Affairs and Trade, Australia, "Russian Sanctions Regime," undated.

[39] For a background discussion on Australia's relations with the United States and Russia, see Paul Antonopoulos, "The Kangaroo, the Bear, and the Dragon: Australia-Russia-China Relations in the 'Asian Century,'" *China Quarterly of International Strategic Studies*, Vol. 3, No. 3, 2017.

[40] Korolev, 2019.

Space for Cooperation

As the preceding sections make clear, the issue of defending U.S. allies and strengthening military cooperation with these partners is seen as directly at odds with the interests of both China and Russia. While the space for cooperation with China and Russia on defending U.S. allies is lacking, and the need for competition is extremely high, it may be worth exploring attempting to extend military-to-military engagement mechanisms developed by the United States for its relations with China and Russia to U.S. allies and partners so as to reduce the prospect of unintentional conflict. Additionally, in the next sections we explore ways in which Chinese and Russian equities are at times overlapping and mutually reinforcing and at others are less aligned, though still providing only minimal prospects of wedges that the United States could conceivably exploit. The overall assessment we make is summarized in Table 4.1.

For the United States, one key concern has been striving to avoid conflict with China over its territorial claims on maritime features occupied and administered by U.S. allies Japan, South Korea, and the Philippines—what Michael E. O'Hanlon has referred to as "the Senkaku paradox" of striving to avoid "great power war over small stakes."[41] This has been achieved in the past at some cost to U.S. credibility, as China has used such deconfliction efforts in an attempt to position U.S. allies as "troublemakers" and the United States as a mediator working essentially toward the goal of legitimating China's claims. While the United States has not faced this challenge over Ieodo (a feature occupied by South Korea in the East China Sea that China claims as Suyanjiao), it did weigh in during the 2010 and 2012 Senkaku crises, encouraging Tokyo to resolve disputes quickly and in ways that Beijing saw as helpful to its efforts to paint Japan as having acted provocatively, even as Tokyo exercised restraint and Washington urged de-escalation on all sides. The most concerning instance of such "cooperation" having failed to achieve its objective was the 2012 effort by the United States to broker a mutual withdrawal of naval and maritime law enforcement forces around the Scarborough Shoal, having believed that both Beijing and Manila would pull out only to find that China refused to leave

TABLE 4.1

Interest in Cooperation on Strengthening Regional Alliance Architectures

Space for Cooperation	China	Russia
Stakes	High	Medium
Rhetorical alignment	Low	Low
Demonstrated willingness to commit resources	Low	Low

[41] Michael E. O'Hanlon, *The Senkaku Paradox: Risking Great Power Wear over Small Stakes*, Washington, D.C.: Brookings Institution, 2019.

even after Filipino forces pulled back.[42] In light of such past experiences, in which China appears to many U.S. national security observers to have broken its word, efforts to cooperate by pursuing confidence-building measures, de-escalation practices, and crisis management have lost a great deal of their credibility and value.

One possible option for the United States would be to encourage U.S. allies to expand existing dialogue mechanisms focused on risk reduction and crisis communications to help avoid the problem of miscommunication, misperception, and accidental or unintentional conflict with the PLA or Russian military forces. Japan, South Korea, and the Philippines (as part of ASEAN) already have hotlines connecting them with the PLA or PRC Foreign Ministry; these should perhaps be bolstered by efforts by the United States to encourage China to extend its coast guard and air annex deconfliction mechanisms to include U.S. allies.[43]

Across the five U.S. allies surveyed here, only Japan and South Korea feel any direct threat from Russia, with Japan by far the more concerned of the two, given the persistence of the dispute over the Northern Territories or Kuril Islands. By contrast, five of the six feel at least some degree of anxiety over the growth of Chinese military power and assertiveness, with Thailand expressing the least concern. While no country in the Indo-Pacific wants to be forced to choose between the United States and China, many have also expressed concern at the notion of Washington and Beijing reaching some sort of modus vivendi at their expense— whether such an agreement goes by the name of a Group of Two, as put forward by former U.S. National Security Advisor Zbigniew Brzezinski, or a "New Type of Great Power Relations," as advanced by China.[44] Such concerns are most prominent in Japanese policymaking but have also appeared from time to time in Korean and Filipino circles. With the growth of U.S.-China tensions in recent years, such worries have fallen aside, even as concerns about U.S. inattention or even abandonment have risen alongside China's continued growth in power. By contrast, U.S. allies evince little to no concern about a U.S.-Russia condominium that might cut deals at their expense. And U.S. allies with few or no major security concerns under threat from China—most notably Thailand but also to some extent Australia (where the threat has largely been one of political subversion and infiltration, with some growing concern about China's power projection capabilities from its South China Sea facilities)— don't particularly worry about U.S.-China security cooperation. Indeed, were U.S. security cooperation with China and/or Russia pursued in such a way as to enhance regional stability

---

[42] Michael Green, Kathleen Hicks, Zack Cooper, John Schaus, and Jake Douglas, *Counter-Coercion Series: Scarborough Shoal Standoff*, Washington, D.C.: Center for Strategic and International Studies, 2017.

[43] Harold, 2019c; Tetsuo Kotani, "Crisis Management in the East China Sea," Stockholm International Peace Research Institute, February 2015; Ankit Panda, "China, South Korea Establish Military Hotline," *The Diplomat*, July 25, 2014; and "China, Southeast Asia to Set Up Hotline for South China Sea Issues," Reuters, July 31, 2015.

[44] Zbigniew Brzezinski, "The Group of Two That Could Change the World," *Financial Times*, January 13, 2009.

without trading this against allies' own equities, most governments in the Indo-Pacific would be in favor of it.

Looking again at the obstacles the three sides face to cooperation on promoting and preserving regional alliance architecture, these can be broken down as trust, audience costs, definitional issues, immediacy problems, and issue linkages. (Third-party problems, legal constraints, and capacity or capability issues do not appear to pose substantial obstacles to cooperation on regional alliance architecture and so are not discussed here.)

Trust. Washington and Beijing harbor deep skepticism about each other's intentions toward the United States' regional alliances. Beijing believes the alliances are intended to contain China's rise, while many in Washington believe Beijing is actively undermining U.S. alliances as a strategy to achieve regional, and potentially future global, hegemony. Moreover, Beijing is constantly working to undermine U.S. alliances.

Similarly, neither the United States nor Russia appear to trust the other country's intentions and engagement with U.S. alliance states in the region. While these assessments may be correct and the three countries' mistrust may be correctly premised on diverging and even conflicting interests, at least some observers have argued that these views reflect misperceptions and worst-casing characteristic of the "security dilemma."[45] Absent a mutual understanding of shared or overlapping goals and willingness to compromise by either country, there will remain obstacles to a productive U.S.-Russia cooperation in this sphere.

Audience costs. For China, memories of Japanese atrocities in World War II and decades of CCP patriotic education about the continued threat of latent Japanese militarism mean that any acceptance by the Chinese leadership of Japan's transition toward becoming a "normal" country with a greater security (military) role in the region would very likely be met with opposition by the Chinese public and Chinese military.

Definitional problem. Dueling views about the inherent value and purpose of alliances as a political construct between Beijing and Washington make it difficult to engage on the issue with a shared conceptual framework.

Immediacy problem. Promoting and preserving the regional alliance architecture—one that is seen by Russia as built toward ensuring the preeminence of U.S. interests—is not an issue of immediate concern, and thus is unlikely to motivate viable U.S.-Russian cooperation.

Issue linkage. For China, the issue of regional alliances is tied closely with its fundamental interests of enforcing its territorial claims—the Diaoyu/Senkakus with Japan and Scarborough Shoal with the Philippines, for example—making it difficult to cooperate. Moscow's skepticism and unwillingness to cooperate with the United States in preserving the regional alliance architecture is linked to its broader strategic ambitions. Therefore, U.S.-Russia cooperation on this front is unlikely to yield substantial benefits.

---

[45] Liberthal and Wang, 2012; John J. Mearshimer, *The Tragedy of Great Power Politics*, 2nd ed., New York: W.W. Norton & Co., 2014; Lyle J. Goldstein, *Meeting China Halfway: How to Defuse the Emerging U.S.-China Rivalry*, Washington, D.C.: Georgetown University Press, 2015; Graham Allison, *Destined for War: Can America and China Escape Thucydides' Trap?* New York: Houghton Mifflin Harcourt, 2017.

Second-Order Effects of Cooperation

Cooperation with China on reducing the threat the PRC poses to U.S. allies in the Indo-Pacific at present appears challenging, given Beijing's hostility to the U.S. alliance system. Similarly, cooperating with Russia to reduce the prospect of unintentional conflict with U.S. allies in the region may prove difficult in any prospective future. Nonetheless, if the United States were to elicit an agreement from Beijing to extend the risk reduction and crisis communication mechanisms it has established with the United States to include Australia, Japan, South Korea, or the Philippines (the four U.S. allies most exposed to PRC coercion at present), it is unclear that it would carry much in the way of implications for competition or cooperation with Russia.

Conclusion

Probably none of the seven U.S. policy goals defined in this report are as difficult to cooperate on, or require as much in the way of competition, as strengthening and defending U.S. alliances in the Indo-Pacific, with the exception of ensuring the peaceful resolution of cross-Strait differences between China and Taiwan (Chapter Six). Both China and Russia tend to regard the U.S. alliance system as the key obstacle to the realization of their ambitions to exercise greater influence in the Indo-Pacific. Nonetheless, the United States may be able to encourage the PRC and Russian Federation, as well as U.S. allies and partners, to establish or expand dialogue mechanisms, risk reduction agreements, and crisis communication channels with the goal of avoiding unintentional conflicts. While U.S. policy should certainly seek ways to alleviate pressure and threats from PRC and Russian foreign policy initiatives and military actions, it is unlikely that any policy steps Washington or its allies could advance would go so far as to substantially transform the views of elites in Beijing or Moscow on this issue. Thus, the balance between competition and cooperation on the goal of strengthening and defending U.S. alliances in the region is heavily tilted in favor of improving U.S. ability to compete.

CHAPTER FIVE

Expanding Strategic Cooperation with Indonesia, Malaysia, and Vietnam

To achieve the goal of a free and open Indo-Pacific, the United States has sought to strengthen and leverage its alliances. These key relationships are certainly critical to any prospect of working with regional nations to help ensure that the Indo-Pacific remains free from coercion or even hegemonic dominance by revisionist actors such as China and Russia. Bolstering the region's ability to resist such coercion, however, requires continually expanding cooperation with powerful local actors so as to gain additional support for this goal. For this reason, a third goal of U.S. policy in the Indo-Pacific has been to expand defense cooperation and partnerships with additional Indo-Pacific nations, such as Indonesia, Malaysia, and Vietnam.

For the United States to do so, it will need to find ways to cooperate more fulsomely with these non-allies even as they continue to maintain long-standing defense ties with Russia. A key issue for U.S. policymakers to consider as they look to deepen engagement with Jakarta, Kuala Lumpur, and Hanoi is whether to compete with Russia in the defense space (and more generally)—and, if so, to what extent—since one possible consequence of U.S.-Russia competition might be to push Russia and China more closely together. Another (and possibly more consequential) consideration is whether the application of the Countering America's Adversaries through Sanctions (CAATSA) sanctions might severely degrade progress in U.S. efforts to cooperate with these three countries.

Understanding the Equities

The United States, China, and Russia each take a differing position on issues related to Indo-Pacific security and the roles of Indonesia, Malaysia, and Vietnam, as well as the defense and security cooperation ties the United States has with these actors.

U.S. Equities

The United States has a deep relationship with Indonesia dating to 1949 and spanning cooperation across diplomatic, economic, and defense affairs.[1] In recognition of the growing confluence of interests between Washington and Jakarta, in 2010 the two sides agreed to establish a "comprehensive partnership,"[2] and in 2015 they agreed to upgrade this to a "strategic partnership."[3] Much of the U.S. interest in security cooperation with Indonesia over the past two decades has centered on intelligence and counterterrorism, especially since the Bali bombings of 2002 and 2005 and the J.W. Marriott bombing of 2003. In the defense realm, U.S. contacts with Indonesia have often centered on professional military educational exchanges, many of them conducted through the International Military Education and Training (IMET) program. In the wake of the Dili Massacre in East Timor in 1991, Indonesia's participation in IMET was suspended by the U.S. side from 1992 to 2005 but was restored thereafter as the two sides shifted their focus to counterterrorism.[4]

Since coming to power in 2014, President Joko Widodo has focused on Indonesia as a "Global Maritime Fulcrum," a policy that, though not heavily focused on the country's navy, has nonetheless sought to bolster Indonesia's maritime law enforcement capabilities.[5] This has increasingly led Jakarta to focus on Chinese poachers and the China Coast Guard's support for their illegal activities, most notably around the Natunas.[6] As tensions over the waters around the Natunas have risen, Indonesia has been forced to deploy more naval vessels and intelligence, surveillance, and reconnaissance (ISR) assets to monitor and respond to Chinese poachers and harassment from Chinese state actors.[7] Against this backdrop of rising tensions, the opportunity for U.S.-Indonesia cooperation to push back on China's assertive behavior and efforts to establish control over the South China Sea has been growing. As a consequence, U.S. defense engagements with Indonesia have increasingly focused on exchanges and assistance, including

---

[1]   U.S. Department of State, Bureau of East Asian and Pacific Affairs, "Bilateral Relations Fact Sheet: U.S. Relations with Indonesia," January 21, 2020a.

[2]   The White House, Office of the Press Secretary, "The U.S.-Indonesia Comprehensive Partnership," June 27, 2010.

[3]   Barack Obama and Joko Widodo, "Joint Statement by the United States of America and the Republic of Indonesia," October 26, 2015.

[4]   Frega Wenas Inkiriwang, "The Dynamic of US-Indonesia Defense Relations: The 'IMET Ban' Period," *Australian Journal of International Affairs*, Vol. 74, No. 4, 2020.

[5]   Lyle J. Morris and Giacomo Persi Paoli, *A Preliminary Assessment of Indonesia's Maritime Security Threats and Capabilities*, Santa Monica, Calif.: RAND Corporation, RR-2469-RC, 2018.

[6]   Hannah Beech and Mukita Suhartono, "China Chases Indonesia's Fishing Fleets, Staking Claim to Sea's Riches," *New York Times*, March 31, 2020.

[7]   Kiki Siregar, "Indonesia Deploys 4 Additional Warships to Natuna Amid Standoff with Chinese Vessels," *Channel News Asia*, January 6, 2020.

- maintaining robust security assistance programs funded at over $10 million per year in the mid-2010s
- increasing Indonesia's patrol capacity, ISR integration, and maintenance capacity to enhance the Indonesian government's ability to protect its maritime areas, safeguard its natural resources, and contribute to regional security and stability
- supporting the Indonesian Coast Guard's organizational development, focusing on human resource capacity, technical skills, and educational partnerships.[8]

Building on the partial lifting in 2010 of a set of restrictions on engagement with the Indonesian Special Forces in place since 1999 as a result of human rights abuses by that service in East Timor, in 2019 the United States announced its intent to remove the last constraints on contacts with that service. Additionally, Washington has moved to transfer defense hardware to Indonesia in the form of eight ScanEagle ISR drones relevant for maintaining maritime domain awareness over Indonesia's massive territorial sprawl.[9]

With respect to ties with Malaysia, U.S. relations are long-standing and diverse, dating to Malaysia's independence from the British Empire and establishment as a separate country in 1957. Today, Washington and Kuala Lumpur cooperate closely on a variety of security dimensions, including "counterterrorism, maritime domain awareness, and regional stability, and participate frequently in bilateral and multilateral training, exercises, and visits. . . . Security cooperation and training builds capabilities among Malaysia's armed forces and coast guard, allowing it to take on an expanded international role including peacekeeping operations."[10] In particular, U.S. efforts to support Malaysia have included the provision of intelligence information about the activities of Chinese fishing, maritime law enforcement, and naval vessels operating in Malaysian waters, especially near James Shoal and South Luconia Shoals, as well as coast guard capabilities.[11] And following the April 2018 elections that toppled the Najib administration, the United States has sought to expand military cooperation, with then–Assistant Secretary of Defense for Indo-Pacific Security Affairs Randall Schriver visiting Kuala Lumpur in August 2018 to discuss training and exercises, capacity building, and Malaysia's participation in the Maritime Security Initiative and Foreign Military Financing programs.[12] U.S. efforts to bolster Kuala Lumpur's situational awareness of and ability to

---

[8] Lightly edited for readability from U.S. Embassy Indonesia, "Fact Sheet: U.S. Building Maritime Capacity in Southeast Asia," undated.

[9] Prashanth Parameswaran, "US Southeast Asia Maritime Security Assistance in the Headlines with New Drones," *The Diplomat*, June 4, 2019.

[10] U.S. Department of State, Bureau of East Asian and Pacific Affairs, "Bilateral Relations Fact Sheet: U.S. Relations with Malaysia," January 21, 2020b.

[11] Joseph Sipalan, "As Beijing Flexes Muscles in South China Sea, Malaysia Eyes Harder Response," Reuters, May 31, 2016.

[12] Dzirhan Mahadzir, "Pentagon Asia Policy Chief Talks South East Asia Military Cooperation, U.S. South China Sea Operations," *USNI News*, August 15, 2018.

respond to China's maritime gray-zone coercion around the disputed Spratly Islands form a core area for prospective U.S.-Malaysia cooperation to counter China.

In many ways, the equities at stake in the U.S.-Vietnam bilateral relationship are the most complex of any country in the region. After having supported the French attempt to salvage its imperial holdings in Indo-China following World War II, the United States then sought to support and defend its ally the Republic of Vietnam from subversion and insurgency in the form of the Viet Cong, and later from invasion by the uniformed forces of North Vietnam. Following the withdrawal of U.S. forces and the collapse of South Vietnam, the country was unified in April 1975, though the United States did not recognize or seek to establish diplomatic ties with the new Socialist Republic of Vietnam. In 1978, following border clashes and massive refugee flows stemming from the Pol Pot regime's genocide in neighboring Cambodia (then called Democratic Kampuchea), Vietnam invaded and toppled the Khmer Rouge regime in Phnom Penh. China, which had been allied with the Khmer Rouge, interpreted this as a Soviet-backed move to further undermine PRC influence in Southeast Asia, and in turn invaded Vietnam just days after China normalized diplomatic ties with the United States, a military action that the Vietnamese defeated relatively easily.

In the early 1990s, Washington and Hanoi began to explore opportunities for nascent contacts and normalization, first over issues of prisoners of war and military personnel deemed missing in action, and later with trade and investment contacts, with formal diplomatic relations established in 1995.

In 2013, the two sides announced the U.S.-Vietnam Comprehensive Partnership, an overarching framework for advancing the bilateral relationship, followed up in 2015 by a bilateral Joint Vision Statement.[13] By 2016, the Obama administration had lifted the ban on sales of defense equipment to Vietnam, which was also deemed eligible for the administration's efforts to bolster regional partners' capabilities via the Maritime Security Initiative.[14] In 2017, with the goal of preventing Chinese dominance over the South China Sea and intimidation of regional counter-claimants to the land features and maritime spaces in that area, the United States transferred six patrol boats and a coast guard cutter to Vietnam, with Trump encouraging Vietnamese officials to purchase American missiles during his November visit to Hanoi.[15] In March 2018, a U.S. aircraft carrier visited Cam Ranh Bay for the first time since the end of the Vietnam War, and in the same month the United States transferred six additional patrol boats to Vietnam.[16] The following February, during his visit to Hanoi for a

---

[13] U.S. Department of State, Bureau of East Asian and Pacific Affairs, "Bilateral Relations Fact Sheet: U.S. Relations with Vietnam," January 21, 2020c.

[14] Scott W. Harold, "Why Has Obama Lifted the Arms Embargo on Vietnam?" *Newsweek*, May 25, 2016.

[15] Donald J. Trump, "Remarks by President Trump Before Bilateral Meeting with Prime Minister Phuc of Vietnam, Hanoi, Vietnam, November 12, 2017b.

[16] Hannah Beech, "U.S. Aircraft Carrier Arrives in Vietnam, with a Message for China," *New York Times*, March 4, 2018; James Pearson, "U.S. Delivers More Patrol Boats to Vietnam amid Deepening Security Ties," Reuters, March 29, 2018.

summit with North Korean leader Kim Jong Un, Trump again urged Vietnamese officials to purchase U.S. weapon systems, and in November 2019 DoD committed to transfer another coast guard cutter to help push back against Chinese efforts to dominate the South China Sea.[17]

All in all, U.S. interests in ties with the three countries largely center around supporting their independence, autonomy, and ability to resist coercion while ensuring that the region's security environment develops in a direction supportive of the vision of a free and open Indo-Pacific outlined in Chapter Three and supported by the U.S. alliances and partnerships discussed in Chapter Four.

Chinese Equities

China's desire to become the dominant power in Asia means that it opposes any regional security and political relationships that could pose a challenge to this vision, especially those with the existing dominant power—the United States. In principle, China professes no objections to countries cooperating with the United States; in practice, it has tended to criticize such cooperation as being driven by ulterior motives, including to stir up trouble and contain China. Beijing's stakes in this issue are of medium importance: It has never indicated a willingness to negotiate with the United States over it, and it has dedicated no resources to the issue.

Historically, China's "periphery diplomacy" has oscillated between emphasizing making gains in its territorial claims to the detriment of its regional relationships and improving those ties through closer economic integration.[18] Under Xi, Beijing has increasingly prioritized its territorial claims, with the apparent belief that existing economic ties regional countries— and military power—are sufficient to outweigh their concerns over the deteriorating security situation.[19] In a 2013 meeting on periphery diplomacy that set Chinese policies for the next ten years, Xi reflected these dueling goals and the desire to increase China's regional influence, stating that the PRC

> needs to protect and make the best use of the strategic opportunities to safeguard China's national sovereignty, security and development interests. China needs to develop closer ties with neighboring countries, with more friendly political relations, stronger economic

---

[17] James Pearson and Jeff Mason, "Trump Pitches U.S. Arms Exports in Meeting with Vietnam," Reuters, February 27, 2019; Wyatt Olson, "U.S. to Give Vietnam Another Coast Guard Cutter Amid Rising Tensions in the South China Sea," *Stars and Stripes*, November 20, 2019.

[18] For a review of U.S.-China-Southeast (ASEAN) relations over 2010–2013, see Bonnie Glaser, "Understanding the evolution of US–China–ASEAN relations: a US perspective," in C. J. Jenner, Tran Truong Thu, eds., *The South China Sea: A Crucible of Regional Cooperation or Conflict-Making Sovereignty Claims?* Cambridge, UK: Cambridge University Press, 2016.

[19] Jacob Stokes, *China's Periphery Diplomacy: Implications for Peace and Security in Asia*, Washington, D.C.: United States Institute of Peace, May 2020.

bonds, deeper security cooperation and closer people-to-people contacts. . . . China needs to make neighboring countries more friendly, stay closer to China, more recognizing and more supportive, and increase China's affinity, magnetism and influence."[20]

As one Western expert summarized, Xi called for China to accomplish this through efforts to "1) enhance political good will; 2) deepen regional economic integration; 3) increase China's cultural influence; and 4) improve regional security cooperation."[21]

China's interests in its periphery reflect many of the CCP's key priorities. At a high level, Beijing wants a stable and prosperous region that accedes to Chinese policy preferences. From perspective of regime security and domestic stability, China's neighboring countries have many overlapping communities with China that could undermine CCP control, whether by passing undesirable information into China or fostering independence movements, among other concerns. Maritime Southeast Asia has a large ethnic Chinese diaspora, and China's Southeast Asia land border with Myanmar has Chinese ethnic minority groups that histori-cally have spanned the border area, with the potential for conflict spillover. China has also successfully sought the extradition of Uyghurs who escaped to Cambodia and Thailand, seeking to cut off any overseas sources of succor for resistance to Chinese rule. Economically, six of China's top 21 trading partners are in Southeast Asia, accounting for roughly 20 percent of China's total trade volume.[22] Southeast Asia is also a crucial corridor for China's energy imports, again making it important to maintain—or shape—positive relations with those countries.

In practice, China opposes intraregional relationships that exclude China and new U.S. relationships in the Indo-Pacific. China's white paper on Asia-Pacific security made clear that Beijing wants to be at the center of future discussions on regional issues: "China is working to construct a community of shared future for countries along the Lancang-Mekong River and between China and the Association of Southeast Asian Nations (ASEAN) as well as in Asia and the Asia-Pacific area as a whole."[23] Beijing is concerned by Hanoi's decision to deepen defense relations with Washington, though it is reported to be relatively confident that the relationship will not progress too far.[24] During Washington's pursuit of improved relations with Myanmar, China also sought to undercut this opening, both for political and geostra-

---

[20] Ministry of Foreign Affairs of the People's Republic of China, 2013.

[21] Timothy Heath, "Diplomacy Work Forum: Xi Steps Up Efforts to Shape a China-Centered Regional Order," *China Brief*, Vol. 13, No. 22, November 7, 2013. For other analysis, see Michael Swaine, "Chinese Views and Commentary on Periphery Diplomacy," *China Leadership Monitor*, July 28, 2014; Bonnie Glaser and Deep Pal, "China's Periphery Diplomacy Initiative: Implications for China Neighbors and the United States," China-US Focus, November 7, 2013.

[22] Authors' calculation (excludes Hong Kong) using data from World Integrated Trade Solution, undated-a.

[23] State Council Information Office of the People's Republic of China, 2017.

[24] Greg Torode and Mai Nguyen, "Vietnam Seeks to Pacify China as Landmark U.S. Carrier Visit Signals Warming Ties," Reuters, March 3, 2018.

tegic concerns. According to China expert Yun Sun of the Stimson Center, "China has perceived new American interest in engaging Myanmar as a threat to their established role in the country, and has tended to view the dynamic in zero-sum, competitive terms."[25]

China has also sought to break ASEAN consensus on China, preferring to deal with ASEAN countries on a bilateral basis to maintain maximum leverage. China's attitude toward ASEAN countries was vividly illustrated by then–Foreign Minister (now director of the Office of the Central Foreign Affairs Work Commission) Yang Jiechi's reported comment to the Singaporean Foreign Minister at a 2010 ASEAN meeting: "China is a big country and other countries are small countries, and that's just a fact."[26] Four years later, the new foreign minister, Wang Yi, similarly commented on the South China Sea, "on issues of principle such as history and territory there is no room for compromise . . . we will never accept unreasonable demands from smaller countries . . . we will defend every inch of territory that belongs to us."[27] China's unwillingness to negotiate in good faith with ASEAN over the territorial dispute between Beijing and several of the organization's members is evident in its slow-rolling of the China-ASEAN South China Sea Code of Conduct, as well as its leveraging of Cambodia's veto against ASEAN's consensus-driven process in 2012.[28] China especially doesn't like the United States involving itself in China-ASEAN issues, as Wang Yi commented in 2019, "We think non-regional countries should not deliberately amplify such differences or disputes. . . . Non-regional countries should also not make use of these differences to sow distrust between China and ASEAN countries."[29]

Overall, in practice, China opposes the United States expanding its relationships in the region, including with Indonesia, Malaysia, and Vietnam.

There is no evidence the Obama or Trump administrations ever directly engaged Beijing on the issue of U.S. relations with Indonesia, Malaysia, and Vietnam.[30] At the Track 1.5 and Track 2 levels, based on available public conference reporting, there has similarly been a dearth of discussion on U.S. ties with Indonesia, Malaysia, and Vietnam. One 2017 Track 2 dialogue did reflect the Chinese side's view of U.S. ties with these new partners as a concern for containment:

---

[25] Yun Sun, *Myanmar in US-China Relations*, Washington, D.C.: Stimson Center, Issue Brief No. 3, June 2014.

[26] John Pomfret, "U.S. Takes a Tougher Tone with China," *Washington Post*, July 30, 2010.

[27] Ministry of Foreign Affairs of the People's Republic of China, "Foreign Minister Wang Yi Meets the Press," March 8, 2014b.

[28] Manuel Mogato, Michael Martina, and Ben Blanchard, "ASEAN Deadlocked on South China Sea, Cambodia Blocks Statement," Reuters, July 25, 2016.

[29] Cate Cadell, "China Warns Outsiders Not to 'Sow Distrust' in South China Sea," Reuters, July 31, 2019.

[30] For a representative sample of U.S.-China strategic dialogues under the last two administrations, see U.S. Department of State, 2016b, 2018b.

In forging defense relationships with countries around China, 'hedging China' seems to be a more important consideration than the traditional calculus of values, political systems, and human rights. For example, the United States views India and Vietnam, both of which have territorial disputes with China, as its defense partners, while Malaysia and Indonesia, which may provide support to future U.S. military presence and operations, as a new focus to expand military cooperation.[31]

Russian Equities

Expanding relations with Indonesia, Malaysia, or Vietnam is of moderate importance to Russia, with Vietnam foremost among these as a long-time partner with robust energy and military ties dating back several decades. Moscow is not aligned rhetorically with Washington on this issue, nor has it articulated interest in negotiating with the United States about pursuing relations with these states. Russia does not appear willing to expend resources to cooperate with the United States on a shared goal in this space.

Russia's 2015 National Security Strategy makes no direct mention of Moscow's position or strategy toward Indonesia, Malaysia, or Vietnam. Notably, the document fails to mention the specific Southeast Asia or Indo-Pacific region in the list of "persisting seats" of regional tensions of concern to Moscow—which include the Near and Middle East, Africa, South Asia, and the Korean Peninsula.[32] Moscow's 2016 Foreign Policy Concept briefly mentions interest in expanding its multidimensional cooperation with Indonesia and Malaysia and strengthening its comprehensive partnership with Vietnam.[33] This, when juxtaposed against the document's more extensive descriptions of Russia's policies toward other states in the Indo-Pacific region, including India, China, and the Korean Peninsula, suggests that Moscow does not have a clearly articulated strategy toward Indonesia, Malaysia, and Vietnam. However, Russia's security exchanges with these countries—however extensive or perfunctory—suggest that, at minimum, Russia derives some value in these relationships in furthering its strategic objectives vis-à-vis China's rise and what Russia considers U.S. hegemonic influence in the region.

Russia may be utilizing its security relations with Indonesia, Malaysia, and Vietnam to secure a market for its arms exports and, by extension, diversify its network of allies and partners in the region to establish a more independent, balancing position against China's influence in the region. In an already profitable market in the Asia-Pacific—which accounts

---

[31] Fu Ying and Wang Jisi, eds., *China-US Relations: Exploring a New Pathway to A Win-Win Partnership*, Beijing, China: Collective Publication, July 2017.

[32] Government of Russia, "O Strategii Nacionalnoy Bezopastnosti Rosiskli Federacii [National Security Strategy of the Russian Federation]," December 31, 2015.

[33] Ministry of Foreign Affairs of the Russian Federation, 2016b.

for roughly 70 percent of Russia's arms exports—Indonesia, Malaysia, and Vietnam are seen as key destinations for Russian weapon and military technology sales.[34]

In 2018, Russia and Indonesia upgraded their relationship to a strategic partnership, with the two countries cooperating in the trade-economic and military spaces.[35] In March 2020, Russia and Indonesia held their first-ever joint naval exercise, Orruda-2020, which has been seen by some observers as a step toward deepening their bilateral relationship and military cooperation.[36] Russia has exported armored personnel carriers, infantry fighting vehicles, assault rifles, planes, helicopters, and other military hardware and technology to Indonesia.[37] In 2019, the two countries signed a new arms deal that included Indonesia's purchase of BT-3F armored personnel carriers and BMP-3F infantry fighting vehicles.[38] Russia and Indonesia are currently negotiating the latter's purchase of Su-35 fighter jets despite U.S. pressure on Jakarta to abandon the deal.[39] Of note, however, is Indonesia's interest in also acquiring U.S. F-16 fighter jets. This may be due to delays in Russia's delivery of the aircraft, as well as Indonesia's concerns about facing sanctions for engaging in defense transactions with Russia under CAATSA.[40]

Russia-Malaysia military cooperation began in 1994, with Russia furnishing fighter jets, assault weapons, helicopters, and other air defenses to help upgrade and strengthen Malaysian armed forces. Malaysia in 2003 purchased 18 Su-30MKM fighter jets from Russia to complement its existing force of Russian MiG-29 fulcrum jets.[41] Malaysia has an outstanding requirement for another 18 fighter jets, which may include purchase of additional Su-30s.[42] Russian sales of fighter jets to Malaysia have faced some criticism, however, amid concerns from Kuala Lumpur about the inoperability and cost of maintaining these fighter jets. Malaysian Defense Minister Mohamad Sabu publicly revealed in 2018 that only four of the

---

[34] Richard Connolly and Cecilie Sendstad, "Russia's Role as an Arms Exporter: The Strategic and Economic Importance of Arms Exports for Russia," Chatham House, March 2017.

[35] "Moscow, Jakarta Embark on Strategic Partnership in their Relations, Lavrov Says," Tass, March 13, 2018.

[36] China Military Online, "First Indonesia-Russia Joint Exercise Has Profound Implications," March 24, 2020.

[37] "Russia's Arms Exports to Indonesia Top $2.5 Bln Over 25 Years," Tass, February 21, 2018.

[38] Prashanth Parameswaran, "New Arms Deals Highlight Indonesia-Russia Military Cooperation," *The Diplomat*, May 1, 2019a.

[39] DefenseWorld.net, "Indonesia, Russia Still Negotiating Su-35 Deal," March 16, 2020.

[40] Public Law 115-44, Countering America's Adversaries Through Sanctions Act (CAATSA), August 2, 2017; Mike Yeo, "Indonesia Eyes American F-16 Jets as It Moves to Secure Russian Su-35 Deal," *Defense News*, November 4, 2019.

[41] "Putin Signs Deal with Malaysia to Provide Jet Fighters—2003-08-05," *Voice of America*, October 26, 2009.

[42] Richard A. Bitzinger, *Russian Arms Transfers and Asian Military Modernisation*, S. Rajaratnam School of International Studies (RSIS), RSIS Policy Report, 2015.

country's 18 Su-30s were able to fly well, with Malaysia being unable to efficiently maintain the airworthiness of the aircraft.[43] Malaysia, however, appears to still be considering upgrading its fighter jets with Russian aircraft. In 2017, it had suspended plans to replace these jets to focus its efforts on dealing with the threat from ISIS; as of late 2019, however, it was still considering a fighter jet exchange deal with Russia to replace its outdated equipment.[44] Outside of their military technical cooperation, Russia and Malaysia maintain normal trade relations, though with neither country occupying the other's top trade partner status.[45] Critically, in March 2020, international prosecutors began the trial of the 2014 missile shootdown of Malaysia Airlines flight MH17 in eastern Ukraine, in which Russian and Ukrainian nationals were held responsible for the killing of almost 300 passengers. Given that the majority of the victims were foreigners and that the incident took place outside Malaysian territory, and perhaps in light of the strategic relations forged with Russia during his tenure, Malaysia's then–Prime Minister Mahatir Mohamad called the accusations "hearsay" and alleged that the investigations were a politically charged maneuver against Russia.[46]

Moscow's relations with Hanoi experienced a setback in the 1990s with the fall of the Soviet Union, but bilateral relations revived over the years, with particular emphasis on military cooperation. In 2018, Russia and Vietnam signed a military cooperation roadmap to highlight achievements in their military partnership and deepen their security relations.[47] Vietnam ranks as the third-largest destination for Russian weapon sales, surpassed only by India and China.[48] In the past decade, Vietnam has purchased Kilo-class Type 636 submarines and T-S90 tanks from Russia and deployed Russian shore-based Bastion missile batteries along its coastal defenses. The two countries have also explored upgrades to Vietnam's military hardware with Russian aircraft, armored vehicles, missile ships, and frigates.[49] With Russia's help, Vietnam has also built its own variant of the Zveda-Strela 3M24 Uran antiship missiles.[50] The Russian armed forces have also provided training to Vietnamese military personnel. Further underscoring Russia-Vietnam military ties is Hanoi's flexible application of its "Three Nos" policy—specifically, no foreign bases in Vietnamese territory—in allowing

---

[43] Prashanth Parameswaran, "Fighter Jet Challenge Spotlights Russia-Malaysia Defense Relations," *The Diplomat,* August 2, 2018.

[44] Joseph Sipalan, "Exclusive: Malaysia Shelves Plan to Buy New Fighter Jets—Defense Source," Reuters, July 13, 2017; Jon Grevatt, "Malaysia Considers 'Fighter Exchange' Offer From Russia," *Jane's,* November 28, 2019.

[45] World Integrated Trade Solution "Trade Summary for Malaysia, 2018," 2018.

[46] Nile Bowie, "Is Malaysia's Position on MH17 Tragedy Shifting?" *Asia Times,* March 9, 2020.

[47] "Russia, Vietnam Ink Military Cooperation Roadmap Until 2020," Tass, April 4, 2018.

[48] Connolly and Sendstad, 2017; Daniel Brown, "The Top 10 Countries That Bought Russia's Most Powerful Weapons in 2017," *Business Insider,* October 6, 2018.

[49] "Russia Offers Most Advanced Types of Military Hardware to Vietnam," Tass, October 4, 2019.

[50] Heydarian, 2019; Anton Tsvetov, "Can US-Vietnam Reconciliation Hurt Russia's Ties With Hanoi?" Russian International Affairs Council, May 27, 2016.

Russia to access its naval base in Cam Ranh Bay since 1978. Russia withdrew from the base in 2002 when Vietnam demanded an annual rent for continued use of the space. In recent years, however, Russia has been refueling its military aircraft from Cam Ranh Bay and training Vietnamese naval personnel on Kilo-class submarine operations and maintenance.[51] When this was discovered, Washington demarched Moscow, and the latter ceased its activities in Cam Ranh Bay, but in 2016 Russia indicated it may reconsider its departure from Vietnam's naval facilities.

Critically, however, the limits of Russia-Vietnam cooperation are manifest in Moscow's unwillingness to choose sides in any territorial disputes between Vietnam and China. While Russia has not expressed clear support for China's Nine-Dash Line claim, it has also consciously avoided taking Vietnam's side or offering to mediate.[52] Moscow insists that non-claimant countries should refrain from getting involved in the dispute—any attempt to portray the conflict as a global problem, it says, is a cynical misrepresentation intended to justify U.S. power grabs.[53] To the United States, this should also send a clear message that Russia is unlikely to be swayed to cooperate with the United States in its effort to strengthen partnerships with Indo-Pacific states. The Russian government refuses to choose sides in any China-related territorial dispute, but Russian-owned corporations are cooperating with Vietnamese companies on resource extraction within the hotly contested Nine-Dash Line space between China and Vietnam, which suggests that Russia may be willing to pursue its own economic interests at a modest price on its relations with China.[54]

As the United States and China compete for influence in the Indo-Pacific, states essentially caught in the middle between the two powers and forced to choose sides may increasingly find utility in Russia's participation and presence in the region. And as Russia seeks to emerge from the shadow of playing "second fiddle" to China into a more independent role,[55] engaging with Indo-Pacific partners through military and security cooperation—which can be considered Russia's strong suit in the region—would seem mutually convenient for Russia and its security partners in Indonesia, Malaysia, and Vietnam. At the same time, dealing with Russia as an effective counterweight to China comes with costs, and thus states may not be readily willing to engage with Russia at a deeper level. For one, the probability of China's economic and military backlash is still a valid concern. Many countries in the Indo-Pacific,

---

[51] Carl Thayer, "Vietnam's Cam Ranh Bay Caught in US-Russia Crossfire," *The Diplomat*, March 13, 2015; "U.S. Asks Vietnam to Stop Russian Use of Cam Ranh Bay," *Voice of America*, March 13, 2015.

[52] Nicholas Trickett, "Working with Vietnam, Russia's Rosneft Draws China's Ire," *The Diplomat*, March 19, 2018; Bennett Murray, "Vietnam's Strange Ally in Its Fight with China," *Foreign Policy*, August 1, 2019b; Bennett Murray, *Russia's Awkward Dance with Vietnam,* Philadelphia, Pa.: Foreign Policy Research Institute, 2019a.

[53] Murray, 2019b.

[54] Murray, 2019b.

[55] Alexander Gabuev, "Bad Cop, Mediator, or Spoiler: Russia's Role on the Korean Peninsula," Carnegie Moscow Center, April 24, 2019.

including Indonesia, Malaysia, and Vietnam, are also involved in economic relations with China and have some stakes in its Belt and Road Initiative. Given China's penchant for economic pressure as a way to force countries to conform with its strategic interests, smaller, less powerful countries whose survival depends significantly on these initiatives may be more sensitive to China's economic and political pressures. In addition, Russia-China ties are no secret, and countries are cognizant of Russia's reputation as one of China's closest partners. Therefore, Indo-Pacific states may harbor suspicions toward Russia's intentions and thus be willing to engage with Russia only to an extent. Finally, those states intent on pursuing greater military and arms cooperation with Russia may be subject to U.S. sanctions under CAATSA, which is intended to dissuade countries not only from purchasing military equipment and hardware from Russia but also deepening their broader relations with Moscow. The effectiveness of these sanctions, however, has been debated by policy analysts who have cautioned that U.S. efforts to curtail nefarious Russian activities in cyberspace and beyond may result in the United States harming its prospects of cultivating deeper ties with Indonesia and Vietnam and, relatedly, fuel anti-U.S. sentiment in these countries.[56] In the worst case, CAATSA sanctions could even drive countries closer to Russia.[57]

The window for U.S.-Russia cooperation on engagement with Indo-Pacific partners in Indonesia, Malaysia, and Vietnam, therefore, seems quite small at best. Russia's security cooperation and engagement with these countries is driven primarily by Russian desires to expand its geographic scale of influence, which are aimed at undermining U.S. strategic goals in the region and beyond. Russia's position of neutrality in territorial disputes between China and Indo-Pacific countries places limitations on prospects for any meaningful U.S.-Russia cooperation to enhance relations with U.S. partners in Indonesia, Malaysia, and Vietnam.

Space for Cooperation

As the discussion of equities in the U.S. relationships with Indonesia, Malaysia, and Vietnam makes clear, Washington's primary goals in seeking to broaden and deepen ties with these partners is to strengthen their air and especially maritime domain awareness and ability to police and defend their own waters and air spaces so as to prevent China from privatizing the South China Sea. Such a goal is not one on which Chinese cooperation can be elicited; competition is unavoidable. With respect to Russia, by contrast, the goals are not funda-

---

[56] Caroline Houck, "A Law Meant to Punish America's Foes Is Hurting Its Partners: Mattis," DefenseOne, April 26, 2018.

[57] DefenseWorld.net, "US to Exempt India, Indonesia, and Vietnam from CAATSA Sanctions," July 24, 2018; Donald Greenlees, "Russia Sanctions Putting Strains on U.S. Relationship with Indonesia," Australian Strategic Policy Institute, June 17, 2019; Stratfor, "With CAATSA, the U.S. Is Trying to Make Russia Hurt," May 28, 2018.

mentally misaligned;[58] rather, it is the ways to reach those goals that are misaligned, since the efforts the United States has made to strengthen regional partners' military capabilities largely involve selling arms that Russia would prefer Indonesia and/or Vietnam buy from Russia. For this reason, some observers suggest seeking cooperation with Russia by waiving the application of CAATSA sanctions on Russian arms sales to Indonesia, Malaysia, and/or Vietnam. Such a step may merit further consideration, but it is unclear that a U.S.-Russia agreement over Moscow's expanding security cooperation with Jakarta, Kuala Lumpur, or Hanoi, would prove to be of much value for Washington's ongoing strategic competition with Beijing. This is due to divergent U.S.-Russian interests in the region, as well as to the lack of trust between Washington and Moscow to establish a foundation for sustainable and productive cooperation in this space. Table 5.1 captures these insights into Chinese and Russian views of the merits of deepening U.S. ties with key regional partner nations.

An additional important point worth noting is that, to date, China and Russia have managed to deepen their strategic cooperation despite the latter's continuing to sell arms to India, Indonesia, and Vietnam—for whom the most likely target of said arms is China. In the short run, allowing Russia's arms sales to proceed in these countries may reduce China's economic, political, and military coercive leverage in the region, as these states seek to arm themselves primarily against China's aggression. If the United States were to waive CAATSA, it is probably more likely to achieve gains (or at least avoid losses) in its relationships with Indonesia, Malaysia, and/or Vietnam than in its ties with Russia or its competition with China. This difference with China over ends and Russia over ways is sometimes taken to imply that perhaps the United States might be able to work with Russia to bolster Indonesia and/or Vietnam against China, but again, to date, no compelling evidence has emerged that Beijing is willing to break with Moscow over the latter's arms sales, nor is it likely that the differences in China's and Russia's positions over U.S. relations with Indonesia, Malaysia, and Vietnam could ever overshadow the broader consensus that Russia and China share on their joint opposition to the U.S.-centric liberal international order.

TABLE 5.1

Interest in Cooperation on Expanding Relationships with Indo-Pacific Nations

Space for Cooperation	China	Russia
Stakes	Medium	Low
Rhetorical alignment	Low	Medium
Demonstrated willingness to commit resources	Low	Low

---

[58] As described above, Russia does not harbor enormous concern about the closure of the South China Sea by China, and it is not seeking to dominate that space itself, nor is it in any meaningful way particularly in favor of Chinese control over those waters.

China regards U.S. efforts to deepen defense ties as largely or even wholly oriented toward constraining its power, contesting its maritime claims, and containing its ambitions to restore China to a position of regional hegemony. For Russia, the issue is less one of broad goals, since Moscow does not aspire to dominate Southeast Asia; instead, Russian concerns center more on broad-gauge opposition to the U.S.-centric order generally, plus more specific concerns about U.S. competition in arms sales markets in Indonesia and Vietnam. (Malaysia has fielded only a limited number of Russian fighter jets; it has also reportedly expressed interest in the Chinese JF-17 and has announced plans to procure a Chinese-made Littoral Mission Ship.) These serve to constrain or complicate any efforts toward cooperation, since the goals and ways are essentially completely misaligned, despite some rhetorical positions by Beijing and Moscow intended to blur or disguise these disagreements.

Looking at the obstacles the United States faces to cooperating with either China or Russia on deepening strategic cooperation with Indonesia, Malaysia, and Vietnam, these include trust, audience costs, third-party problems, and legal constraints. By contrast, definitional problems, immediacy, issue linkages, and capacity or capability issues do not appear as substantial obstacles to cooperation on improving ties with regional partners, and so we do not discuss them further here.

Trust. China views U.S. efforts to improve ties with regional countries—especially defense ties with its neighbor, Vietnam—as part of Washington's larger containment effort. For Russia, neither the United States nor Russia trust the other country's intentions in dealing with Indonesia, Malaysia, and Vietnam. This mutual skepticism will likely pose challenges to constructive U.S.-Russia cooperation in strengthening a mutually beneficial security cooperation with these states.

Audience costs. Chinese elites could well take issue with expanded U.S.-Russia cooperation on Vietnam if Xi tolerates it. Despite elevating ties with Russia to a "comprehensive strategic partnership of coordination for a new era" in June 2019, the fact that Russia still sells weapons to Vietnam and other rival claimants to China (such as India) is seen as unhelpful in Beijing national security policymaking circles.[59] For example, the United States' waiving of CAATSA sanctions on Russia for arms sales—and Russia's decision to follow through on future sales—would likely be met with displeasure in China. However, China has so far accepted such sales and is unlikely to change this anytime soon.

Third-party problems. U.S.-Russia cooperation on expanding security relationships with Indonesia, Malaysia, and Vietnam carries the risk of Chinese retaliation against these countries, or even against Russia. The undesirability of coping with the scale and intensity of China's backlash may hinder any efforts at productive U.S.-Russia cooperation.

Legal constraints. U.S.-Russia cooperation on Indonesia, Malaysia, and Vietnam faces legal constraints under CAATSA, as it aims to penalize and discourage countries from engaging in arms purchase transactions with Russia.

---

[59] "China, Russia Agree to Upgrade Relations for New Era," Xinhua, June 6, 2019.

Second-Order Effects of Cooperation

Insofar as competition with China forms one of the core motivations for the United States to seek closer security relations with Indonesia, Malaysia, or Vietnam, it may be worth exploring how Russia would respond to a waiver of CAATSA sanctions. It would also be important to gauge what reaction (if any) China might take in response to such a step; it is possible that China might simply place a substantial order of its own for Russian military hardware, and in so doing cancel any hoped-for improvements in U.S.-Russian ties (even if doing so would not necessarily offset the gains Indonesia, Malaysia, or Vietnam would see from additional hardware). At the same time, U.S. efforts to compete with Russia by selling arms to Southeast Asian nations, if successful in displacing Russia from these markets, might make Russia's defense industry more vulnerable and in need of arms sales, and hence a more pliable target for PRC pressure to transfer the few remaining capabilities that the PLA's own defense industrial firms cannot produce indigenously. What is less clear is whether or not, assuming continued growth in PRC power and assertiveness, Indonesia, Malaysia, and/or Vietnam might be able to credibly message Russia about the importance of working together to constrain China in ways that the United States struggles to do effectively. At any event, at present, the threat that Moscow and Beijing perceive from Washington appears to overwhelm any possible incentives that might lead to a split in their relations.

Conclusion

As the foregoing analysis suggests, neither China nor Russia are likely to be interested in cooperating with the United States to help strengthen cooperation with Indonesia, Malaysia, or Vietnam—China because doing so would affect its ultimate ability to achieve the goal of claiming all the air and maritime space within their self-proclaimed Nine Dash Line, and Russia because it seeks to contest the U.S. role in the world and needs to retain a lead in certain arms markets to sustain its defense industrial base. China and Russia both sell arms and engage in defense cooperation with these three countries on some level, but this is usually to woo their militaries, reduce their willingness to balance against China (in the case of Beijing), or simply achieve commercial gains (for Moscow). Neither China nor Russia evinces any interest in helping encourage these countries to further consolidate their democracies (in the cases of Indonesia and Malaysia) or to transition away from communism (in the case of Vietnam), nor do they seek to bolster their ability to deter or defeat external aggression or coercion such as China employs.

CHAPTER SIX

Managing Cross-Strait Differences Between China and Taiwan

The Republic of China was founded in 1912 at the fall of the Great Qing Manchu Empire and was first led, at least nominally, by the Kuomintang (KMT), or Nationalist Party.

Initially disinclined to commit resources to trying to preserve the KMT regime after its flight from China to Taiwan in 1949, the Truman administration ultimately changed its mind and intervened to preserve Taiwan independence in the wake of the North Korean invasion of South Korea on June 25, 1950.[1] From 1954 to 1979, the United States and the Republic of China were treaty-bound allies, with Washington stationing military forces in Taiwan and helping the Republic of China fight off communist aggression aimed at seizing offshore islands in both 1954 and 1958.

With the establishment of formal U.S. relations with the PRC in 1979, Beijing made it clear that it expected Washington to ultimately wind down its ties with and commitment to Taipei; Washington, by contrast, made clear that its policy of engagement with the PRC and its management of its continuing ties to Taiwan were premised on an assumption that Beijing would resolve its differences with Taipei peacefully. This history and the differences in the two powers' central assumptions constitute the relevant backdrop to the United States' goal of ensuring that the key issues in the cross-Strait relationship are resolved peacefully and free from coercion.

Understanding the Equities

The policy goals that the three sides have at stake in this issue are stark for the United States and China and virtually nonexistent for Russia.

---

[1] David M. Finkelstein, *Washington's Taiwan Dilemma, 1949–1950: From Abandonment to Salvation,* Annapolis, Md.: Naval Institute Press, 1993.

U.S. Equities

Since the cessation of formal diplomatic recognition and the termination of the Mutual Defense Treaty upon the establishment of ties with the PRC in 1979, the United States has not maintained a formal security commitment to Taiwan. Successive U.S. administrations, elected representatives, and the broader policy community have made clear, however, that the United States has an abiding interest in the peaceful resolution of Beijing's differences with Taipei free from coercion. U.S. administrations have sought, since 1979, to find ways to work around the issue of Taiwan's status in the U.S. relationship with the PRC, looking to focus on issues of perceived common ground. U.S. policy has also sought to explicitly set bounds on the extent to which U.S.-Taiwan ties might be pressured by China, most notably through the 1982 Six Assurances, in which Washington committed to Taipei that it

- had not agreed to set a date for ending arms sales to the Republic of China
- had not agreed to hold prior consultations with the PRC regarding arms sales to the Republic of China
- would not play a mediation role between the PRC and the Republic of China
- would not revise the Taiwan Relations Act
- had not altered its position regarding sovereignty over Taiwan
- would not exert pressure on the Republic of China to enter into negotiations with the PRC.[2]

Taiwan's democratic transition in 1986, and its democratic consolidation over the subsequent three and a half decades, has only further deepened American attention to, interest about, and investment in Taiwan's importance. Over the same period, China's growing military capabilities, domestic repressiveness, and external aggressiveness and ambition have drawn an increasingly stark contrast with the ever-more liberal and globally integrated Taiwan. In particular, Taiwan's geographic position astride the First Island Chain and the PRC's claims to the Senkaku Islands mean that Taiwan's security carries direct implications for Japan and the U.S.-Japan alliance.[3] Chinese conquest of and control over Taiwan would also put at severe risk the U.S.-Philippines alliance and the U.S. ability to base forces in Guam.[4] An additional equity for the United States, beyond the geostrategic location of Taiwan, is the growing prominence of the Taiwan Semiconductor Manufacturing Corpora-

---

[2] Harvey Feldman, "President Reagan's Six Assurances to Taiwan and Their Meaning Today," Heritage Foundation, October 2, 2007.

[3] Nancy Bernkopf Tucker, "If Taiwan Chooses Unification, Should the United States Care?" *Washington Quarterly*, Vol. 25, No. 3, 2002.

[4] Andrew S. Erickson and Joel Wuthnow, "Barriers, Springboards and Benchmarks: China Conceptualizes the Pacific 'Island Chains,'" *China Quarterly*, Vol. 225, March 2016.

tion (TSMC) in global electronics and critical technology supply chains, meaning that PRC control over Taiwan could imperil the U.S. economy and defense industrial base.[5]

As a consequence of Taiwan's continuing and growing importance to the security, interests, and values of the United States, Congress has weighed in again in recent years, passing the 2018 Taiwan Travel Act and the 2020 Taiwan Allies International Protection and Enhancement Initiative (TAIPEI) Act.[6] In addition to these repeated signals of concern for the security of Taiwan and its importance to both U.S. interests and values, the United States has repeatedly sold Taiwan substantial volumes of defensive systems intended to complicate or defeat any PLA attempt to invade or coerce Taiwan.[7] These commitments to Taiwan's security, when combined with the politics of U.S.-Taiwan relations in the United States and the implications for U.S. national security in the region more generally, and especially when set against a backdrop of continuing PRC efforts to coerce Taiwan into unification and that could be used as a springboard for further regional power projection, make U.S.-China cooperation on this goal virtually unimaginable.

Chinese Equities

China has immense stakes in the issue of Taiwan and consistently signals its willingness to use force to unify (or, in China's view, "reunify") Taiwan with China. Because the PRC has at times managed around the issue in its ties with the United States, and to the extent that it emphasizes peaceful dialogue, it is possible to say that the issue is at least rhetorically aligned at times—but in practice, China has never indicated a willingness to bargain with the United States over its claims to Taiwan, much less to strengthen Taiwan's security, nor has it ever dedicated any resources to the issue.

Taiwan is viewed as a near-existential interest to Beijing, owing to CCP perceptions of regime legitimacy, regional security, nationalism, and great power status. Perhaps most importantly, the CCP has always sought reunification with Taiwan as an important part of its claim to govern all of China, and for its own security. In the years after the Chinese civil war, the CCP leadership feared that Chiang Kai-shek was plotting an invasion of the mainland to defeat the CCP. Now that Taiwan is a democracy, the concern is that Taiwan represents a direct threat to CCP regime security and domestic control as an alternative model to what Beijing claims is the only suitable form of government for "Chinese" culture. The CCP has staked its legitimacy on its claim to govern all of China, including the recovery of "lost" territories. This narrative extends back to the Chinese civil war but has been especially emphasized since the 1989 Tiananmen Square protests, with potential audience costs for PRC

---

[5] Chen Cheng-Hui, "TSMC Key to U.S. Supply Chains, Fitch Says," *Taipei Times*, May 25, 2020.

[6] Public Law 96-8, Taiwan Relations Act, January 1, 1979; Feldman, 2007; Public Law 115-135, Taiwan Travel Act, March 16, 2018; Public Law 116-135, Taiwan Allies International Protection and Enhancement Initiative (TAIPEI) Act, March 26, 2020.

[7] Kan, 2014.

leaders from generations of Chinese citizens who now expect the CCP to fulfill this promise, making the Chinese leadership walk a fine line about overzealous public opinion and Taiwan. From a geopolitical and security perspective, Beijing views Taiwan as an important stepping-stone—or hindrance—for its ambitions in Asia.

The CCP has never set a specific timeframe on unification, but Xi has made a point of creating a sense of urgency. In 2013, he told a visiting Taiwan official that "the issue of political disagreements that exist between the two sides must reach a final resolution, step by step, and these issues cannot be passed on from generation to generation."[8] In his 2017 speech, Xi further stated, "Resolving the Taiwan question to realize China's complete reunification is the shared aspiration of all Chinese people, and is in the fundamental interests of the Chinese nation," adding that "achieving China's full reunification is essential to realizing national rejuvenation."[9] This linkage between unification and national rejuvenation suggests that Xi's timeline for reunification could be sometime within the next three decades, when China is supposed to complete its transformation into a "great modern socialist country" and make progress toward national rejuvenation. It is important to note that there has always been speculation by some of an impending Chinese invasion of Taiwan, and it so far has not come—this may well reflect the immense military operational challenge such a decision would entail, and the risks of failure for the CCP.[10]

The CCP generally emphasizes peaceful unification as its preferred approach, but it clearly reserves the right to use force if necessary. Most importantly, Beijing's 2005 Anti-Secession Law explicitly states that if Taiwan moves toward independence or if "possibilities for a peaceful reunification should be completely exhausted," then "the state shall employ non-peaceful means and other necessary measures to protect China's sovereignty and territorial integrity."[11] However, Chinese official documents usually call for peaceful means, such as Xi's 2017 call that "We must . . . advance the process toward the peaceful reunification of China."[12] Xi made a similar point in January 2019, saying "We Chinese should not fight each other. We will work with the greatest sincerity and exert utmost efforts to achieve peaceful reunification, because this works best for the people on both sides and for our whole nation."[13] Indeed, it is noteworthy when the use of force is highlighted as an option or a call for peaceful means is left out of significant statements on cross-Strait issues, such as the May

---

[8] James Pomfret and Ben Blanchard, "China's Xi Says Political Solution for Taiwan Can't Wait Forever," Reuters, October 6, 2013.

[9] Xi, 2017.

[10] Peter Gries and Tao Wang, "Will China Seize Taiwan?" *Foreign Affairs*, February 15, 2019; Tanner Greer, "Taiwan Can Win a War With China," *Foreign Policy*, September 25, 2018; Drew Thompson, "China Is Still Wary of Invading Taiwan," *Foreign Policy*, May 11, 2020.

[11] Ministry of Foreign Affairs of the People's Republic of China, "Anti-Secession Law," March 15, 2005.

[12] Xi, 2017.

[13] Xi Jinping, "Working Together to Realize Rejuvenation of the Chinese Nation and Advance China's Peaceful Reunification," speech at the Meeting Marking the 40th Anniversary of the Issuance of the Mes-

2020 government work report, since this is generally interpreted as signaling Beijing's frustration at that moment in time.[14]

Of all issue areas explored in this report, the Chinese leadership's long-term dedication of massive resources toward the goal of ensuring the ability to unify Taiwan by force makes clear that it is not interested in compromise on this issue. From the perspective of defense expenditures, as the driving planning scenario for PLA military modernization, a large part of the PLA's current $178 budget for 2020 will go toward this express goal.[15] With an estimated defense spending of nearly $1.5 trillion since 2010, this is a substantial dedication of resources in opposition to a key U.S. policy priority.[16] It is impossible to actually quantify the amount of PLA resources dedicated to Taiwan, but as the "main strategic direction," it likely absorbs a majority of resources.

Beyond military preparation for the use of force against Taiwan, the CCP is also using means below the threshold of military force (i.e., gray-zone coercion) to force Taiwan into unification. These include leveraging economic ties that were strengthened under Taiwan's previous president, Ma Ying-Jeou. China is also leveraging cross-Strait social ties via its United Front Work Department (UFWD). Politically, China has likely always sought to interfere in Taiwanese elections. Most recently, China has also begun using social media for such political interference, including in the 2018 local elections and 2020 Taiwan presidential election.

The Chinese leadership is aware of the risks of a U.S.-China war arising from any attempt it might make to compel Taiwan's unification, further clarifying its lack of willingness to compromise on this issue. In Xi's January 2019 speech on Taiwan, he said, "We do not renounce the use of force and reserve the option of taking all necessary measures. This is to guard against external interference and a tiny number of separatists and their separatist activities for 'Taiwan independence.'"[17] The Chinese Ministry of Foreign Affairs reiterated, "We make no promise to renounce the use of force. This does not target compatriots in Taiwan, but the interference of external forces and the very small number of 'Taiwan independence' separatists and their activities. In fact, you should note that China's stance on this has never changed."[18] This aligns with authoritative PLA strategy documents, such as the 2013 *Science of Military Strategy*, which says that a Taiwan scenario is unlikely but most risky for its potential for war with the United States.

---

sage to Compatriots in Taiwan, January 2, 2019. For analysis, see Richard C. Bush, "8 Key Things to Notice from Xi Jinping's New Year Speech on Taiwan," Brookings Institution, January 7, 2019.

[14] Chun Han Wong, "China Breaks with Taiwan Precedent, Omitting Call for 'Peaceful' Policy," *Wall Street Journal*, May 22, 2020.

[15] Mike Yeo, "China Announces $178.2 Billion Military Budget," *Defense News*, May 22, 2020.

[16] Center for Strategic and International Studies, "What Does China Really Spend on Its Military?" undated (data as of June 1, 2020).

[17] Xi, 2019.

[18] Ministry of Foreign Affairs of the People's Republic of China, "Foreign Ministry Spokesperson Lu Kang's Regular Press Conference on January 2, 2019," January 2, 2019a.

The United States and China have never officially engaged in direct discussions over Taiwan's fate or the nature of U.S.-Taiwan relations. An example of typical engagement came in the most recent U.S.-China Diplomatic and Security Dialogue, in November 2018, with the U.S. side's readout simply reiterating the long-standing U.S. position:

> The United States reaffirmed its commitment to the United States. One China policy, based on the Taiwan Relations Act and the three joint communiques, and called on China to restore cross-Strait stability and respect Taiwan's international space. The United States opposes unilateral actions by any party aimed at altering the status quo, including any resort to force or coercion.[19]

Unofficially, however, Washington has engaged with Beijing on at least some aspects of the U.S.-Taiwan relationship. For example, the Obama administration was widely believed to time at least some U.S. arms sales to Taiwan based on larger trends in U.S.-China relations, and informal understandings have limited U.S. official visits to Taiwan.[20] More importantly, cross-Strait tensions and the mutually acknowledged risk of a U.S.-China conflict over Taiwan have been the biggest driver in U.S.-China military-to-military dialogue over crisis management and crisis communication, discussed in Chapter Three. At the Track 1.5 and Track 2 levels, Taiwan has been a topic of discussion for decades, and a constant topic since the Taiwan Strait Crisis of 1995–1996.[21] However, mirroring the official U.S.-China discussions, there is no evidence U.S. and Chinese interlocutors have ever negotiated over Taiwan's fate. Rather, much of the conversation centers on cross-Strait relations and crisis stability.

Russian Equities

Ensuring a peaceful resolution to China-Taiwan issues is not an issue of high importance to Russian interests. Russian statements do not in any way endorse or express unity with U.S. objectives in Taiwan. Furthermore, Moscow has not expressed any interest in bargaining or cooperating with Washington over cross-Strait issues, nor has it articulated a willingness to commit significant resources to achieve a shared goal in this space.

On cross-Strait issues, Russia has placed premium on its strategic partnership with China over cultural and trade relations with Taiwan and unequivocally upheld Beijing's position on matters dealing with Taiwan's status. The 2016 Foreign Policy Concept makes no explicit mention of Taiwan or the China-Taiwan issue, but it underscores cooperation in all areas with Beijing and common principled approaches to address key issues on the global agenda.[22]

---

[19] U.S. Department of State, 2018b.

[20] David Brunnstrom and Patricia Zengerle, "Obama Administration Authorizes $1.83-Billion Arms Sale to Taiwan," Reuters, December 17, 2015.

[21] For an early Track 2 dialogue in December 2001 that covered Taiwan, see Harvard University Belfer Center, "U.S.-China Track II Dialogue," undated.

[22] Ministry of Foreign Affairs of the Russian Federation, 2016b.

Russia's position on the Taiwan issue is pegged to the 2001 Treaty of Good Neighborliness and Friendly Cooperation Between the People's Republic of China and the Russian Federation, wherein Moscow affirmed the PRC's One China Policy, acknowledged the PRC as the sole legal government representing the whole of China, and opposed any form of Taiwanese independence from China.[23] Russia has continually articulated this position and called out Taiwan's efforts to seek liberalization and independence as "dangerous political games" that are categorically unacceptable to Moscow.[24] Likewise, Russia has consistently supported China's position in blockading Taiwan's attempts to secure a legitimate presence at multilateral or international organizations, including Taiwan's bid for a seat at the United Nations and membership to the International Civil Aviation Organization.[25]

Further underscoring Russian unity with China's position on Taiwan are Moscow's military activities and arms sales. Russian warplanes have allegedly joined the PLA Air Force in flying in and around Taiwan's airspaces.[26] And Russia has sold China the S-400 surface-to-air missile system, antiaircraft guided missiles, and the Su-35 fighter aircraft, all of which have contributed to Beijing's ability to threaten the airspace over Taiwan.[27]

Russia's support for China on the Taiwan issue suggests that there is little, if any, room for Moscow to cooperate with Washington on policies toward Taipei. Moscow-Taipei ties, while they exist, appear limited in scope and circumscribed by Russia's interest in currying favor with the PRC. Therefore, any U.S. efforts to persuade Russia to split from China's position on cross-Strait security issues—for instance, a gradual shift toward supporting Taiwan's independence—are unlikely to be successful or benefit Washington's strategic position in the Indo-Pacific domain. Shortly after Taiwan introduced visa waivers for Russian citizens, in May 2019, the two sides established direct flights between Moscow and Taipei.[28] Bilateral trade relations are mutually beneficial for the two parties—Taiwan struggles with limited natural resources, and Russia, though resource-rich, lags behind in manufacturing

---

[23] Ministry of Foreign Affairs of the People's Republic of China, "Treaty of Good Neighborliness and Friendly Cooperation Between the People's Republic of China and the Russian Federation," communiqué, July 24, 2001.

[24] Ministry of Foreign Affairs of the Russian Federation, "Briefing by Foreign Ministry Spokesperson Maria Zakharova, Sochi, May 19, 2016," May 19, 2016a; "China Values Russia's Support on Taiwan—Foreign Ministry," Tass, May 20, 2016.

[25] Ministry of Foreign Affairs of the Russian Federation, "Statement by Mikhail Kamynin, the Spokesman of Russia's Ministry of Foreign Affairs, Regarding Taiwan Preparations for Referendum on UN Entry," December 17, 2007; "Russia Against Taiwan's Membership in Int'l Civil Aviation Organization, Tass, October 3, 2019.

[26] John S. Van Oudenaren, "Why Are Russian Military Planes Flying Around Taiwan?" *The Diplomat*, January 16, 2020.

[27] Elizabeth Shim, "Report: Russia Delivers S-400 Missile System to China," *UPI*, January 27, 2020; Vassily Kashin, "Why Is China Buying Russian Fighter Jets?" Carnegie Moscow Center, September 2, 2016.

[28] Duncan DeAeth, "Relations Between Taiwan and Russia Are Steadily Improving: VOA," *Taiwan News*, June 5, 2019.

daily necessities. Neither country ranks as a top trade partner for the other, however. According to information from Taiwan's Ministry of Economic Affairs, Russia accounts for a mere 0.76 percent of Taiwan's total trade and ranks as Taiwan's 21st largest trade partner.[29] This pales significantly in comparison to Taiwan-U.S. trade relations, with the United States ranking as the second-largest trading partner, and of course, Taiwan's top trading relationship, which is with China.[30] Perhaps a silver lining in Russia-Taiwan trade relations can be found in the significant increases in total bilateral trade (up 26.74 percent), Taiwan's exports to Russia (up 25.76 percent), and Russia's imports to Taiwan (up 27.06 percent) between 2016 and 2017.[31] As with Taiwan, China also occupies the top trade partner status for Russia, further constraining Moscow's willingness to consider deeper ties in defense of Taipei.[32] Critically, it should be noted that with many of Taiwan's manufacturing facilities relocating to China, goods produced at these sites follow the pattern of "receiving orders in Taiwan and shipping goods from China."[33] This means the goods are calculated as part of China-Russia trade instead of Taiwan-Russia trade, which, according to experts, means that the actual trade volume between Moscow and Taipei may be larger than official statistics indicate.

Space for Cooperation

The issue of Taiwan's status and security is a difficult one for the United States to cooperate with China or Russia on, as Table 6.1 makes clear.

TABLE 6.1
Interest in Cooperation on the Peaceful Resolution of the Cross-Strait Dispute

Space for Cooperation	China	Russia
Stakes	High	Low
Rhetorical alignment	Low	Low
Demonstrated willingness to commit resources	Low	Low

[29] Ministry of Economic Affairs, Bureau of Foreign Trade, Republic of China, "Taiwan-Russia Economic Relations," revised December 5, 2018.

[30] See Taiwan's statistics on trade with the United States and China, respectively: Ministry of Economic Affairs, Bureau of Foreign Trade, Republic of China, "Taiwan-U.S. Economic Relations," revised January 23, 2019; Ministry of Economic Affairs, Bureau of Foreign Trade, Republic of China, "Cross-Straits Economic Relations," revised May 12, 2020.

[31] Ministry of Economic Affairs, Bureau of Foreign Trade, of the Republic of China, 2018.

[32] World Integrated Trade Solution, "Russia Trade," undated-b.

[33] Anton Tang, "Are Closer Taiwan-Russia Relations Possible? How?" *The Commonwealth*, February 5, 2018.

It is sometimes said that while China cares about Taiwan in terms of substance (i.e., wanting to absorb it by any means possible), the United States cares about Taiwan in terms of process, being willing to countenance any outcome so long as it is mutually agreed upon and peacefully arrived at. China has consistently indicated that the "Taiwan question" is the central, unresolved issue in U.S.-China relations, but it has nonetheless been able to find a modus vivendi with the United States for almost all of the 40 years following derecognition of the Republic of China and recognition of the PRC. Despite U.S. arms sales, contemplated legislation that would upgrade U.S.-Taiwan security cooperation, Taiwan presidential "stopover diplomacy," and U.S. expressions of support for Taiwan's security (which even went as far as dispatching two U.S. carrier action groups toward the Taiwan Strait in 1995–1996), Beijing has managed to focus on areas of mutual interest with Washington. Washington, too—despite its concerns about PLA aggression against Taiwan in the mid-1990s, in the run-up to the 2000 and 2008 elections, and since 2016—has for the most part been able to engage with the PRC on other issues and venues even if the two sides clearly hold to fairly diametrically opposed positions on Taiwan.

As a policy matter, the way in which Taiwan's status is resolved will carry critical implications for the future of U.S.-China relations.[34] And apart from both the political impossibility of "trading away" Taiwan and the patent immorality of any attempt to abandon 24 million people who have built a functioning and consolidated democracy out of communist tyranny, because the PRC defines Taiwan as an internal affair in which outsiders have no right to say anything, it is unlikely that the United States would gain anything from the PRC in terms of cooperation on other issues were it to abandon Taiwan. Instead, it would be more likely to embolden China and demoralize other U.S. allies and partners in the region and around the world.[35]

Of course, were Beijing to downplay or abandon its pressure on and threats to Taiwan, reform its political system, and formulate a more attractive policy that appealed to and had credibility with the people of Taiwan, Washington would likely counsel caution but might not object (or have grounds to oppose such a move). At present, given the PRC's manifest betrayal of its promises to the United Kingdom in the Sino-British Joint Declaration of 1984 and the evisceration of its "one country, two systems" promise to the people of Hong Kong (always intended to serve a demonstration effect for Taiwan) through the introduction of a harsh new National Security Law, such a development seems unlikely. To the extent that China seeks

---

[34] Roger Cliff and David A. Shlapak, *U.S.-China Relations After the Resolution of Taiwan's Status*, Santa Monica, Calif.: RAND Corporation, MG-567-AF, 2007.

[35] J. Michael Cole, *Convergence or Conflict in the Taiwan Strait: The Illusion of Peace?* New York: Routledge, 2017; J. Michael Cole, *Cross-Strait Relations Since 2016: The End of the Illusion*, New York: Routledge, 2020; Nancy Bernkopf Tucker and Bonnie Glaser, "Should the United States Abandon Taiwan?" *Washington Quarterly*, Vol. 34, No. 4, 2011; for an alternative, but marginal, view that the United States could and should abandon Taiwan to appease China, see Charles Glaser, "A U.S.-China Grand Bargain? The Hard Choice Between Military Competition and Accommodation," *International Security*, Vol. 39, No. 4, Spring 2015.

to compel Taiwan's unification or absorption through coercion or force, then, it is necessary under both long-standing U.S. policy and U.S. national interests to compete with China.

Inasmuch as Russia plays little role in, has no concrete equities around, and is largely indifferent to the fate of Taiwan and supportive of Beijing's position, the United States is unlikely to benefit from cooperating with Russia over Taiwan's security issue, nor does it need to compete with Russia over this matter. However, it is worth noting that in the 1950s, Soviet policy sought to encourage Beijing to exercise restraint and to avoid the possibility of a broader conflict that could conceivably have led to a Soviet-American clash and potentially even a nuclear war. From this experience, Mao and the CCP began to grow concerned that Moscow would not stand on its side in a crisis, contributing to the ultimate fracturing of their alliance and the Sino-Soviet split. Such a development is unlikely to recur and Russia's importance to China is relatively limited on Taiwan, but it is worth bearing such historical precedents in mind in case unexpected developments occur down the road. Clearly though, Moscow today values its ties with Beijing over any prospective cooperation with Taipei or Washington. Russia's military role in the Taiwan Strait is dwarfed by that of China, and Russia is virtually if not entirely irrelevant to the resolution of the cross-Strait dispute from the perspective of the United States.[36] For this reason, Russia is unlikely to have much to offer to U.S. efforts to ensure the peaceful resolution of differences between China and Taiwan.

The United States faces serious obstacles to cooperation with China or Russia on managing cross-Strait differences between China and Taiwan. These include trust, audience costs, third-party problems, immediacy, issue linkages, and legal constraints. Definitional problems and capacity or capability did not appear to substantially impede cooperation with China and/or Russia on the peaceful resolution of the cross-Strait dispute, and hence we do not discuss them further here.

Trust. China and the United States have deep fundamental issues of trust on the issue of Taiwan, with Beijing framing any U.S. support for Taiwan's self-defense or international status as an attack on China's sovereignty, whereas Washington views Chinese efforts to challenge these actions as undermining U.S. principles of freedom and democracy, as well as a direct threat to U.S. national security interests in the Western Pacific area, as described in the 1979 Taiwan Relations Act.

Audience costs. Both Chinese elites and the broader Chinese public view Taiwan as part of China and U.S. support for Taiwan as undermining China's sovereignty, meaning any acceptance of U.S. support for Taiwan would be very likely unpopular domestically. On the U.S. side, Taiwan—once a nondemocratic ally dating back to World War II, now a democratic partner and one of the richest and freest countries in the Indo-Pacific—enjoys both historical and continuing U.S. public support. Such support is reflected in the halls of Congress, with bipartisan measures including the Taiwan Travel Act and the TAIPEI Act having passed in recent years to further develop U.S. contacts with and commitment to Taiwan. Additionally, the Taiwanese-American community, while small, is well organized and resourceful and can

---

[36] Van Oudenaren, 2020.

draw on intellectual support from think tanks such as the Global Taiwan Institute and the Project 2049 Institute, both of which are dedicated to deepening U.S.-Taiwan ties and have connections to high-level former policymakers.

Definitional problems. Beijing has defined cross-Strait relations as a domestic issue with no role for external powers. Washington, however, views Taiwan as an international issue, not China's domestic concern, making this fundamental difference of view a major obstacle to tangible cooperation. For Russia, although Moscow's interests are not immediately affected by cross-Strait dynamics, its support for Beijing's position indicates that Moscow's definition—and by extension, policy position—differs from that of Washington.[37] There does not appear to be much room for U.S.-Russia cooperation in this sphere.

Third-Party problems. For the United States and China, cross-Strait issues cannot be managed strictly bilaterally—Taiwan has agency and could take steps that might prompt responses by either Beijing or Washington, as it did in the 2000s when the Chen Shui-bian administration pursued referenda on cross-Strait ties and rejoining the United Nations. For Moscow, should the United States and Russia attempt to cooperate on cross-Strait issues, their efforts would likely to entail Chinese retaliation against Russian equities that Moscow values more than it might gain from any cooperation with the United States over Taiwan's security.

Immediacy problem. Taiwan is generally considered the biggest risk factor for a U.S.-China war. An action by Taipei that Beijing determines requires the use of force, or an accident between the PLA and the U.S. or Taiwanese military, could make the issue urgent enough to prompt serious U.S.-China dialogue on cross-Strait issues.

Issue linkage. For the United States and its allies, the issue of Taiwan is also linked to broader regional security issues. This is especially true for Japan, which looks at the fate of Taiwan both as a key marker of Chinese intensions and a key buffer against Chinese military aggression. For Russia, Moscow's cooperation with the United States on cross-Strait issues will likely affect Russia's broader interests—most critically, its relations with China. Russian apprehensions about a potential Chinese backlash, coercion, or withdrawal of support for Moscow's policy positions would likely impede meaningful U.S.-Russian cooperation over cross-Strait issues.[38]

Legal constraints. For China, although the CCP is not in practice actually constrained by Chinese law, it did enact a 2005 Anti-Secession Law that reserves the right to "employ non-peaceful means and other necessary measures to protect China's sovereignty and territorial integrity" in the event of Taiwan's succession.[39] For the United States, the 1979 Taiwan Relations Act states that "the future of Taiwan will be determined by peaceful means and that any effort to determine the future of Taiwan by other than peaceful means, including by boycotts

---

[37] Ministry of Foreign Affairs of the Russian Federation, 2007.

[38] Tang, 2018.

[39] Ministry of Foreign Affairs of the People's Republic of China, 2005.

or embargoes is considered a threat to the peace and security of the Western Pacific area and of grave concern to the United States."[40] In turn, it requires the United States to "maintain the capacity of the United States to resist any resort to force or other forms of coercion that would jeopardize the security, or social or economic system, of the people of Taiwan." In theory, this means that a Taiwanese action that Beijing interprets as a move toward independence—a referendum on changing Taiwan's name to the Republic of Taiwan (instead of Republic of China), perhaps—could "force" Beijing's use of force for unification and thus then trigger U.S. intervention in support of Taiwan's self-defense.

Second-Order Effects of Cooperation

Were the United States to dramatically enhance its confrontation with China in defense of Taiwan, it is entirely possible that Russia might opportunistically seek to take advantage of this confrontation by advancing its interests at the expense of American equities in Europe, the Middle East, Central Asia, or elsewhere. By contrast, if the United States and China were somehow to find ways to reduce or even amicably resolve their differences over Taiwan, this would presumably result in a greater ability for the United States to focus on the defense of Europe against Russian aggression, adversely affecting Russia's interests and influence.

By contrast, there is little in the way of options for the United States to cooperate with Russia on the security of Taiwan, and any such cooperation as might be envisioned would result in little impact on the challenge China poses to this goal. And since Russia is largely irrelevant to the security threat posed to Taiwan, there is little to discuss in terms of competing with Russia over the defense of Taiwan.

Conclusion

As the foregoing analysis shows, the issue of ensuring the peaceful resolution of differences between China and Taiwan is an issue near or at the center of U.S.-China relations for nearly five decades; certainly this has been Beijing's perspective and many, perhaps even most, U.S. policymakers would agree. The United States has sought ways to coexist with China without resolving the question of Taipei's relationship with Beijing, hoping that over time China might develop economically as well as liberalize and even democratize, possibly with the effect of reducing or eliminating the differences across the Strait—but this development has not come to pass.[41] Instead, competition over Taiwan's status and security has intensified substantially over the past four decades, and especially since the assumption of power by Xi in 2012 and as his administration has sought to coerce Taipei ever more openly since the elec-

---

[40] Pub. L. 96-8.

[41] Kurt M. Campell and Ely Ratner, "The China Reckoning," *Foreign Affairs*, March/April 2018.

tion of Tsai Ing-wen in 2016. All this suggests that the room for cooperation, if it ever existed, has shrunk dramatically, while the imperative of competition has grown ever more central.

By contrast, Russia is largely, if not entirely, irrelevant to the issue of Taiwan's status and security, and on this issue at least Russia can for all intents and purposes be treated as a marginal actor with minor ability to make things worse by competing and little to offer in terms of making things better through cooperation, with Moscow's position shaped almost exclusively by its interest in supporting Beijing and countering Washington.

CHAPTER SEVEN

Achieving the Denuclearization of North Korea

Preventing the Democratic People's Republic of Korea (DPRK; North Korea) from acquiring nuclear weapons and the associated ballistic missile delivery systems that would enable it to directly threaten the U.S. homeland or the Republic of Korea (ROK; South Korea), Japan, or other allies and partners has been a high priority U.S. policy goal since the mid-1980s, and deterring a North Korean attack on the U.S.-ROK alliance dates back even further, to the mid-1950s. The acquisition of such weapons and the ability to reliably deliver them to targets as distant as the continental United States could both put at risk Americans in the homeland and fuel the erosion of the U.S. strategic extended deterrent (often referred to as the *nuclear umbrella*) to South Korea and Japan, potentially leading those states to acquire their own weapons or to strategic decoupling and the destabilization of Northeast Asia. In this chapter, we explore the possibility of cooperating with as compared with the necessity of competing with China and Russia on this nonproliferation goal.

Understanding the Equities

The United States, China, and Russia all appear, at least on the surface, to share a similar goal of preventing North Korea from acquiring a nuclear arsenal and associated delivery systems. Pursuit of complete, verifiable, and irreversible denuclearization should therefore be an area where cooperation among the three parties should be easy and competition entirely unnecessary. Unfortunately, this expectation has been repeatedly dashed. To understand why, it is important to explore the various equities the three sides have at stake. In this section, we lay those out in detail.

U.S. Equities

The United States seeks to defend U.S. allies South Korea and Japan from North Korea. Since the end of the Korean War, the North's threat has evolved beyond a simple ground invasion to include special operations missions and subversion, missile strikes, cyber attacks, and proliferation.

From the mid-1980s, as South Korea pulled definitively into the lead on economic and industrial wealth and began to transition from a military dictatorship to a liberal democracy, the North began to prioritize acquisition of nuclear weapons. When the United States detected this development, it reached out to the Soviet Union from the mid-1980s onward in an attempt to work together to head off North Korean nuclear weapon development.[1]

Although Soviet-American cooperation initially appeared to be a promising approach to preventing North Korea from acquiring the nuclear fuel cycle, by the early 1990s, with the collapse of the USSR and the Chinese decision to recognize South Korea and stop blocking its accession to the United Nations, the North moved forward aggressively to develop a plutonium pathway to the bomb, precipitating the first North Korean nuclear crisis.[2] That crisis was initially resolved through the 1994 Agreed Framework, under which North Korea agreed to abandon its plutonium production in exchange for heavy fuel oil and two proliferation-resistant light-water reactors, but the North continued provocative conventional activities, including a 1998 Taepodong-1 intermediate-range ballistic missile test that overflew Japan, as well as a number of attacks on South Korea, including clashes in the West Sea in 1998 and 2002. In October 2002, North Korea admitted to having a clandestine uranium enrichment program, leading the United States to withdraw from the Agreed Framework and the North to expel the International Atomic Energy Agency (IAEA).[3]

By the time it tested its first nuclear explosive device in October 2006, the United States had already reached out to China to bring the United States, South Korea, Japan, China, Russia, and North Korea together under the Six-Party Talks format. Previous engagements in the late 1990s had centered around four parties—the United States, DPRK, ROK, and PRC—but by the mid-2000s the recovery of the Russian economy and the growing involvement of Japan in regional security affairs suggested that a collective effort by the five main parties affected by Pyongyang's actions might prove an effective approach to countering the spread of WMD in North Korea.[4] Unfortunately, across several rounds of nuclear negotiations and despite a series of North Korean commitments, Pyongyang showed no substantive willingness to abandon its nuclear weapon program and development of relevant delivery vehicles, and it instead began accelerating its efforts under Kim Jong Un.[5]

---

[1] Michael J. Mazarr, *North Korea and the Bomb: A Case Study in Non-Proliferation*, New York: St. Martin's Press, 1995.

[2] Joel S. Wit, Daniel B. Poneman, and Robert L. Gallucci, *Going Critical: The First North Korean Nuclear Crisis*, Washington, D.C.: Brookings Institution Press, 2005.

[3] Charles L. Pritchard, *Failed Diplomacy: The Tragic Story of How North Korea Got the Bomb*, Washington, D.C.: Brookings Institution Press, 2007.

[4] Yoichi Funabashi, *The Peninsula Question: A Chronicle of the Second North Korean Nuclear Crisis*, Washington, D.C.: Brookings Institution Press, 2007.

[5] Jonathan D. Pollack, *No Exit: North Korea, Nuclear Weapons, and International Security*, New York: Routledge, 2011.

Over the past decade, the United States has sought to characterize, slow, halt, and ultimately reverse North Korea's nuclear program.[6] Most U.S. experts regard this last goal as desirable, but serious questions exist about its feasibility, with some observers arguing it may still be possible through a campaign of Maximum Pressure 2.0 and others arguing for shifting to an approach focused on "accepting reality and managing a nuclear-armed North Korea."[7] The United States has sought to do so through unilateral and United Nations Security Council sanctions on North Korea; striving to cut off the regime's ability to export arms, coal, minerals, and other products; and working to restrict its ability to import fuel and ban its imports of luxury goods that the regime uses to reward its supporters.[8]

As part of its growing pressure campaign throughout the past decade, the United States has also sought to deter North Korea from advancing its weapon programs by enhancing ballistic and cruise missile defenses together with its ISR and counterstrike capabilities in tandem with South Korea and Japan. These moves have included strategic deterrent signaling in the form of fighter and bomber packages, enhanced use of surveillance platforms over the Korean peninsula, movement of naval strike assets into Guam and elsewhere in theater, and emplacement of a THAAD ballistic missile defense battery in South Korea. This last move has been opposed by both China and Russia, which have objected to the system even as they field their own weapons that can strike Korea, as well as their own defenses against ballistic missiles.

Since 2017, the United States has combined an escalating degree of pressure under the "maximum pressure and engagement," reportedly briefly considering a "bloody nose" option to dissuade Pyongyang from further developing its strategic capabilities before settling on an approach premised on summitry and assurance.[9] Despite personal entreaties from the North Korean leadership, the Trump administration opted to leave sanctions in place, although it canceled regular large-scale U.S.-South Korean military exercises. Additionally, the Trump administration ceded a substantial degree of control over the negotiation process to the Moon Jae-in administration in South Korea, but this did not result in any substantive advances in North Korean denuclearization.[10]

---

[6] Arms Control Association, "Chronology of U.S.-North Korea Nuclear and Missile Diplomacy," May 2020.

[7] Bradley Bowman and David Maxwell, *Maximum Pressure 2.0: A Plan for North Korea*, Washington, D.C.: Foundation for Defense of Democracies, 2019; Michael D. Swaine, *Time to Accept Reality and Manage a Nuclear-Armed North Korea*, Washington, D.C.: Carnegie Endowment for International Peace, 2017.

[8] Arms Control Association, "UN Security Council Resolutions on North Korea," April 2018.

[9] "Panmunjom Declaration on Peace, Prosperity and Reunification of the Korean Peninsula, issued by the Republic of Korea and the Democratic People's Republic of Korea," April 27, 2018; Donald J. Trump and Kim Jong Un, "Joint Statement of President Donald J. Trump of the United States of America and Chairman Kim Jong Un of the Democratic People's Republic of Korea at the Singapore Summit," June 12, 2018; Ankit Panda and Vipin Narang, "The Hanoi Summit Was Doomed from the Start," *Foreign Affairs*, March 5, 2019.

[10] Harold, 2020a; John Bolton, *The Room Where It Happened: A White House Memoir*, New York: Simon & Schuster, 2020.

Chinese Equities

China shares the United States' desire to denuclearize North Korea but is unwilling to align its approach with the United States' "maximum pressure" approach to force North Korea to the negotiating table. For China, stability on the Korean peninsula still supersedes denuclearization. Beijing has occasionally facilitated pressure on Pyongyang, but it has usually come against the backdrop of U.S.-DPRK tensions that risk war and threaten China's security. Beijing's preferred approach is to focus on dialogue and economic development, along with a rollback of the U.S.-ROK alliance. Overall, China has medium stakes in DPRK denuclearization and some degree of rhetorical alignment with the United States. There has been substantial bilateral dialogue on the issue, and China has shown some willingness to commit resources, but ultimately the prospects for more substantial cooperation are slim.

China's interests in DPRK denuclearization are mainly centered around regional stability and its great power status. From a security perspective, North Korea's location on China's border and the Korean Peninsula's historical status as a geopolitical stepping-stone for adversaries invading China (Japan in World War II, as well as a fear that the United States intended to do so during the Korean War) means that Beijing views DPRK security and stability as highly important to its own security.[11] North Korea's nuclear program specifically is a concern to China for two reasons. First, Beijing is very worried that the United States will conduct a preemptive strike on DPRK nuclear facilities, or otherwise start a war on the Korean Peninsula that spills across the border into China, potentially even in terms of nuclear fallout.[12] A second, much less emphasized but equally dangerous concern is that the Kim regime could use its nuclear weapons against China.[13] Although China and North Korea have always touted positive ties, in reality there has always been a high degree of mistrust and enmity in the relationship and these have gotten worse under Xi and Kim.[14] Another indirect but strong

---

[11] Nathan and Scobell, 2012.

[12] Qiao Zhongwei, Wang Jiasheng, and Zou Hao, eds., 边境危机应急控制 [*Border Crises Emergency Response and Control*], Beijing: Academy of Military Science, 2013. Chinese references to this concern appeared starting in 2004–2005. For example, see 霍丽杰 [Huo Lijie], 金贞顺 [Jin Zhenshun], 李莉 [Li Li], 何梅芳 [He Meifang], and 陈淑敏 [Chen Shumin], "边境地区未来核袭击后的护理特点及应解决的问题 [The Characteristics of Future Nursing and the Problems to Be Solved After Nuclear Attacks in Frontier Regions]," 护理管理杂志 [*Journal of Nursing Administration*], October 2005. For an early discussion of this concern and mission by foreign researchers, see Bonnie Glaser, Scott Snyder, and John Park, "Keeping an Eye on an Unruly Neighbor," Center for Strategic International Studies, January 3, 2008.

[13] This is not generally acknowledged by Chinese sources, but for one foreign analysis, see Katsuji Nakazawa, "Pyongyang Missile Footage Is a Dagger to Xi's Throat," *Nikkei Asian Review*, August 21, 2017.

[14] Jane Perlez and Peter Baker, "Trump Eyes China Sanctions While Seeking Its Help on North Korea," *New York Times*, August 12, 2017; Jane Perlez, "North Korean Leader, Young and Defiant, Strains Ties with Chinese," *New York Times*, April 13, 2013.

interest is the risk of DPRK refugees crossing the border into China, arising from any number of DPRK policies or contingencies, any of which could threaten China's domestic stability.[15]

Beijing has had difficulty balancing its desire for security against its desire for DPRK denuclearization. China's North Korea policy is often described as "no war, no instability and no nuclear weapons" (不战, 不乱, 无核), reflecting China's main interests in order of priority.[16] Analysts have sometimes believed Beijing was prioritizing denuclearization over "no war, no instability," but, overall, Chinese actions suggest denuclearization is still a secondary goal.[17] Chinese Foreign Minister Wang Yi has made clear that any Chinese support for denuclearization is indeed conditioned on the other two interests first. In March 2014, Wang described China's "red line" as "China will not allow war or instability on the Korean peninsula," and in February 2016 he expanded this to explain three principles for the DPRK nuclear issue:

> Firstly, under no circumstances could the Korean Peninsula be nuclearized, whether the DPRK or the ROK, self-produced or introduced and deployed. Secondly, there is no military solution to the issue. If there is war or turbulence on the Peninsula it is not acceptable for China. Thirdly, China's legitimate national security interests must be effectively maintained and safeguarded.[18]

This has been echoed by Xi, reinforcing the message.[19]

Beyond the narrow issue of DPRK denuclearization, China's broader interests on the Korean Peninsula extend to its economic relationship with South Korea and opposition to the U.S.–South Korea alliance. Economically, China's trade with North Korea ($2.4 billion) is dwarfed by trade with South Korea ($314 billion), including high-tech components from

---

[15] Li Xiaodong, ed., 朝鲜半岛危机管理研究 [*A Study of Crisis Management on the Korean Peninsula*], Military Science Publishing House, 2010; Qiao, Wang, and Zou, 2013. For analysis of Chinese planning for DPRK refugees, see Drew Thompson and Carla Freeman, *Flood Across the Border: China's Disaster Relief Operations and Potential Response to a North Korean Refugee Crisis*, US-Korea Institute at the Johns Hopkins School of Advanced International Studies (SAIS), April 2009.

[16] Li Xiaodong, 2010, p. 4; Bonnie Glaser and Brittany Billingsley, "Reordering Chinese Priorities on the Korean Peninsula," Center for Strategic International Studies, 2012, p. 1.

[17] Stephanie Kleine-Ahlbrandt, "China's North Korea Policy: Backtracking from Sunnylands?" 38 North, July 2, 2013; Stephanie T. Kleine-Ahlbrandt, "China's Relations with North Korea," testimony before the U.S.-China Economic and Security Review Commission, June 5, 2014.

[18] "王毅: 中国在朝鲜半岛问题上有"红线" 绝不允许生战生乱 [Wang Yi: China Has a "Red Line" on the Korean Peninsula Issue and Will Never Allow War and Chaos]" People.cn, March 8, 2014; "China Will Not Allow War or Instability on Korean Peninsula," Xinhua, March 8, 2014; Ministry of Foreign Affairs of the People's Republic of China, "Wang Yi Talks About Principles China Upholds in Dealing with the Korean Peninsula Nuclear Issue," February 13, 2016a.

[19] "Xi Jinping Speaks with South Korean President Park Geun-Hye," Xinhua, February 5, 2016.

ROK companies such as Samsung.[20] Beijing seeks to woo Seoul away from Washington, with the goal of weakening, if not ending, the alliance.[21] Because Seoul prioritizes DPRK denuclearization, Beijing's maintenance of positive relations with Seoul thus requires that it provide at least a modicum of rhetorical support to Seoul for this goal.

Although China is rhetorically aligned with the United States on the shared goal of denuclearizing North Korea, its preferred approach emphasizes political dialogue free from pressure or sanctions, with the U.S.-ROK alliance urged to make concessions to reassure Pyongyang. China was a signatory of the Six-Party Talks joint statement in 2005 that called for DPRK denuclearization, and it consistently reiterates this point.[22] China's 2017 white paper on Asian security issues states,

> China is committed to the denuclearization of the peninsula, its peace and stability, and settlement of the issue through dialogue and consultation. . . . China has made clear its opposition to such actions and supported the relevant Security Council resolutions to prevent the DPRK's further pursuit of nuclear weapons. China will continue to work with the international community and strive for denuclearization.[23]

However, China's emphasis is always on political dialogue and the importance of economic development. Moreover, during Xi's 2019 visit to North Korea, he hinted at siding with North Korea on its demands, saying he support Pyongyang's "reasonable concerns."[24]

Beijing's main diplomatic proposal to resolve the DPRK nuclear issue is a dual-track approach between Washington and Pyongyang. First proposed by Foreign Minister Wang Yi in March 2017, this would entail

> as a first step, the DPRK suspend its missile and nuclear activities in exchange for a halt of the large-scale U.S.–ROK exercises. This suspension-for-suspension can help us break out of the security dilemma and bring the parties back to the negotiating table. Then we can follow the dual-track approach of de-nuclearizing the peninsula on the one hand and establishing a peace mechanism on the other.[25]

---

[20] Authors' calculation using 2018 trade data, excluding Hong Kong, from World Integrated Trade Solution, undated-a.

[21] Jae Ho Chung and Jiyoon Kim, "Is South Korea in China's Orbit? Assessing Seoul's Perceptions and Policies," *Asia Policy* No. 21, January 1, 2016.

[22] "Joint Statement of the Fourth Round of the Six-Party Talks," September 19, 2005.

[23] State Council Information Office of the People's Republic of China, 2017.

[24] Yun Sun, "The Real Agenda of Xi Jinping's First Trip to North Korea," 38 North, June 25, 2019.

[25] Ministry of Foreign Affairs of the People's Republic of China, "Foreign Minister Wang Yi Meets the Press," March 8, 2017a.

North Korea and Russia have also supported this proposal in various forums, including the UN.[26] From Beijing's point of view, the basic contours of the U.S.-DPRK plan announced at the two countries' bilateral summit in Singapore aligned well with China's proposal.[27] Of note is that this proposed approach is not unique, as Pyongyang has offered a variation of this plan since at least 2015, though as one analyst noted, "Beijing and Pyongyang hope to achieve different things through the same proposal. China views the 'dual freeze' as an interim step for denuclearizing the Korean Peninsula, but North Korea does not."[28] China has left the door open for other proposals, at least rhetorically, as the Chinese Foreign Ministry spokesperson said in August 2017: "If the United States or other parties have better and more effective proposals, we will remain positive and open to them as long as they are conducive to the peaceful settlement of the Korean Peninsula nuclear issue and the early resumption of talks."[29]

Of all the issues addressed in this report, the prospects and path forward on DPRK denuclearization have been subject to the greatest amount and most substantive dialogue and negotiation between Washington and Beijing. Beijing's decision to host the Six-Party Talks in 2003 represented a breakthrough in China's more proactive approach to regional affairs. However, of note, this decision was made against the backdrop of the Bush administration's invasion of Iraq and Afghanistan, and the specific threat by Bush to Jiang Zemin in February 2003 that "if we could not solve the [North Korea nuclear] problem diplomatically, I would have to consider a strike against North Korea."[30] Subsequent U.S. administrations have all considered the possibility of conflict with North Korea, something China has been mindful of.

U.S.-China discussions over DPRK denuclearization during the Bush, Obama, and Trump administrations have all revolved around debates over clashing preferred solutions: U.S. sanctions versus Chinese engagement. At the last U.S.-China Strategic and Economic Dialogue under the Obama administration, in June 2016, following the North's fourth nuclear test that January, the two sides

> reiterated their commitment to achieve the verifiable denuclearization of the Korean Peninsula in a peaceful manner and concurred on the importance of safeguarding the peace and stability of the Korean Peninsula. The two sides called on all relevant parties to make joint efforts and take the necessary actions to create the conditions for an early resump-

---

[26] Son Daekwon, "What Does North Korea Think of China's 'Dual Freeze' Proposal?" *The Diplomat*, July 25, 2017.

[27] Ministry of Foreign Affairs of the People's Republic of China, "Foreign Ministry Spokesperson Geng Shuang's Regular Press Conference on June12, 2018," June 12, 2018a.

[28] Son, 2017.

[29] Ministry of Foreign Affairs of the People's Republic of China, "Foreign Ministry Spokesperson Hua Chunying's Regular Press Conference on August 17, 2017," August 17, 2017b.

[30] George W. Bush, *Decision Points*, New York: Broadway Paperbacks, 2011, p. 424.

tion of the Six-Party Talks. The two sides decided to continue close communication and coordination on relevant issues.[31]

In 2018, at the last round of the U.S.-China Diplomatic and Security Dialogue under the Trump administration, the two sides "emphasized their continued commitment to achieving the final, fully verified denuclearization of the Korean Peninsula, as committed to by Trump and Kim. The United States and China committed to continue coordination and to fully, strictly implement the relevant UN Security Council resolutions."[32]

At the Track 1.5 and Track 2 levels, U.S.-China conversations have long similarly revolved around the best approach to denuclearize North Korea. However, in more recent years, as Chinese concern over U.S. military action has increased, there has been a slow and small, but marked, improvement in the willingness of Chinese interlocutors to discuss crisis management. These conversations have generally been off the record but have included some discussion of DPRK contingencies, U.S.-China cooperation (or deconfliction), and challenges therein.[33]

China's commitment of resources toward the objective of DPRK denuclearization has been limited, but it has occasionally played a useful role in applying pressure on North Korea. Beijing's sanctions enforcement has been at best inconsistent over the years, and its enforcement and scrutiny of cross-border trade usually goes up during times of tension on the Peninsula and recedes as the situation improves. This reflects the PRC's preferred approach of economic engagement, as well as concerns over the fragility of the DPRK economy and risks of cutting off China-North Korea trade for too long. Beyond sanctions enforcement, Beijing has also called for sanctions relief over 2019 and 2020 as a way to jump-start the denuclearization process, after the failure of the Singapore and Hanoi summits.[34]

Reflecting inconsistent sanctions enforcement, the U.S. government has sanctioned Chinese companies on many occasions for continued trade with North Korea. One early notable instance was the Bush administration's 2005 sanctioning of Banco Delta Asia, a Macao-based bank that was a key node for DPRK financial flows, for money laundering.[35] This provided an initial shock to Chinese banks, and 12 years later the U.S. government sanctioned another Chinese bank, the Bank of Dandong, for doing the same thing.[36] There have been some

---

[31] U.S. Department of State, 2016b.

[32] U.S. Department of State, 2018b.

[33] Authors interviews.

[34] Josh Smith, "U.S.-Led Pressure Fractures as China, Russia Push for North Korea Sanctions Relief," Reuters, December 17, 2019.

[35] David Lague and Donald Greenlees, "Squeeze on Banco Delta Asia hit North Korea Where It Hurt," *New York Times*, January 18, 2007. For a recounting of this by a former U.S. official, see Juan Zarate, *Treasury's War: The Unleashing of a New Era of Financial Warfare*, New York: Public Affairs, 2013.

[36] U.S. Department of Treasury, "Treasury Acts to Increase Economic Pressure on North Korea and Protect the U.S. Financial System," June 29, 2017.

financial sanctions enforcement by Beijing, such as Bank of China's 2013 decision to cut ties with North Korea's main foreign banking arm.[37] However, Chinese experts admit that these actions have more to do with political calculations and the risks of U.S. sanctions than Beijing's actual desire to pressure North Korea toward denuclearization.[38] In the end, the Kim regime has been fairly successful at sustaining foreign trade and banking activities, and much of this routes through China to this day.[39]

China's opposition to sanctions comes from three main factors. First, China has always been against sanctions as a foreign policy tool in principle, in part because it has been under sanctions itself for much of its history.[40] Second, and likely most importantly, China fears that full sanctions enforcement could cause the collapse of North Korea, which Beijing believes will seriously undermine its own security. Third, some Chinese analysts view North Korea as a useful tool for imposing asymmetrical costs on the United States.[41]

China's relatively high commitment to facilitating a diplomatic solution to the DPRK nuclear issue is evident in the fact that Beijing's proposed action-for-action plan actually has some details, in contrast to vague principles proffered by Chinese diplomats for far-flung issues of little actual interest, such as New Asian Security Concept offered at the Conference on Interaction and Confidence-Building Measures in Asia (see Chapter Five).

Beijing is also preparing to commit military resources—if necessary—to DPRK denuclearization.[42] Although Beijing is very unlikely to preemptively enter North Korea for a WMD elimination (WMD-E) mission, the Chinese military is actively planning and training for conducting WMD-E inside North Korea.[43] As discussed below, there is space for cooperation, discussed with China for WMD-E in a DPRK collapse scenario.

---

[37] Heng Xie and Megha Rajagopalan, "Bank of China Closes Account of Key North Korean Bank," Reuters, May 7, 2013.

[38] Xie and Rajagopalan, 2013.

[39] Niharika Mandhana and Aruna Viswanatha, "North Korea Built an Alternative Financial System Using a Shadowy Network of Traders," *Wall Street Journal*, December 28, 2018.

[40] Despite its purported belief that sanctions are illegitimate, Beijing has not hesitated to engage in economic coercion of its own in recent years, whether against South Korea over the deployment of a THAAD battery, the Philippines over a territorial row and lawsuit at the International Tribunal on the Law of the Sea, Norway over the awarding of the Nobel Peace Prize to Chinese dissident Liu Xiaobo, or Australia over its calls to investigate the origins of the COVID-19 pandemic, to list just a few examples.

[41] Shen Dingli, "North Korea's Strategic Significance to China," *China Security*, Autumn 2006.

[42] Oriana Skylar Mastro, "Conflict and Chaos on the Korean Peninsula: Can China's Military Help Secure North Korea's Nuclear Weapons?" *International Security*, Vol. 43, No. 2, Fall 2018.

[43] For one example of reported training, see Jun Ji-Hye, "China Conducted Large-Scale Drill in Preparation for Sudden Change in NK," *Korea Times*, December 18, 2017. For early acknowledgement of PLA planning for seizing DPRK nuclear sites, see Liu Xuefeng, Kong Xiangsong, and Hao Hongjun, "区域核辐射监测及安全风险评估系统研究 [Regional Nuclear Radiation Monitoring and Safety Risk Assessment System]," *2013 Proceedings of the China Command and Control Conference*, 2013. For more detailed planning, see 王海燕 [Wang Haiyan], 周慧贞 [Zhou Huizhen], 姜晓峰 [Jiang Xiaofeng], and 王秀华 [Wang Xiuhua], "参与处置周边国家核事故行动装备保障初探 [Preliminary Study on Emergency Disposal Equipment Support

Russian Equities

The North Korean nuclear issue is of medium importance to Russian interests. Moscow's official statements support objectives that run counter to U.S. strategic goals in the Korean Peninsula. Russia has demonstrated willingness to bargain with the United States for a solution to mitigate the North Korean nuclear threat—but on terms that ultimately contradict Washington's aims to achieve a complete, verifiable, and irreversible denuclearization. In this vein, Moscow has not expressed a desire to commit significant resources to achieve a shared goal of the denuclearization of North Korea.

Russia's official rhetoric on regional cooperation to solve the North Korean nuclear issue and emphasis on preventing war on the Korean Peninsula creates an impression that its interests converge with U.S. strategic goals in North Korea.[44] Russia's 2016 Foreign Policy Concept prioritizes easing confrontation and tensions between the two Koreas and achieving a nonnuclear status for the Korean Peninsula through the Six-Party Talks framework.[45] Putin has stated that Russia cannot live with a nuclear North Korea, has called for diplomacy and the resumption of the Six-Party Talks, and has underscored the imperative for trust-building measures and inter-Korean dialogue.[46] Furthermore, as a signatory to the UN Security Council resolutions on the DPRK's nuclear weapon program and illicit activities, Moscow has maintained its support for these international measures in its public statements.

A closer reading of Russian leaders' comments and decisionmaking, however, reveals inconsistencies between Moscow's stated goals and its policy choices. Fundamentally, although Russia supports denuclearization, it subscribes to a more generic goal of removing nuclear weapons from the totality of the Korean Peninsula—not the complete, verifiable, irreversible denuclearization of North Korea, which is the goal of the United States.[47] Furthermore, Moscow supports a reduction—as opposed to complete dismantlement and disablement of Pyongyang's nuclear assets—in the DPRK's nuclear and ballistic missile capabilities, and views this goal as only attainable through a concerted multilateral effort and with economic incentives and other benefits in exchange, including sanctions easing and security guarantees.[48] In addition, Russia holds an inconsistent record on implementing and enforcing sanctions against the DPRK, with Russian companies complicit in reexporting

---

for Neighboring Countries' Nuclear Accidents]," 装备学院学报 [*Journal of Equipment Academy*], February 2016; and 沈同强 [Shen Tongqiang] and 张文宇 [Zhang Wenyu], "认清当前核安全威胁形势, 提升军队核应急处置能力 [Recognize the Current Nuclear Security Threat Situation and Enhance the Military's Nuclear Emergency Response Capability]," 核安全 [*Nuclear Safety*], June 2018.

[44] Elena Ponomareva and Georgij Rudov, "Russia-North Korea: State of Affairs and Trends," *Journal of Asian Public Policy,* Vol. 9, No. 1, 2015.

[45] Ministry of Foreign Affairs of the Russian Federation, 2016b.

[46] Putin, 2012.

[47] Gabuev, 2019.

[48] Artyom Lukin, "Russia's Policy Toward North Korea: Following China's Lead," 38 North, December 23, 2019; Ministry of Foreign Affairs of the Russian Federation, "Foreign Minister Sergey Lavrov's Remarks and

North Korean coal and hiring DPRK forced labor and Russian financial institutions serving as conduits for Pyongyang's illicit financial activities.[49]

From Russia's perspective, the burden of responsibility for dealing with the North Korean nuclear issue does not fall entirely on the DPRK regime. Putin has suggested that there are external aggravators—coded language for the United States and its allies—compelling countries such as North Korea and Iran to pursue nuclear weapons. In his words, "Armed outside interference in the domestic affairs of countries may prompt authoritarian regimes to possess nuclear weapons."[50] Other Russian officials have also spoken out in criticism of the United States' approach to dealing with the North Korean nuclear issue, at times even defending Pyongyang's actions as a legitimate response to Washington's aggressive actions. Days after North Korea launched its Hwasong-15 ballistic missile in November 2017, Russian Foreign Minister Lavrov accused the United States of provoking North Korea to pursue this course of action and demanded that the United States explain its intentions to the international community clearly so that Russia and other countries can respond accordingly.[51] On a separate occasion, Lavrov called for a more flexible approach in the implementation of sanctions against North Korea and criticized the United States for its "imprecise and inaccurate" use of the term "denuclearization of North Korea."[52]

Russia's position on North Korea's denuclearization is similar to, but not identical to, China's stance on the issue, but it differs in a few key dimensions. First, Russia has a greater stake in resolving tensions on the Korean peninsula in order to implement its long-held plan for the gasification of the Korean Peninsula and the building of a trans-Korea gas pipeline with links to the Russian Far East. Additionally, Russian scholars have pointed out that Russia's limited economic leverage has enabled it to play the role of honest broker periodically, especially when ties between the DPRK and China become more fraught. Though Russia has expressed interest in developing relations with the two Koreas so as to facilitate gasification of the Korean Peninsula, it has not made consistent or sufficient efforts to make progress in these areas or to reduce inter-Korean tensions.[53]

Answers to Media Questions at a News Conference Following His Visit to the U.S., Washington, December 10, 2019," December 11, 2019b.

[49] "Russia Resumes Coals Supplies Via North Korea: Ifax Citing Official," *Reuters*, September 5, 2018; United Nations, *2019 Midterm Report of the Panel of Experts Submitted Pursuant to Resolution 2464 (2019)*, S/2019/691, August 30, 2019; Christy Lee, "Experts: Russia Skirts Sanctions on N. Korean Workers to Defy US-Led Pressure," *Voice of America*, February 1, 2020; Scott A. Snyder, "Where Does the Russia–North Korea Relationship Stand?" Council on Foreign Relations, April 29, 2019.

[50] Putin, 2012.

[51] "US Should Come Clean if It's Looking for Pretext to Destroy N. Korea–Russian FM Lavrov," *RT*, November 30, 2017.

[52] Ministry of Foreign Affairs of the Russian Federation, 2019b.

[53] We thank Elizbeth Wishnick for several comments in this and the next paragraph, which we have adapted from her review.

Finally, Russia is less affected by the U.S. deployment of a THAAD battery on the Korean peninsula and did not follow China in retaliating economically for that deployment against South Korea. This may be attributed to the greater weight China places on DPRK issues in its regional foreign policy—for instance, a humanitarian spillover into China's border appears to be a consistent concern for Chinese decisionmakers in dealing with North Korea.[54]

In the realm of similarities, Moscow has been supportive of Beijing's position on a "freeze for freeze" initiative, wherein the United States and South Korea, as a trust-building, reciprocal measure, would suspend certain joint military exercises while North Korea would freeze its missile tests.[55] In November 2019, Moscow and Beijing drafted a proposal for solving the long-standing security dilemma on the Korean Peninsula and announced plans to submit this document to North Korea's Vice Minister of Foreign Affairs Choe Son Hui, as well as to the stakeholders involved in the nuclear negotiations.[56] Details of the China-Russia joint proposal have not been revealed, but the terms of the plan likely support the long-standing positions of Beijing and Moscow on the need to lift sanctions, pursue dialogue through a multilateral construct that considers the interests of all concerned parties, and compromise on the key issue of North Korea's denuclearization via a partial dismantlement of its nuclear facilities or a freeze on its nuclear activities.[57]

China's growing weight and impact in the region and its ongoing strategic competition with the United States have increased the asymmetry of power in Russia's own relations with China. On the North Korea issue, the DPRK regime clearly views Beijing as the more effective card than Moscow to use against Washington as leverage in negotiations over its nuclear weapon program and sanctions easing. Russia, for its part, has been willing not only to cooperate with China and support its position on the nuclear issue but also come to terms with Russia's own waning leverage over North Korea and tacitly acknowledge the Korean Penin-

---

[54] Richard C. Bush, "China's Response to Collapse in North Korea," Brookings Institution, January 23, 2014; Steve Mollman, "It's Time to Start Considering What a North Korean Refugee Crisis Would Look Like," *Quartz*, May 17, 2017.

[55] For background reading on the arguments for or against a "freeze-for-freeze" or "double-freeze" proposal, see "North Korea 'Dual Freeze' Plan Working, Russia's UN Envoy Says," Tass, February 9, 2018; Jong Chul Park, "How to Promote Peace On the Korean Peninsula After PyeongChang Winter Olympics," Korea Institute for National Unification, February 8, 2018; Andrei Lankov, "North Korea, Nuclear Weapons, and the Search for a New Path Forward: A Russian Response," *Bulletin of the Atomic Scientists*, Vol. 72, No. 5, 2016.

[56] "Россия и Китай согласовали новый проект плана по корейскому урегулированию [Russia and China Agreed on a New Draft Plan for a Korean Settlement]," Tass, November 19, 2019.

[57] For discussions on North Korean nuclear negotiations and Russia-China positions on the issue, see Sangtu Ko, "International Sanctions on North Korea: A Two-Level Solution," *Pacific Focus*, Vol. 34, No. 1, April 2019; Michelle Nichols, "Russia, China to Hold More U.N. Talks on Lifting North Korea Sanctions: Diplomats, Reuters, December 29, 2019.

sula as China's sphere of influence.[58] This also suggests that the North Korea issue is less of a foreign policy priority for Russia than it is for China.

For the United States, this likely implies that the space or desire for Moscow to cooperate with Washington on the North Korean denuclearization issue is at best limited. Russia appears to lack the motivation or determination to compete seriously with China on influence over North Korea. That Russia depends on its relations with China to support its own strategic ambitions likely discourages Moscow from stoking Beijing's ire by challenging the latter's position on the DPRK.

Space for Cooperation

As noted at the outset, in principle neither China nor Russia should welcome a nuclear-armed North Korea on its border, given the Kim family regime's penchant for risk manipulation and provocative actions that could risk a wider conflagration, potentially with nuclear weapons. Additionally, both Beijing and Moscow are signatories to and have ratified the Nuclear Non-Proliferation Treaty and should therefore feel an international legal obligation reinforcing the self-interested proposition that having North Korea acquire the bomb lessens its relative dependence on them and their relative advantage over it. And the two countries have joined with the United States at times—in the Six-Party Talks and at the United Nations Security Council—to pass resolutions sanctioning North Korea when it has engaged in highly provocative actions.

Yet, as the discussion of U.S., Chinese, and Russian equities laid out above makes clear, although Beijing and Moscow publicly hold to the line that they oppose North Korean nuclear weapon acquisition and missile development, these positions are substantively undercut by Beijing's and Moscow's perceptions that (1) the most significant problems in their external security environments stem from the power of the United States and its allies and partners and (2) that the value of liberal democracy as a norm that threatens the CCP and Putin regimes' holds on power. Additionally, for Beijing and likely for Moscow as well, there is simply no plausible pathway to compel North Korean denuclearization that does not run at least some risk of regime instability and collapse or war. For this reason, neither Beijing nor Moscow is willing to undertake much in the way of substantial, costly, or irreversible steps to impose costs on North Korea for its actions and efforts to build nuclear weapons, since both prioritize stability over denuclearization and see upsides to tying the United States down. Table 7.1 reflects these difficult-to-bridge differences.

Some U.S. observers have noted that the upcoming renewal of the 1961 Sino–North Korean Mutual Aid and Cooperation Friendship Treaty in 2021 gives Beijing some additional

---

[58] Lukin, 2019; Gabuev, 2019; Rozman, 2007; Jamie Tarabay, "Russia's Foreign Minister Is Headed to North Korea," CNN, May 31, 2018.

TABLE 7.1

Interest in Cooperation on DPRK Denuclearization

Space for Cooperation	China	Russia
Stakes	Medium	Medium
Rhetorical alignment	High	High
Demonstrated willingness to commit resources	Low	Low

leverage in pushing Pyongyang to recommit to denuclearization.[59] However, analysts note that Beijing is unlikely to actually recognize its commitment under that treaty (instead, Chinese action will be determined at the time based on political calculations) and that Pyongyang is unlikely to similarly expect a Chinese commitment, so the treaty's symbolic nature makes this leverage rather hollow.

Highly destabilizing North Korean actions, and U.S. willingness to take steps that might lead to war, have been the two most obvious factors that have moved China and Russia to sanction Pyongyang in the past, particularly after nuclear tests and missile launches or during 2017, when the United States appeared to be preparing a "bloody nose" option. At times, the two sides have acted in something like coordination, most notably in their joint 2017 "dual suspension" proposal and again in their 2019 joint proposal to lift sanctions on the North at the UN.[60]

At other times, China and Russia have existed in a state of some competition with each other over influence in Korea. Sino-Russian competition in Korea dates back at least as far back as the late 19th century but also existed throughout the period of the Kim family regime's establishment and the Korean War;[61] throughout the Cold War, most notably in the two countries' 1961 security treaties with Pyongyang; at the point of recognition of the South from 1990 to 1992; over port access in North Korea in the mid-2000s and 2010s; and over provision to the North of external internet servers.[62] Despite these historical tensions, for the most part Russia has recognized PRC dominance on Korea and effectively subordinated its competition with China for influence in Korea to the broader goal of working with Beijing to counter the United States; for this reason, it is unlikely Russia will work at cross-purposes to China on North Korean denuclearization.[63]

---

[59] Joseph DeTrani, "China Can Push North Korea for Complete and Verifiable Denuclearization," *Washington Times*, August 17, 2020.

[60] "China Says 'Dual Suspension' Proposal Still Best for North Korea," Reuters, November 16, 2017; Smith, 2019.

[61] Sergei Goncharov, John Lewis, and Xue Litai, *Uncertain Partners: Stalin, Mao, and the Korean War*, Stanford, Calif.: Stanford University Press, 1995.

[62] "Russian Firm Provides New Internet Connection to North Korea," Reuters, October 2, 2017.

[63] Lukin, 2019.

One common interest that may provide space for cooperation is technical cooperation over WMD-E. This is most likely to occur in a DPRK collapse scenario, raising the prospect that any or all of the U.S., PRC, and Russian militaries will be entering North Korea. As previous RAND work has found, in a North Korea collapse scenario "the window for seizing WMD, materials, technologies, and scientific and technical personnel before they can be dispersed or proliferated may be quite short," and the demand for U.S. forces could run as high as 188,000 persons or more, meaning that cooperation and deconfliction with China and Russia to find and fix North Korean WMD is likely to be an urgent mission.[64] Rendering safe nuclear weapons, especially those of foreign countries, is extremely difficult. The United States is the only country that has experience in handling foreign nuclear weapons, as part of its cooperation with former Soviet Union states in the 1990s. It is perhaps possible (even if not likely) that if the geopolitical climate changes substantially, Beijing and Moscow may welcome U.S. expertise for this mission.

The single greatest stumbling block on the path to the complete, verifiable, and irreversible denuclearization of North Korean is, of course, the determination of the regime in Pyongyang that it must have nuclear weapons and ballistic missiles.

Chinese and Russian views of the nature of the North Korean threat and its place in their national narratives also represent a challenge for U.S. policy. For example, despite the fact that the Korean War started when the North invaded the South, official PRC views of the Korean War continue to paint the conflict in patriotic tones and associate it with the founding of the Chinese state as a heroic resistance by Asian nations against American imperialism.[65] Indeed, even down to the present, many Chinese analyses continue to paint the North's nuclear program as a response to threats from the United States; oppose the use of sanctions; imply at times that the issue is a bilateral U.S.-North Korea problem; and argue that the United States, as the more powerful country, should take steps first and should seek to meet the North's demands.

A related challenge that further complicates matters is that the North's proliferation procurement channels and methods for evading sanctions are deeply intertwined with criminal networks in both China and Russia, a strategy that the Kim regime has adopted as a hedge against the possibility that Beijing or Moscow might seek to cooperate with Washington and the rest of the world in containing its nuclear development.[66] This suggests that policing, intelligence, and, possibly, military cooperation among the three countries—as unlikely as that may be—would be needed in order to unravel and roll up North Korea's clandestine proliferation efforts, alongside economic sanctions and a political-military pressure campaign.

---

[64] Timothy M. Bonds, Eric V. Larson, Derek Eaton, and Richard E. Darilek, *Strategy-Policy Mismatch: How the U.S. Army Can Help Close Gaps in Countering Weapons of Mass Destruction*, Santa Monica, Calif.: RAND Corporation, RR-541-RC, 2014.

[65] Abraham Denmark and Lucas Myers, "Eternal Victory," *Wilson Quarterly*, Summer 2020.

[66] John Park and Jim Walsh, *Stopping North Korea, Inc.: Sanctions Effectiveness and Unintended Consequences*, Cambridge, Mass.: Massachusetts Institute of Technology, 2016.

Unfortunately, it is not clear that Beijing or Moscow is unaware of North Korean oil bunkering, illegal coal exports, or other criminal or sanctions-violating activities, and hence eliciting official cooperation from China and Russia to counter these activities is likely to prove difficult or even impossible.[67]

Achieving the denuclearization of North Korea is thus a challenging policy goal made all the more complicated by the serious obstacles the United States faces in eliciting cooperation toward this end from either China or Russia. The reasons for this include distrust, audience costs, definitional problems, third-party problems, and issue linkages. By contrast, immediacy, legal constraints, and capacity or capability do not appear as major obstacles to cooperation with China and/or Russia on the denuclearization of North Korea, and hence we do not discuss them further here.

Trust. For China and the United States, mistrust on DPRK issues is long-standing and deep. Some in China believe that the United States and its allies exploit the DPRK threat as a way to cover their military buildup against China, and that their efforts toward denuclearization are a covert way to push the collapse of the Kim regime and unification of the Korean peninsula under South Korean rule. On the other side, in Washington, some believe Beijing uses North Korea as a "proxy" to distract U.S. attention in Asia, and even secretly supports the North's WMD and missile programs, in part through lax enforcement of UN sanctions. For Russia and the United States, mistrust of the other party's intentions and policy interests over North Korea is likely to impede meaningful U.S.-Russian cooperation over the DPRK nuclear issue. Russia has condoned, overlooked, and even participated in North Korea's sanctions violating activities, including illegal ship-to-ship transfers of oil and the transport of luxury vehicles to the Kim regime, casting doubts about its commitment to resolving the North Korea threat.[68]

Audience costs. For China, some in elite circles support North Korea out of nostalgia and pride over their country's performance against the superior U.S. military in the Korean War and sympathize with North Korea's "oppression" and "coercion" by the United States. This is most prominent—though not a dominant view—among the Chinese military and some CCP elites whose families made political advancement during the war. Some in the Chinese public also support North Korea as a truer form of communism that harkens back to the days of Mao. As one 2017 report noted,

> The Party's prestige is on the line. Among the People's Liberation Army, in particular, North Korea still evokes a revolutionary nostalgia; Mao's son died in the 1950–53 Korean War, in which Chinese forces fought the Americans to a standstill, a proud boast to this day . . . letting North Korea go would give encouragement to political forces in China that

---

[67] "How North Korea Evades Sanctions," *New York Times*, video, September 22, 2017; "How Kim Jong-Un Gets His $500,000 Mercedes," *New York Times*, video, July 16, 2019.

[68] U.S. Department of the Treasury, "Treasury Targets Russian Shipping Companies for Violations of North Korea-Related United Nations Security Council Resolutions," August 21, 2018; Edward Wong and Christoph Koettl, "How North Korea's Leader Gets His Luxury Cars," *New York Times*, July 16, 2019.

Mr. Xi spent his first term ruthlessly crushing—dissidents, human rights activists and others who might read in Mr. Kim's demise a message about the vulnerabilities of their own socialist leaders.[69]

Definitional problems. Differences in the definition of North Korea's "denuclearization"—and ultimately, the desired end states in the issue—are likely to pose obstacles to U.S.-China and U.S.-Russia cooperation. Whereas the United States adheres to and defines the desired end state with North Korea as complete, verifiable, and irreversible denuclearization, China and Russia define the process and end goal of the denuclearization issue in much broader terms, with U.S. incentives and reciprocity to correspond with North Korean steps toward nuclear restraint. As Stephanie Kleine-Ahlbrandt of the United States Institute of Peace testified to Congress in 2014, "From Beijing's perspective, denuclearization is a long-term endeavor, which first requires Pyongyang to receive security assurances that create stability around it. Chinese conventional wisdom holds that no amount of pressure will induce Pyongyang to give up its nuclear weapons program without fundamental concessions from the U.S."[70] Instead, China views denuclearization as the end result of a broader process that changes "will ultimately alter North Korea's strategic calculus regarding the role of nuclear weapons."[71] Russia is in lockstep with China's position of preserving regional stability and a reciprocal, step-by-step approach to reducing the North Korean nuclear threat. Moscow also appears skeptical about the viability of Washington's goals of North Korea's complete, verifiable, and irreversible denuclearization and advocates greater "flexibility" in dealing with North Korea, including the easing of sanctions on the Kim regime's nuclear and ballistic missile programs and activities.[72]

Third-party problems. For the United States and China, the issue of DPRK denuclearization cannot be solved simply bilaterally—North Korea is an actor in its own right with the ability to accelerate, or even use, its WMD and missile programs, or conduct attacks on South Korea or Japan that force a U.S.-allied military response against China's wishes. Chinese businesses that trade with North Korea are another group of actors that could complicate U.S.-China cooperation on the issue.[73] Although this is as much about Beijing's dedication of resources to actually enforce sanctions, Pyongyang recognizes the challenges of doing business in China and thus makes it very lucrative for Chinese companies to partner with it. For Russia, North Korea and/or China may seek to thwart successful U.S.-Russian cooperation

---

[69] For comments on the PLA and North Korea, see Andrew Browne, "China Won't Help: It's Paralyzed by North Korea," *Wall Street Journal*, September 6, 2017. For the general public and ideological inspiration from North Korea, see "Paradise Lost: Chinese Maoists in North Korea," *The Economist*, November 24, 2012.

[70] Kleine-Ahlbrandt, 2014.

[71] Kleine-Ahlbrandt, 2014.

[72] Ministry of Foreign Affairs of the Russian Federation, 2019b.

[73] Park and Walsh, 2016.

over the DPRK nuclear issue through nuclear and missile provocations, conventional military aggression, and other forms of coercion that are meant to discourage progress over the denuclearization of North Korea. The estrangement of Russia–North Korea relations following Moscow's reduction of financial assistance to Pyongyang in the 1980s diminished Russia's influence over North Korea, to the extent that Pyongyang was able to pressure Moscow into restructuring—essentially forgiving—Pyongyang's financial debt to Moscow incurred during the Soviet years.[74] Given North Korea's tendency to resort to pressure and provocations against countries pursuing policies that constrain the regime's mobility, it is likely that U.S.-Russia cooperation over the North Korean nuclear issue will elicit responses from Pyongyang designed to complicate and frustrate any emerging U.S.-Russia coordination.

Issue linkage. For at least some elites in Beijing, the fate of North Korea is viewed as interlinked with broader U.S.-China competition. This is true both in terms of using North Korea as a convenient cost-imposition strategy against the United States to distract resources away from its assumed intention of containing China's rise and in terms of the related concern that if DPRK denuclearization is pursued with too much zeal and forces the collapse of the Kim regime, a unified Republic of Korea under Seoul's leadership would increase U.S. influence and potentially bring U.S. military power to China's doorstep. As one 2017 report noted,

> There are even perverse benefits to Beijing from Mr. Kim's nuclear brinkmanship: It keeps the U.S. military pinned down in Northeast Asia, and to the extent that it casts doubt on Washington's resolve to defend South Korea and Japan—would Mr. Trump risk San Francisco for Seoul or Tokyo?—it drives a wedge between the U.S. and its two key Asian allies.[75]

Second-Order Effects of Cooperation

Were the United States to achieve the complete, verifiable, and irreversible denuclearization of North Korea (CVID) with Chinese cooperation, it would likely make Pyongyang more likely to turn to other sources of assistance, possibly including Russia. Moscow, recognizing that a North Korea under pressure from China and the United States would likely be open to greater cooperation, could try to restore or expand its influence in Pyongyang, while also expanding its ability to bargain with Washington as a result of any such expanded leverage. Still, even under such an unlikely scenario, Moscow would likely still seek to subordinate its ties with Pyongyang to the broader goal of keeping closely aligned with China for the purposes of competing with the United States. By contrast, were the United States to achieve CVID through cooperation with Russian cooperation and without Chinese assistance, Pyongyang

---

[74] Maya Dyakina and Lidia Kelly, "Russia Writes Off 90 Percent of North Korea's Debt," Reuters, September 18, 2012.

[75] Browne, 2017.

would presumably become even more dependent on, and probably resentful of, China, reducing Beijing's leverage to some extent over the United States, South Korea, and Japan. Such an outcome could conceivably result in friction in the China-Russia relationship, though in some sense it would simply be a recognition that Moscow's influence in Pyongyang has long been and will likely long be less than Beijing's.

If the United States were forced to compete more with China on CVID in North Korea, this could conceivably take one of two forms.

First, China could continue to put forward alternative proposals deemed unlikely to succeed by the United States, such as advocating for talks without sanctions or a "freeze-for-freeze" formula. Such a development would likely be seen as desirable by Russia, which might seek to join in such calls, as, indeed, it has to date.

Second, Chinese officials could move a step further, more openly providing support to North Korea in the form of state visits, diplomatic cover at the UN, food aid and energy assistance, or even technological support. The most extreme variant of this approach would be a more fulsome embrace of the North by China as a military ally, reducing or eliminating compliance with international sanctions and reiterating support for defending the North. While not consonant with how China has behaved to date—it has largely sought to retain leverage with all parties as opposed to placing all its chips on Pyongyang, an actor it does not trust that has some interests that are at odds with those of the CCP—such an outcome may not be impossible if Beijing concludes that the Sino-U.S. relationship has devolved into outright confrontation and containment.

U.S. competition with Russia over North Korean CVID is likely a lesser case of that described above for China. Russia has far fewer resources and influence to bring to bear on defending North Korea either against sanctions or in a physical, military sense. With that said, Russia has shown its willingness to introduce proposals the United States regards as unhelpful, has enabled Pyongyang's cyber attacks by establishing an additional internet server outside the country, and would not have to provide large amounts of defense technology to complicate U.S. force planning against the North. Support for Pyongyang has not traditionally provided Moscow with as much leverage vis-a-vis Washington, Seoul, and Tokyo as it has given Beijing, but were Moscow to come under sustained pressure and perceive its economic and geopolitical positions to be growing dire, it may come to regard Pyongyang as a relatively low-cost way to push back and regain some influence, especially if cooperation with Beijing were seen as less feasible or desirable for some reason.

Conclusion

Overall, despite an apparent commonality of interests between Washington, Beijing, and Moscow on countering North Korea's efforts to acquire nuclear weapons and associated ballistic missile delivery systems, at present the prospects for such cooperation appear remote. Both China and Russia regard North Korea as troublesome but also useful inasmuch as it gives them leverage vis-à-vis the United States and complicates Washington's ability to focus on the challenges that China and Russia pose to U.S. interests in other areas. Moreover, even if the three sides were to genuinely share the goal of denuclearizing North Korea, the approaches that each has historically preferred to achieving that goal are deeply contradictory. Therefore, it is highly likely that the United States will have to compete—at least at times—with Chinese and Russian approaches to achieving North Korean CVID, and any cooperation Washington is able to elicit is likely to be compelled, not freely given; come only after some egregious North Korean provocation; and be walked back as soon as possible.

CHAPTER EIGHT

Countering Terrorism and Violent Islamist Extremism in Afghanistan and Southeast Asia

As with the goal of seeking CVID in North Korea, so too when the United States seeks to counter terrorism and violent extremism in Afghanistan and Southeast Asia (primarily Indonesia, Malaysia, the Philippines, Singapore and Thailand), it would appear on the surface to be a promising area where American, Chinese, and Russian interests overlap and may present opportunities for cooperation. Yet this has rarely proven to be the case, for reasons explored in the following analysis.

Understanding the Equities

Three primary factors—domestic concerns for human rights, strategies for how best to counter terrorist groups, and views of the international system and geopolitical competition within it—are the most critical factors shaping the views each country has of its equities at stake in the issue of counterterrorism/countering violent extremism (CT/CVE).

U.S. Equities

U.S. counterterrorism policy, as laid out in the Trump administration's 2018 *National Strategy for Counter-Terrorism* (NSCT), identifies radical Islamist groups such as al Qaeda and the Islamic State as the primary nonstate actors that the United States seeks to disrupt, deny, degrade and destroy.[1] To do so, the United States prioritizes using "all available instruments of United States power" and anticipates "building strong borders, strengthening security at all ports of entry . . . protecting critical infrastructure, and facilitating preparedness."[2] U.S. policy also emphasizes the need to "broaden our range of partners to combat radical Islamist

---

[1] The White House, *National Strategy for Counterterrorism of the United States of America*, Washington, D.C., 2018. See also Nathan A. Sales, "Keeping the Pressure on al-Qaida," U.S. Department of State, Office of the Coordinator for Counter-Terrorism, September 12, 2019.

[2] The White House, 2018.

terrorism . . . encourage capable partners to play a larger role . . . and assist other partners so that they can eventually address terrorist threats independently."[3]

Four key defining features of U.S. CT/CVE policy stand out as different from those of China and Russia.

First, as the NSCT notes, in the quest to defeat radical Islamist terror groups and the threat they pose to U.S. national security, the approach guiding U.S. CT/CVE policy will "continue to protect American freedoms." This is a key first key difference from the approaches of China and Russia, where civil liberties, the rule of law, an independent media and legislative oversight are weak or nonexistent.

Second, the U.S. strategy references a key line of effort that has not been a traditional part of Chinese or Russian CT/CVE efforts, noting that the United States will "pursue terrorist threats to their source . . . conducting military, intelligence, and law enforcement operations and employing financial measures against discrete targets."[4]

Third, the U.S. approach, focused on an aggressive response to dismantle terror networks *in toto*, including overseas, is described as being pursued in partnership with foreign nations that the United States will seek to bolster and provide intelligence to, another key divergence from the approaches of China and Russia, which have primarily sought to engage in counterterrorism within their own borders. On those occasions when they pursue targets abroad, their actions have generally revolved around seeking extradition of Uyghurs, propping up states that actively support terrorism (Iran and Syria—something both the PRC and Russia do), or actually engaging in the use of WMD to assassinate the regime's political enemies who have fled abroad (as Russia has on multiple occasions).[5]

Fourth and finally, the U.S. view is that, by taking action to defeat terrorist groups and ideologies where they seek to take root, it is making manifest America's "special role among nations as a vanguard of freedom, democracy, and constitutional governance" and that "as fascists and communists did before them, terrorists seek to use our openness, tolerance, and freedoms against us. They will fail."[6] Such language is unlikely to appeal to either China (led by a Communist Party that displays increasingly national-socialist or fascist tendencies) nor Russia (led by Putin, who has described the fall of Soviet communism as the greatest tragedy of the 20th century), both because it positions them as adversaries and compares them to terrorists, and also because it reflects a commitment to a political order they regard as an obstacle to the realization of their ambitions and threatening to their continued hold on power.

---

[3]   The White House, 2018.

[4]   The White House, 2018.

[5]   U.S. Department of State, Bureau of Counter-Terrorism, "State Sponsors of Terrorism," undated, accessed June 26, 2020; Alan Cowell, "Putin 'Probably Approved' Litvinenko Poisoning, British Inquiry Says," *New York Times*, January 21, 2016; "UK Says Nerve Agent Used to Poison Ex-Russian Spy Was in Liquid Form: BBC," Reuters, April 17, 2018.

[6]   The White House, 2018.

In practical terms for the Indo-Pacific region, the United States has equities in CT/CVE in Afghanistan and Pakistan in South-Central Asia and also in supporting the efforts of Indonesia, Malaysia, the Philippines, Singapore and Thailand.

In South and Central Asia, U.S. CT/CVE policy has focused on Afghanistan, where the United States has been seeking to deny al Qaeda and ISIS-Khorasan a base from which to operate while also seeking to counter the violent extremism of the Taliban and working toward a peace deal that would permit the withdrawal of most U.S. forces while preserving the viability of the Afghan national government.[7] Closely linked to U.S. efforts to counter al Qaeda and ISIS-Khorasan in Afghanistan are efforts to engage the government of Pakistan on CT/CVE policy. U.S. efforts seek to encourage Pakistan to "take decisive and irreversible action against . . . externally-focused militant groups and UN-designated terrorist organizations operating from its territory," and urge the Pakistani government to sever ties with other militant groups that have often served as proxies in Islamabad's long-running struggle with India.[8]

In Southeast Asia, U.S. CT/CVE policy seeks to bolster the ability of governments in Indonesia, Malaysia, the Philippines, Singapore and Thailand, which face challenges with terrorism, insurgency, and political violence. The groups the United States has focused on most notably from Jemaah Islamiyyah (JI) in Indonesia, the Abu Sayyaf Group (ASG) in the Philippines. Gerakan Mujahidin Islam Pattani in Thailand, and Kumpulan Mujahidin Malaysia, as well as efforts by al Qaeda and ISIS to expand their influence within the region.[9] U.S. efforts to support local governments in countering these violent extremist groups have included information- and intelligence-sharing, police work, airborne and maritime monitoring, training, arms sales, and even direct support to ongoing counterterrorism operations, such as those related to the siege of Marawi in the Southern Philippines in 2017, as well as assistance to the Philippines with rebuilding in the wake of that crisis. The United States also signed a counterterrorism memorandum of understanding with Indonesia in 2018 to facilitate expanded information-sharing, training, and exchanges of best practices.[10]

Overall, the United States seeks to counter, deny, degrade, and destroy violent extremist groups while at the same time bolstering U.S. security and respect for global norms such as

---

[7] U.S. Department of State, Bureau of South and Central Asian Affairs, "Bilateral Relations Fact Sheet: U.S. Relations with Afghanistan," July 8, 2019c.

[8] U.S. Department of State, Bureau of South and Central Asian Affairs, "Bilateral Relations Fact Sheet: U.S. Relations with Pakistan," June 21, 2019b.

[9] It should be noted that many of the groups in the Southeast Asia terrorism scene change affiliations or carry more than one affiliation, and hence the boundaries between these should be seen as fuzzy rather than fixed. For example, JI has at one point in time affiliated with al-Qaida, as has ASG; more recently, ASG associated itself with ISIS. Additionally, geographic boundaries are highly but not rigidly correlated with where these groups operate; such groups move regularly across borders as needed and as feasible to avoid law enforcement and intelligence or to procure resources and execute plans.

[10] U.S. Department of State, Office of the Spokesperson, "Media Note: Ambassador Sales Signs MOU to Strengthen Counterterrorism Cooperation with Indonesia," September 14, 2018.

human rights and the rule of law. It does this by engaging the totality of its own capabilities while also assisting overseas partners in establishing control over their own borders and encouraging them to take steps that would cut off both the resources terrorist groups need to thrive and the ideational or normative spaces they need to operate.

Chinese Equities

China shares a rhetorical position in common with the United States and other regional countries seeking to counter terrorism in South-Central and Southeast Asia, but the prospects for substantial cooperation with the United States are low because of China's problematic definition of terrorism and frequent use of counterterrorism cooperation as a way to improve its security relationships in the region.[11] China's increased interest in counterterrorism efforts in recent years reflects Beijing's growing concerns over domestic terrorism and a greater willingness to undertake military operations abroad in service of Chinese interests. Overall, although China began "marching Westward" with its Belt and Road Initiative in the 2012–2013 timeframe, it has taken a relatively low-key approach to counterterrorism in South-Central and Southeast Asia and has mixed rhetorical alignment with the United States, in part because of U.S. concerns about China's human rights record and its approach to counterterrorism.[12] U.S.-China dialogue on the issue has been long-standing, and China has demonstrated at least some willingness to commit resources toward these shared interests.

China's interests against terrorism in the Indo-Pacific are rooted in the CCP's key interest in maintaining domestic stability, because of concerns that terrorism abroad could foment attacks within China. In his 2017 speech to the 19th Party Congress, Xi said, "We must rigorously protect against and take resolute measures to combat all acts of infiltration, subversion, and sabotage, as well as violent and terrorist activities, ethnic separatist activities, and religious extremist activities."[13] One important related interest for China is economic growth, since terrorism in South Asia may have spillover effects into China that disrupt Xinjiang's economic growth and, more importantly, the BRI. The Xinjiang Uyghur Autonomous Region is one of several key hubs in China's BRI plan and is the gateway for China's Silk Road Economic Belt as it extends through Central Asia into the Middle East and eventually Europe. Xinjiang is also where much—perhaps close to 50 percent—of China's imported liquid natural gas from Central Asia enters the country, adding another reason to prioritize stability in the territory.[14] As one U.S. analyst noted in 2018,

---

[11] For a recent overview of China's position in Afghanistan, see "Envoy Elaborates China's Position on Afghanistan," Xinhua, November 28, 2019.

[12] 王缉思 [Wang Jisi], "西进, 中国地缘战略的再平衡 [Marching West: China's Geo-Strategic Re-Balancing]," 环球时报 [Huanqiu Times], October 17, 2012.

[13] Xi, 2017.

[14] Office of the Secretary of Defense, Military and Security Developments Involving the People's Republic of China 2018: Annual Report to Congress, Washington, D.C.: U.S. Department of Defense, May 2018, p. 56.

The US and Chinese governments recognize their shared interest in a stable, peaceful, and increasingly prosperous (or, at least, increasingly self-sufficient) Afghanistan. Perhaps most clearly, for the United States, achieving a stable outcome in Afghanistan would allow it to end its long, costly military involvement there; but China too would benefit enormously from reduced instability on its border.[15]

Beijing has always been concerned about maintaining control of its border regions, including Xinjiang.[16] This concern was accentuated at the outset of Xi's rise to power by both foreign and domestic events.[17] The outbreak of instability in the Middle East, especially concerns over Chinese citizens fighting in Syria and returning to launch attacks at home, coupled with the U.S. withdrawal from Afghanistan, made China's periphery looks rather perilous to the leadership in Beijing.[18] In a series of secret speeches in 2014 obtained by the *New York Times*, Xi said,

> After the United States pulls troops out of Afghanistan, terrorist organizations positioned on the frontiers of Afghanistan and Pakistan may quickly infiltrate into Central Asia. . . . East Turkestan's terrorists who have received real-war training in Syria and Afghanistan could at any time launch terrorist attacks in Xinjiang.[19]

These fears were spurred on by a spate of domestic terror attacks in 2013–2015, including a 2013 car attack in Tiananmen Square in downtown Beijing, as well as a 2014 knife attack in a southwestern China train station that killed 29 and injured 143.[20]

China's response under Xi has been to double down on repression to an unprecedented degree and to pursue greater "counterterrorism" cooperation abroad. In one secret speech, Xi called for the CCP to "struggle against terrorism, infiltration and separatism" and show

---

[15] David Rank, *Leveraging US-China Cooperation to Build a Regional Consensus on Afghanistan*, Washington, D.C.: United States Institute of Peace, March 2018.

[16] For a review of China's past approaches to terrorism concerns, see Murray Scot Tanner and James Bellacqua, *China's Response to Terrorism*, Washington, D.C.: U.S.-China Economic and Security Review Commission, June 2016.

[17] Sheena Chestnut Greitens, Myunghee Lee, and Emir Yazici, "China's Changing Strategy in Xinjiang: Counterterrorism and Preventive Repression," *International Security*, Vol. 44, No. 3, 2020. For a critique of this framing, see Matthew Robertson, "Counterterrorism or Cultural Genocide? Theory and Normativity in Knowledge Production About China's 'Xinjiang Strategy,'" *Made in China Journal*, June 12, 2020.

[18] Jacob Zenn, "An Overview of Chinese Fighters and Anti-Chinese Militant Groups in Syria and Iraq," *China Brief*, Vol. 14, No. 19, October 10, 2014; Joseph Hope, "Returning Uighur Fighters and China's National Security Dilemma," *China Brief*, Vol. 18, No. 13, July 25, 2018; Mathieu Duchâtel, "China's Foreign Fighters Problem," *War on the Rocks*, January 25, 2019.

[19] Austin Ramzy and Chris Buckley, "'Absolutely No Mercy': Leaked Files Expose How China Organized Mass Detentions of Muslims," *New York Times*, November 16, 2019.

[20] Andrew Jacobs and Chris Buckley, "China Blames Xinjiang Separatists for Stabbing Rampage at Train Station," *New York Times*, March 2, 2014.

"absolutely no mercy."[21] Even though the CCP often frames economic development as the best solution to solve the problem of terrorism, Xi rejected that notion for China's northwest, saying, "In recent years, Xinjiang has grown very quickly and the standard of living has consistently risen, but even so ethnic separatism and terrorist violence have still been on the rise . . . economic development does not automatically bring lasting order and security."[22] Xinjiang Party Secretary Chen Quanguo, installed in 2016, has implemented a centrally approved crackdown that is estimated to have imprisoned upward of 3 million people in what U.S. officials have described as "concentration camps" that are a part of China's "genocide" in the region.[23]

This has been coupled with more efforts for cooperation abroad. Xi made this an explicit part of the BRI and the Community of Common Destiny, his overarching proposal for revising the international order, by saying in his 2017 speech,

> We call on the people of all countries to work together to build a community with a shared future for mankind, to build an open, inclusive, clean, and beautiful world that enjoys lasting peace, universal security, and common prosperity . . . [and to] oppose terrorism in all its forms.[24]

The Shanghai Cooperation Organization (SCO), co-founded by China, Russia, and several Central Asian states in 1995 as the Shanghai Five and upgraded in 2001 with the addition of more participants, focuses on common security concerns, including China's preferred formula of "countering terrorism, separatism and extremism."[25] Early Chinese security operations abroad for counterterrorism include joint military exercises under the SCO's "Peace Mission" series, reflecting a broader emphasis on counterterrorism for China's foreign military exercises.[26]

Afghanistan has been the biggest terrorism-related topic discussed between Washington and Beijing over the years, with mixed results. In 2017, Trump and Xi "discussed the Middle East, Afghanistan, and other issues, and agreed to deepen cooperation on counterterrorism," and Trump said the two leaders agreed that "terrorists are a threat to all of humanity, and we will stop radical Islamic terrorism."[27] However, in the most recent U.S.-China dialogue,

---

[21] Ramzy and Buckley, 2019.

[22] Ramzy and Buckley, 2019.

[23] Phil Stewart, "China Putting Minority Muslims in 'Concentration Camps,' U.S. Says," Reuters, May 3, 2019.

[24] Xi, 2017.

[25] Shanghai Cooperation Organization, "General Information," undated.

[26] Kenneth Allen, Phillip C. Saunders, and John Chen, *Chinese Military Diplomacy, 2003–2016: Trends and Implications*, Washington, D.C.: National Defense University, July 2017.

[27] Donald J. Trump and Xi Jinping, "Remarks by President Trump and President Xi of China in Joint Press Statement," November 9, 2017.

in November 2018, Afghanistan wasn't even mentioned.[28] China participated in the Quadrilateral Group, along with the United States, Pakistan, and Afghanistan, over 2016–2017 to coordinate on Afghanistan issues.[29] China also joined a similar effort in 2019 with the United States, Russia, and Pakistan.[30] Some U.S.-China endeavors have highlighted superficial cooperation, such as "joint training of Afghan diplomats, health workers, and agricultural specialists."[31] However, as one U.S. analyst noted,

> Concrete US-China cooperation on Afghanistan has been notable primarily for its limited ambition. . . . Increasingly, given the largely symbolic nature of these programs, they also unintentionally serve to highlight the dearth of more fundamental Sino-US cooperation on Afghan issues. Public statements from both parties at recent international gatherings have expressed an interest in cooperation but have yet to translate into demonstrable joint or tightly coordinated action.[32]

At the Track 2 level, a 2004 U.S.-China dialogue on failing states addressed Afghanistan, but there has been scant in-depth dialogue on the issue since—it was not addressed in a 2018 Track 2 dialogue on prospects for cooperation on global issues.[33] A 2017 Track 2 dialogue on global governance is revealing in that the U.S. side did not mention Afghanistan, but the Chinese side did address it, saying "China is committed to the realization of Afghan peace and stability through political reconciliation and economic reconstruction so as to prevent the country from becoming a terrorist hideout."[34] Reflecting the Chinese view of economics as a key solution to security concerns, the Chinese representative added, "The Belt and Road Initiative will help countries along the belt and road routes to address the root causes of terrorism."

Beijing has committed some resources to counterterrorism in the region, both financially and with its military, but only very directly for its domestic security. An early and ongoing commitment of resources is China's joint patrols along the Mekong River with Laos, Myan-

---

[28] U.S. Department of State, 2018b.

[29] U.S. Department of State, "Joint Press Release of the Quadrilateral Coordination Group on Afghan Peace and Reconciliation," January 11, 2016a.

[30] "China, Russia, U.S., Pakistan hold talks on Afghan peace process," Xinhua, October 26, 2019.

[31] Rank, 2018.

[32] Rank, 2018.

[33] Banning Garrett and Jonathan Adams, *U.S.-China Cooperation on the Problem of Failing States and Transnational Threats*, Washington, D.C.: United States Institute of Peace, September 2004. For 2018 dialogue, see Council on Foreign Relations, "Managing Global Disorder: Prospects for U.S.-China Cooperation," April 18, 2018.

[34] For the U.S. and Chinese reports on the 2017 dialogue, see Richard C. Bush et al., *Joint US-China Think Tank Project on the Future of US-China Relations: An American Perspective*, Washington, D.C.: Center for Strategic and International Studies, July 2017; and Fu and Wang, 2017.

mar, and Thailand since 2011.[35] Beyond its militarized outposts in the South China Sea, China's first foreign deployment—before it opened its first official military base in Djibouti in 2017—was sending People's Armed Police to Tajikistan so they could patrol Afghanistan's Wakan corridor.[36] Dating to at least 2016, China built a secret military outpost in Shaymak, Tajikistan. This is clearly part of the PLA's broader mission, as its 2019 defense white paper calls on the military to "fulfill [its] international responsibilities and obligations, and provide more public security goods" in part by countering the growing threat of terrorism.[37] Financially, China has also committed $70 million to the Afghan military.[38] This is a rare grant for China, which has only given more military aid to Cambodia. On its own, China appointed a special envoy for Afghanistan issues in 2014 as the U.S. military was withdrawing, and Beijing has engaged with the Taliban and regional players, with little success.[39] This financial and personnel commitment shows that Beijing is willing to dedicate at least some resources to pressing counterterrorism missions on its border when its interests—in this case, domestic stability in its Xinjiang minority region—are under threat. However, the lack of coordination with Washington suggests that Beijing's willingness to cooperate on this issue should not be taken for granted. Moreover, China has long resisted using its leverage over Pakistan to improve Islamabad's support for Afghan stability, reflecting a narrow appetite for incurring diplomatic costs for this issue.[40]

For any U.S.-China counterterrorism cooperation, there are likely to be at least two problems.[41] First is China's definition of terrorism. The CCP's framing of its domestic crackdown against those who oppose its rule and policies, especially in the wake of 9/11, as "counterterrorism" has led to concerns about U.S. cooperation with China on the issue, and U.S. offi-

---

[35] "88th Joint Patrol on Mekong River Completed," *Global Times*, November 23, 2019.

[36] Gerry Shih, "In Central Asia's Forbidding Highlands, a Quiet Newcomer: Chinese Troops," *Washington Post*, February 18, 2019. For earlier and corroborating reporting, see Nazarali Pirnazarov and Olzhas Auyezov, "China to Build Outposts for Tajik Guards on Tajikistan-Afghanistan Border," Reuters, September 26, 2016; Charles Clover, "Mystery Deepens over Chinese Forces in Afghanistan," *Financial Times*, February 26, 2017; Craig Nelson and Thomas Grove, "Russia, China Vie for Influence in Central Asia as U.S. Plans Afghan Exit," *Wall Street Journal*, June 18, 2019.

[37] State Council Information Office of the People's Republic of China, "China's National Defense in the New Era," July 2019a.

[38] Jessica Donati and Ehsanullah Amiri, "China Offers Afghanistan Army Expanded Military Aid," *Wall Street Journal*, March 9, 2016.

[39] Ben Blanchard, "China Appoints Special Envoy for Afghanistan," Reuters, July 18, 2014; Ahmad Bilal Khalil, "Afghanistan's 'China Card' Approach to Pakistan, Part 1: 1991–2014," *The Diplomat*, April 11, 2019a; Ahmad Bilal Khalil, "The Afghan National Unity Government's 'China Card' Approach to Pakistan: Part 2," The *Diplomat*, April 12, 2019b.

[40] Rank, 2018.

[41] Shirley A. Kan, *U.S.-China Counterterrorism Cooperation: Issues for U.S. Policy*, Washington, D.C.: Congressional Research Service, July 15, 2010.

cials in recent years have made this criticism explicit.[42] This is a change from 2002, when the United States designated the East Turkmenistan Independence Movement (ETIM) as a terrorist organization, though the United States still holds some Uyghurs in Guantanamo.[43] This exploitation of the "counterterrorism" framing for legal cooperation has also been an issue for Turkey, as China requested extradition of a Uyghur refugee on apparently unsubstantiated terrorism grounds.[44] China has also supported other countries' problematic crackdowns, including Filipino President Duterte's counterterrorist campaign in Mindanao.[45] This is notable because China filled a vacuum left by the United States when the latter stopped cooperating on humanitarian grounds.

Another major complicating factor is the U.S. military presence in Afghanistan. According to one China expert, "Beijing instinctively sees American troops in China's 'backyard' as a serious strategic threat."[46] This has occasionally led to more outright Chinese opposition to the U.S. military presence, as Chinese diplomats reportedly attempted to pay the Kyrgyzstan government to close the U.S. airbase there early in the Afghan war, though Beijing denied these attempts.[47] Yet, so far at least, "China believes that it has benefited from the security that the United States has provided there, especially in terms of curtailing the growth and spread of anti-China terrorist groups."[48] As U.S.-China relations deteriorate further and the Chinese military is increasingly able to conduct these counterterrorism missions on its own, Beijing's desire to allow U.S. military forces near its border may decrease.

Russian Equities

Russia assigns low importance to countering terrorism and violent extremism in Afghanistan, Pakistan, and Southeast Asia, though it does watch developments in these areas closely for their impact on Russian equities in Central Asia. Russia's official statements and rhetoric have been mixed in its positions supporting or countering U.S. objectives in the CT/CVE space. Its willingness to negotiate with the United States on the counterterrorism issue has been mixed. Moscow does not appear willing to commit significant resources to contribute to the United States goal of combating radical Islamic terrorism in the region.

---

[42] Lisa Schlein, "US Warns China's Detention of Uighurs to Counter Terrorism Will Backfire," *Voice of America*, March 14, 2019.

[43] Richard Bernstein, "When China Convinced the U.S. That Uighurs Were Waging Jihad," *The Atlantic*, March 19, 2019.

[44] Bethany Allen-Ebrahimian, "Documents Show China's Secret Extradition request for Uighur in Turkey," *Axios*, May 20, 2020.

[45] Sarah Zheng, "China Arms Philippine Police for Counterterrorism Mission," *South China Morning Post*, October 5, 2017.

[46] Sun, 2020. For a similar view, see Rank, 2018.

[47] Bill Gertz, "Inside the Ring: China in Kyrgyzstan," *Washington Times*, December 2, 2010.

[48] Sun, 2020.

On CT/CVE, Russian official statements acknowledge the threat posed by terrorist elements through provocations fomenting instability and interstate conflicts. Yet, Moscow seems to find fault in "the policy of double standards to which some states adhere to"—code for U.S. policy—as the underlying cause or impetus for the emergence of ISIS and the strengthening of its influence.[49] Russia's 2016 Foreign Policy Concept outlines its position on CT/CVE—creating a broad international counterterrorist coalition with a solid legal foundation based on effective and consistent international cooperation without any political considerations or "double standards."[50] Yet, again, Moscow appears to be calling for the international community to look inward to its "systemic development problems" and challenging the ideological values and prescriptions imposed from countries outside the regions relevant to terrorism.[51]

Russia's role in the fight against terrorism—however much it claims rhetorically to be in support of global counterterrorism efforts—seems aligned with the United States' objectives on counterterrorism in theory only. As scholars have noted, Moscow's contributions to the global fight against terrorism seem geared more toward weakening and dividing the West's solidarity and undermining U.S. interests.[52] Moscow's deployment of air and naval assets to the fight against ISIS in Syria was geared largely toward expanding its presence and power while distracting and limiting the West's ability to maneuver in the region.[53] With regard to the fight against terrorism in Afghanistan, the Russian government maintains that Afghanistan is a close neighbor and that Moscow has an interest in seeing its stable and peaceful development. Yet, the Kremlin has expressed no objections to Afghanistan's national reconciliation being joined by "participants of the armed opposition," including the Taliban.[54] In demonstration of this position, Moscow in 2018 convened a meeting with an Afghan delegation, where Taliban representatives were present for the first time. Moscow believes that a lasting solution to the issue of terrorism in Afghanistan cannot be realized without involving the Taliban.[55] Russian support for the Taliban may appear to contravene its previous record of providing military equipment and allowing U.S. troops and logistics to transit over its territory. Here, it should be pointed out that Russia's current positions on Afghanistan and the

---

[49] Government of Russia, 2015.

[50] Ministry of Foreign Affairs of the Russian Federation, 2016b.

[51] Ministry of Foreign Affairs of the Russian Federation, 2016b.

[52] Mariya Y. Omelicheva, "Russia's Counterproductive Counter-Terrorism: An Overview and Assessment of Trends in Russia's Counterterrorism Policy and Moscow's Efforts to Promote It Internationally," testimony before the U.S. Helsinki Commission, Washington, D.C., June 12, 2019.

[53] Anna Borshchevskaya, "Russia's Questionable Counterterrorism Record: Why Moscow Is an Unreliable Partner for the West," *Foreign Affairs*, November 23, 2017.

[54] Putin, 2012.

[55] Aleksei Zakharov, "The Geopolitics of the US-India-Russia Strategic Triangle," *Strategic Analysis,* Vol. 43, No. 5, 2019; Aleksei Zakharov, *Exploring New Drivers in India-Russia Cooperation,* Observer Research Foundation, ORF Occasional Paper No. 124, October 2017; Uma Purushothaman, "India-Russia Relations Are Evolving and Strengthening," London School of Economics, January 18, 2018.

Taliban are to an extent driven by the Russia-Western discord over the conflicts in Ukraine and Syria, a key difference from their relationship earlier in this century, when bilateral cooperation over counterterrorism was a higher priority.

To Russia, the presence of ISIS in Afghanistan and the potential spillover effects on its influence in Central Asian states justifies its "limited" contact with the Taliban, when in fact its support—which appears far from being limited—for the group is largely aimed toward reducing U.S. influence and using this card as a hedge in case the Taliban returns to power.[56] Russia has been suspected of counterintelligence operations against the United States and providing the Taliban with weapons and military equipment, which, as terrorism experts point out, only enable the Taliban and supporting militants to directly target U.S. and NATO service members.[57] As a recent example to further illustrate this point, U.S. intelligence agencies recently told the press that a Russian military intelligence unit linked with the Skripal poisoning incident and other assassination attempts and covert operations in Europe had offered Taliban-linked militants bounties to kill coalition forces in Afghanistan, including American troops.[58] Motivations are unclear at this point, but officials speculate that Moscow may be seeking revenge on NATO for the killing of pro-Syrian forces, including Russian mercenaries, in the 2018 battle in Syria, or attempting to thwart progress in U.S.-Taliban peace talks, seeking to keep the United States bogged down in Afghanistan. Indeed, it's even plausible that Russia may be seeking a measure of revenge for the U.S. support for the mujahideen that helped defeat the Soviet Union in Afghanistan in the 1980s.

Russia cooperates with ASEAN collectively on efforts to reduce ISIS and other militant threats in their regions. In 2016, Moscow hosted the Russia-ASEAN summit, where the parties agreed to cooperate on counterterrorism and drug trafficking under their shared goal of promoting a new security architecture in the region.[59] In 2019, Russia and Thailand signed a military cooperation agreement to enhance counterterrorism cooperation, intelligence exchange, and military personnel training.[60] Russia has also provided counterterrorism training and assistance to the Philippines. In 2017, Russia and the Philippines signed a memorandum of understanding on security cooperation, wherein Moscow offered Manila access to its intelligence database to help the latter fight transnational crime and terrorism.[61] In the

---

[56] Zakharov, 2019; Carpenter, 2019.

[57] Carpenter, "2019; Colin P. Clarke, "Russia Is Not a Viable Counterterrorism Partner for the United States," *Russia Matters*, February 8, 2018.

[58] Charlie Savage, Eric Schmitt, and Michael Schwirtz, "Russia Secretly Offered Afghan Militants Bounties to Kill U.S. Troops, Intelligence Says," *New York Times*, June 26, 2020.

[59] Dmitry Gorenburg and Paul Schwartz, *Russia's Relations with Southeast Asia*, Paris: Institut Français des Relations Internationales (IFRI), Russie.NEI.Reports No. 26, March 2019.

[60] "Russia, Thailand Sign Military Cooperation Agreement," Tass, September 14, 2017.

[61] "Russia to Share Intelligence with Philippines, Train Duterte Guards," Reuters, February 16, 2017; Department of Foreign Affairs of the Republic of the Philippines, "Key PH-Russia Security Agreement Enters into Force," January 16, 2018.

words of Putin and Russia's ambassador to the Philippines, Moscow is ready to provide assistance "of any kind" to Manila in its counterterrorism and national security efforts, including arms deliveries, staff training, and sharing of best practices.[62] Although Russian training and services may serve some utility in states' efforts to manage the threat of terrorism, Moscow's provision of assistance and access to its military and law enforcement resources are likely driven by its designs of expanding its global arms sales market as well as reasserting its strategic importance to the region.

Conflicting U.S.-Russia interests, Moscow's inconsistent record on counterterrorism efforts, and its underlying aim to use its counterterrorism policy as a crutch to reassert its regional influence and establish itself as a more prominent player to weaken U.S. interests leave little space for meaningful and effective U.S.-Russia cooperation on counterterrorism. With Russia viewing the United States as an adversary, any counterterrorism cooperation with Moscow portends costs to U.S. strategic interests, as well as ongoing counterterrorism and peacekeeping operations.

Space for Cooperation

In view of the strong divergences between Chinese and Russian views of and interests in CT/CVE and those of the United States, the space for cooperation on this topic is likely to be highly constrained, as Table 8.1 lays out.[63]

For example, American, Chinese, and Russian representatives have met on the Afghan peace process, but such meetings have been largely symbolic, with no real impact in terms of degrading al Qaeda or ISIS or pressuring the Taliban to moderate its demands and lay down its arms.[64] Moreover, in light of credible reporting that Russian intelligence operatives were offering bounties to the Taliban for killing U.S. military personnel, cooperation with Russia

TABLE 8.1

Interest in Cooperation on Countering Terrorism in South and Southeast Asia

Space for Cooperation	China	Russia
Stakes	Low	Low
Rhetorical alignment	Medium	Medium
Demonstrated willingness to commit resources	Low	High

[62] Franco Luna, "Russia Willing to Help with Nuclear Energy, Counterterrorism Should Philippines Ask— Envoy," *PhilStar Global*, October 18, 2019; "Russia Ready to Help Philippines Fight Against Terrorism, Says Putin," Tass, October 3, 2019.

[63] For one view of the prospects for U.S.-China cooperation on Afghanistan in 2018, see Rank, 2018.

[64] U.S. Department of State, Office of the Spokesperson, "Media Note: Joint Statement on Trilateral Meeting of Afghan Peace Process," April 26, 2019.

on Afghanistan seems unlikely. Similarly, with China having detained more than 1 million Uyghurs, cooperation with China on CT/CVE would serve little more than to tarnish the U.S. reputation by associating it with a regime that is committing genocide.[65] It is unclear that any past instance of cooperation with China or Russia ever yielded substantial operational intelligence or impact on reducing or defeating terrorist groups in South-Central or Southeast Asia; thus, reducing U.S. expectations of or hopes for trilateral CT/CVE cooperation may not be giving up much in the way of benefits forgone.

Because China trades with and has substantial investments in Afghanistan (for example, at the Aynak Copper Mine), Pakistan, and most of Southeast Asia, China's influence is greater than Russia's, and therefore China might feel it has more to lose if any of these countries were to fall under terrorist control. This is especially true of Pakistan, with its nuclear arsenal, border with Xinjiang, and centrality in China's strategy to pen in rival India, and this is reflected in China's roughly $62 billion in infrastructure investments associated with the China-Pakistan Economic Corridor.[66] As for Russia, its counterterrorism efforts in Afghanistan and Pakistan appear to be concerned primarily with limiting or countering U.S. influence and counterterrorism successes so that Moscow's own interests are preserved. Russia's core concerns are likely distant from the actual goal of reducing the threat of terrorism and violent extremism to bring stability to South and Southeast Asia. Moscow maintains its strategic interest in a stable Afghanistan, but its motivations for doing so appear largely self-serving. More clearly, Russia's support for the Taliban appears to be a means to ensure that the Afghan peace process tracks consistently with Moscow's own strategic cost-benefit assessment. Russia may judge that its support for the Taliban prevents the collapse of Afghanistan and, furthermore, gives pretext for the presence of U.S. troops to maintain stability. It may not be in Russia's interests to have U.S. forces stationed in the region indefinitely; however, a premature U.S. troop withdrawal may only inflict greater costs on Moscow's interests by precipitating the collapse of Afghanistan and the return to civil war. The differences in how vested China and Russia are in these areas might appear on the surface to present a possible fissure or seam that the United States might seek to exploit, but it is unclear that Russia cares enough about CT/CVE as an issue—or has enough influence in these spaces—to make any sort of substantive difference in terms of outcome that China might care about and that the United States could leverage.

---

[65] Stephanie Nebehay, "1.5 Million Muslims Could Be Detained in China's Xinjiang," Reuters, March 13, 2019; Human Rights Watch, "Interpol: Address China's 'Red Notice' Abuses," September 25, 2017; Azeem Ibrahim, "China Must Answer for Cultural Genocide in Court," *Foreign Policy*, December 3, 2019.

[66] For more on China's relationship with Pakistan, see Andrew Small, *The China-Pakistan Axis: Asia's New Geopolitics*, Oxford, UK: Oxford University Press, 2015. For recent assessments of the CEPC, see Jonathan Hillman and Maesea McCalpin, *The China-Pakistan Economic Corridor at Five*, Washington, D.C.: Center for Strategic and International Studies, April 2020; Madiha Afzal, *"At All Costs": How Pakistan and China Control the Narrative on the China-Pakistan Economic Corridor*, Washington, D.C.: Brookings Institution, June 2020.

The primary obstacles to cooperation with China and Russia on CT/CVE, as noted above, are the human rights abuses of the two regimes domestically; their differing approaches to CT/CVE, treating it primarily as an issue within their own territory but not one where they bring substantial political-military power to bear outside their own borders; and their penchant for seeing it as an issue they can use to bog the United States down or one where they can present a cooperative face on the surface to mask the extent to which they actually seek to compete with the United States.

Neither China nor Russia therefore appears to be a promising partner for cooperation in countering terrorism and violent Islamist extremism in Afghanistan, Pakistan, or Southeast Asia, owing to factors that include distrust, definitional problems, and issue linkages. Because issues of audience costs, third parties, immediacy, legal constraints, and capacity or capability did not appear to be important obstacles to counterterrorism cooperation with China and/or Russia, we do discuss them further here.

Trust. For China and the United States, mistrust is likely to complicate efforts to cooperate on CT/CVE. Washington has long been suspicious of Beijing's definition of *terrorism* and its self-serving designation of Uyghur groups as terrorists in the post-9/11 era. This means that there is broad skepticism in Washington for any tangible cooperation, such as Chinese intelligence, that would support U.S. action against Chinese-suspected terrorists.

The United States does not trust Russian intentions and objectives in CT/CVE efforts, and Moscow likely does not trust Washington's underlying motivations behind CT/CVE operations in the region. The recent revelation of a Russian intelligence unit providing bounties to Taliban-linked operatives to assassinate coalition forces in Afghanistan casts doubts about the viability and durability of productive U.S.-Russia CT/CVE cooperation in the region.[67] Unless these issues of mistrust are resolved, the two countries are unlikely to successfully cooperate on CT/CVE.

Definitional problems. As noted above, China's problematic definition of *terrorism* is a challenge for cooperation with the United States. Beijing has tended to treat opposition to the CCP's rule and support for ethnic separatism (even peacefully pursued) as grounds for labeling its political opponents terrorists, and China's behavior inside the country routinely violates U.S. and global norms of human rights. As a 2016 report noted,

> In some cases, acts of violence that Chinese officials and state media have labeled as terrorism do not meet the definitions of the term that are widely accepted outside of China. ... To date, when discussing events within the People's Republic of China (PRC), China's official use of the term 'terrorist' appears to be reserved almost exclusively for describing people and groups tied to Xinjiang.[68]

---

[67] Savage, Schmitt, and Schwirtz, 2020.

[68] Tanner and Bellacqua, 2016.

One example of a conflicting definition of *terrorism* is that, in 2003, China designated the World Uighur Congress as a terrorist organization, but the organization has not been designated a terrorist organization by the United States and, on the contrary, receives grant funding from the National Endowment for Democracy.[69]

Issue linkage. For China, counterterrorism cooperation abroad relates directly to its domestic stability. Moreover, cooperation on regional counterterrorism issues relates directly to the U.S. relationship with Pakistan and Philippines, areas where China is striving to undercut U.S. influence. As one 2016 report noted, "Historically, China appears to have focused far more on the domestic dimensions of its terrorism challenge . . . its primary emphasis has been the impact that jihadists and separatists outside China's borders might have on extremism in Xinjiang."[70] However, in recent years, Beijing has at times stepped up foreign counterterrorism cooperation at the expense of the United States. For example, Beijing in 2017 donated over $7 million in small arms to the Philippines for counterterrorism during the siege of Marawi, which was reportedly used to replace U.S. sales that were withdrawn over human rights concerns under Duterte.[71]

Second-Order Effects of Cooperation

CT/CVE is simply not a consequential enough issue for either China or Russia that cooperation with either one would substantially open a gap or create severe complications for the other. If the United States and Russia were to initiate major cooperation on CT/CVE, it likely would not substantially change China's view that it should present a generally amenable public face while also criticizing the U.S. practice of CT/CVE and leveraging any real or perceived U.S. missteps to its advantage owing to the competition the United States and China face for influence in the Indo-Pacific. Similarly, were the United States and China to institute some substantial new initiative on CT/CVE cooperation, the implications for Russia would be relatively marginal to the broader questions of tensions over Ukraine and NATO-Russia relations. If the United States and China fail to achieve cooperation on CT/CVE and instead are in a more competitive position, Russia will gain marginally, inasmuch as Moscow will have Beijing to amplify its criticisms of the U.S. role in the world, but this is unlikely to present Russia with any dramatic new openings. And should the United States and Russia fail to achieve a commonality of purpose, it will potentially give China opportunities to see the United States remain bogged down Afghanistan or elsewhere, but this was likely to be the case even absent Russian meddling and efforts to promote the assassination of U.S. troops by the Taliban, as nearly two decades of war have shown.

---

[69] Tanner and Bellacqua, 2016.

[70] Tanner and Bellacqua, 2016.

[71] Prashanth Parameswaran, "What's in the New China Military Aid to the Philippines?" *The Diplomat*, October 5, 2017.

Conclusion

Unfortunately, despite what might on the surface appear as a collective interest with the United States in countering terrorism and violent extremism, China and Russia, for reasons tied to the nature of their regimes and their hostility to the U.S. role in the world, do not appear likely to cooperate to any substantial degree on CT/CVE in Afghanistan, Pakistan, or Southeast Asia. Neither China nor Russia field forces in any numbers in these areas, and the regimes' hostility to the United States, as well as their overall abuses of human rights, make it both impractical and unappealing to pursue cooperation with either Beijing or Moscow on the issue.

CHAPTER NINE

India's Regional Role and Strategic Orientation

The final U.S. objective in the Indo-Pacific is in some ways a subset of the third objective of expanding partnerships with Indo-Pacific nations (see Chapter Five), but with a country that is so large and consequential that it merits its own category as being of geostrategic importance: India. In this chapter, we begin by exploring U.S., Chinese, and Russian equities before turning to the space for cooperation and competition and then the practicalities of cooperative and competitive behavior before offering some final thoughts.

Understanding the Equities

India, a democratic country with 1.35 billion people, a rapidly growing economy, a nuclear-armed military, and a hugely geostrategic location astride major sea lines of communications between Europe, Africa, and the Middle East and East and Southeast Asia, has long been an attractive partner for the United States, China, and Russia.

American interest surged after the conclusion of the Cold War while Russian ties waned, and though Moscow's contacts date back to the early Cold War, Russia has been slipping in influence in recent years as U.S. and European arms and trade and investment ties deepen. China, despite its proclamations of "friendship" and promises to embody the *Hindi-Chini bhai-bhai* ("Indian-Chinese brotherhood") spirit, has fought a 1962 war with India; was purportedly the reason India developed its nuclear arsenal (according to India's then–Minister of Defense Georges Fernandez in 1998); and has recently clashed repeatedly along the two countries' shared border while continually bolstering Pakistan and other South Asian neighbors as counterweights to India. As the next sections show, cooperation points are likely to be few and far between among the three great powers as Washington courts New Delhi.

U.S. Equities

U.S. outreach to India was limited during the Cold War, during which New Delhi adopted a socialist domestic economic policy and a foreign policy in favor of national liberation and opposed to European imperialism and great power alignment. By contrast, the United States had a warm and cooperative relationship with India's archnemesis, Pakistan, for which reason

U.S.-India ties remained cool until the mid- to late-1990s. Initially in 1974, and then again on a larger scale in 1998, India tested nuclear weapons, with then–Defense Minister Fernandes quoted as saying that the latter tests were motivated by the threat of a rising China.[1] In spring 2000, then-President Bill Clinton took a six-day trip to India, dramatically advancing U.S.-India relations and focusing them on shared interests, values, and strategic cooperation.[2]

The George W. Bush administration deepened counterterrorism cooperation with India in the wake of 2001 and the 2002 Indian Lok Sabha attacks and moved to expand patrolling of sea lines of communication and intelligence-sharing, as well. Following the December 26, 2004, Indian Ocean tsunami, the United States, Japan, Australia, and India formed the Quadrilateral Contact Group, bringing India into more regular and structured cooperation with key U.S. allies. Then, in 2005, the Bush administration moved forward on a Civil Nuclear Cooperation agreement with India that signaled the effective end of the sanctions imposed on New Delhi for its 1998 nuclear tests and the more fulsome embrace of India as a strategic partner and counterweight to a more assertive China and an increasingly authoritarian and aggressive Russia.[3] The Bush administration also signed a ten-year defense cooperation agreement that initiated "collaboration in multilateral operations, expanded two-way defense trade, increased opportunities for technology transfers and co-production, and expanded collaboration related to missile defense."[4] From 2007, the United States and India began to regularly include Japan in the Malabar naval exercises, thereby building links between India and the U.S. alliance system.

During the Obama administration, U.S.-India cooperation increasingly came to be incorporated into the overall strategy of the "pivot" or "rebalance" to the Asia-Pacific. Ties were elevated in the wake of state visits by Prime Minister Manmohan Singh to Washington and President Barack Obama to New Delhi, with defense secretaries Leon Panetta, Chuck Hagel, and Ashton Carter all focusing on deepening arms sales and strategic cooperation, including the sales of U.S. P-8 Poseidon maritime patrol aircraft. From 2015 onward, the United States, India, and Japan inaugurated a trilateral foreign ministers' meeting, laying the groundwork for the revival of the Quadrilateral Dialogue ("the Quad") during the Trump administration (the arrangement had fallen into disuse from 2008–2017). Additionally, in 2016, the Obama administration designated India as a "major defense partner," a step that allowed India to receive "license-free access to dual-use American technologies."[5]

In 2018, the United States and India signed a Communications Compatibility and Security Agreement and inaugurated a "2+2" foreign and defense ministers' dialogue, leading

---

[1] John F. Burns, "India's New Defense Chief Sees Chinese Military Threat," *New York Times*, May 5, 1998.

[2] U.S. Department of State, "U.S.-India Relations: A Vision for the 21st Century," March 21, 2000.

[3] U.S. Department of State, "U.S.-India Civil Nuclear Cooperation," undated.

[4] K. Alan Kronstadt and Shayerah Ilias Akhtar, *India-U.S. Relations: Issues for Congress*, Washington, D.C.: Congressional Research Service, R44876, June 19, 2017.

[5] Kronstadt and Akhtar, 2017.

Indian Defense Minister Nirmala Sithamaran to state at its conclusion that defense cooperation has come to be "the most significant dimension of our strategic partnership and as a key driver of our overall bilateral relationship."[6] The two countries have continued since that time to exchange defense ties, agreeing to tri-service joint exercises and welcoming the Indian defense minister to the United States in December 2018 for a visit to the Pentagon, as well as the Defense Innovation Unit in California and USINDOPACOM in Hawaii.[7]

As a U.S. Department of State Bureau of Political-Military Affairs fact sheet notes, the United States has authorized weapons sales to India via Foreign Military Sales, including

- MH-60R Seahawk helicopters ($2.6 billion)
- Apache helicopters ($2.3 billion)
- P-8I maritime patrol aircraft ($3 billion)
- M777 howitzers ($737 million).[8]

The same fact sheet also notes that India was the first nontreaty partner to be offered a MTCR Category-1 Unmanned Aerial System (the Sea Guardian UAS manufactured by General Atomics), and points out that since 2008, the United States has sold India over $6.6 billion in defense articles via the Direct Commercial Sales process.

In short, as then–Secretary of Defense James Mattis said in 2018, the U.S.-India partnership is "a natural partnership between the world's oldest democracy and the world's largest democracy . . . [that share] the same principles, values and respect for the rules-based international order," a view that the State Department has echoed in noting that "India plays a vital role in the U.S. vision for a free and open Indo-Pacific."[9]

Chinese Equities

Beijing seeks to discourage India from joining a U.S.-led coalition to contain China but balances this desire for neutralizing or even building positive relations with New Delhi against its security concerns and disagreements relating to the on-going border dispute. The June 2020 border clash near Aksai Chin once again highlighted the volatility of the relationship. Overall, China has medium stakes in India's future regional role and strategic orientation. Although China has some rhetorical alignment with the United States on the issue, there has been limited engagement on the topic, and there is no indication Beijing is willing to compromise or commit resources to the issue.

---

6   Jim Garamone, "U.S.-India Defense Cooperation a 'Key Driver' of Overall Relationship," *DOD News*, September 6, 2018a.

7   Jim Garamone, "U.S., India Strengthen Defense Cooperation," *DOD News*, December 3, 2018b.

8   U.S. Department of State, Bureau of Political-Military Affairs, 2019.

9   Garamone, 2018b; U.S. Department of State, Bureau of Political-Military Affairs, 2019.

China's interests in India are tied to both security and economic interests. India's hosting of the Dalai Lama in Dharamshala presents a challenge to Beijing's domestic stability because of the CCP's desire to control the Tibetan Buddhist religion, which is Tibet's predominant religion and a key facet of its historical and cultural identity.[10] Additionally, Beijing accuses the Dalai Lama of supporting Tibetan independence, though His Holiness has described his goal as meaningful autonomy. Economically, India is China's 11th-biggest trading partner, with bilateral trade in 2018 at $95.7 billion, with a $58 billion trade surplus for Beijing.[11] China, on the other hand, has been India's biggest trading partner since 2008, accounting for roughly 15 percent of total trade.[12] With just $5 billion in cumulative Chinese investment in India and less than $1 billion from India into China, the two sides are only minimally linked by investment.[13] Border disputes over several areas are a major interest for China's emphasis on territorial integrity, making India China's last problematic land border. As China expands its ambitions outside East Asia, its interest in great power status is intimately related to its relationship with India, as the Chinese military expands its presence in the Indian Ocean region.

Security issues have plagued the relationship historically and once again came to a head with the June 2020 border clash. Since the short 1962 war that Beijing won, skirmishes along the border have occurred off and on, most notably with a two-month standoff near Doklam in 2017.[14] These border clashes raise the risk of escalation, since the PLA considers a war with India one of its major strategic priorities and actively trains it.[15] Outside the border dispute, China is also pushing its naval presence into India's backyard, with submarine deployments into the Indian Ocean that New Delhi considers provocative.[16] There is speculation that China could establish military bases in Pakistan and/or Sri Lanka, which would worsen

---

[10] Krishna N. Das and Sunil Kataria, "Dalai Lama Contemplates Chinese Gambit After His Death," *Reuters*, March 18, 2019; Krithika Varagur, "The Coming Fight for the Dalai Lama's Soul," *Foreign Policy*, January 22, 2019; Eric Baculinao and Jason Cumming, "China Spends Big in Tibet to Avert a Crisis When the Dalai Lama Dies," *NBC News*, August 30, 2018; Sudha Ramachandran, "Rivalries and Relics: Examining China's Buddhist Public Diplomacy," *China Brief*, Vol. 19, No. 5, March 5, 2019.

[11] Authors' calculation using 2018 data, excluding Hong Kong, from World Integrated Trade Solution, undated-a; Embassy of India in Beijing, China, "India-China Trade And Economic Relations," undated.

[12] Embassy of India in Beijing, China, undated.

[13] Embassy of India in Beijing, China, undated.

[14] Joel Wuthnow, Satu Limaye, and Nilanthi Samaranayake, "Doklam, One Year Later: China's Long Game In The Himalayas," *War on the Rocks*, June 7, 2018.

[15] Larry M. Wortzel, "PLA Contingency Planning and the Case of India," in Andrew Scobell, Arthur S. Ding, Phillip C. Saunders, and Scott W. Harold, eds., *The People's Liberation Army And Contingency Planning in China*, Washington, D.C.: National Defense University Press, 2015.

[16] Fu and Wang, 2019.

security concerns in India.[17] Despite all this strategic attention on India's backyard, China often overlooks India's relevance in broader regional issues.

Rhetorically, China supports India playing a regional role in South Asia and seeks a positive relationship built on a shared identity as developing countries, away from alignment with the United States. In 2018, Foreign Minister Wang Yi said, "China and India must do everything to empathize with and support each other and to avoid mutual suspicion and attrition. . . . Our shared understandings far outstrip our differences and our common interests far outweigh our frictions. . . . Let us replace suspicion with trust, manage differences through dialogue, and build a future through cooperation."[18] Following the October 2019 meeting between Xi and Indian Prime Minister Narendra Modi meeting, the Chinese Foreign Ministry released a statement saying, "The two leaders affirmed the importance of an open, inclusive, prosperous and stable environment and better connectivity for the prosperity and stability of the region. On this basis, the Chinese side is ready to actively promote cooperation between China, India, Myanmar and Bangladesh with India and other relevant countries."[19]

India has been receptive to improving ties with China on the surface, mostly on economic development issues, but is slowly moving closer to the United States and its allies and partners. Early on in the 2000s, China and India were grouped together under the BRICS framework, reflecting their shared status as developing powers and marked by attending the annual leadership summits since 2009. India joined the BRICS-backed New Development Bank in 2014 and China's Asia Infrastructure Investment Bank as a founding member in 2015, reflecting common dissatisfaction with the global financial order.[20] New Delhi has not, however, joined China's BRI. At the leadership level, Modi and Xi have had two informal working summits, with Modi visiting Wuhan, China, in April 2018 and Xi visiting Mamallapuram, India, in October 2019. However, neither leadership summit led to a joint statement, suggesting limited areas of agreement.[21]

Beijing opposes expanding India's role in East Asian affairs and was thus concerned by the Trump administration's renewed emphasis on increasing India's engagement with other East Asian countries through the Quad. On the surface, Foreign Minister Wang Yi in 2018 dismissed the Quad as "like the sea foam in the Pacific or Indian Ocean," because it "may get some attention, but soon will dissipate," adding that "stoking a new Cold War is out of sync

---

[17] U.S. Department of Defense, *Assessment on U.S. Defense Implications of China's Expanding Global Access*, Washington, D.C., December 2018c.

[18] Ministry of Foreign Affairs of the People's Republic of China, "Foreign Minister Wang Yi Meets the Press," March 9, 2018b.

[19] Ministry of Foreign Affairs of the People's Republic of China, "The Second Informal Meeting Between Chinese and Indian Leaders Has Yielded Fruitful Results," October 13, 2019c.

[20] Alonso Soto, "BRICS Bank to Defy Western Clout in Global Finances," Reuters, July 11, 2014.

[21] Geeta Mohan, "Modi-Xi meet: India, China to issue separate statements today," *India Today*, October 12, 2019.

with the times and inciting block confrontation will find no market."[22] However, Western analysts believe that Beijing is definitely opposed to the Quad.[23] It is clear that China seeks to keep India out of East Asian affairs, evident in Wang Yi's intentional separation of the "Pacific or Indian Ocean," which reflects an implicit refutation of the U.S. "Indo-Pacific" framing that brings India into East Asian affairs.[24] One analysis finds that

> Chinese analysts are especially focused on developments in military cooperation between Washington and New Delhi, including the U.S. sale to India of 22 Sky Guardian unmanned aerial vehicles in June 2017, the first to a non-ally; pledges to increase defense cooperation during Modi's July 2017 U.S. visit; and frequent exchanges between the two countries' defense ministers.[25]

Fears of encirclement further drive Chinese opposition to India's alignment with the United States. "Geographically, it is not lost on Chinese observers that the Quad countries occupy important positions across China's eastern, southern, and western flanks or that these countries tend to align with the United States on matters such as opposing China's expansive territorial claims," one recent study notes.[26]

At the same time, Chinese observers have expressed doubts over the staying power of the Quad, with several scholars portraying India as "the weakest link in the Quad, arguing that New Delhi's aversion to alliances and policy differences with the United States on matters such as India's arms relations with Russia, energy ties to Iran, and U.S. visa restrictions would prevent [it] from siding with the United States."[27] This leads Chinese scholars to consider what steps Beijing can take to mollify Indian concerns and complaints about China's rise, with some supporting a positive approach such as joint China-India cooperation in Myanmar to "force India to acknowledge the reality of China's entrance into the Indian Ocean region."[28]

The United States and China have not discussed India's regional role and strategic orientation in depth. Perhaps the most high-level statement on the issue came in a 2009 joint statement following a meeting between Obama and then–Chinese President Hu Jintao: "The two sides welcomed all efforts conducive to peace, stability and development in South Asia. . . . The two sides are ready to strengthen communication, dialogue and cooperation on issues related to South Asia and work together to promote peace, stability and development

---

[22] Ministry of Foreign Affairs of the People's Republic of China, 2018b.

[23] Wuthnow, 2020; Feng Liu, "The Recalibration of Chinese Assertiveness: China's Responses to the Indo-Pacific Challenge," *International Affairs*, Vol. 96, No. 1, January 2020, pp. 9–27.

[24] Feng, 2020, pp. 9–27.

[25] Wuthnow, 2020, p. 6.

[26] Wuthnow, 2020, p. 8.

[27] Wuthnow, 2020, p. 8.

[28] Ye Hailin, quoted in Wuthnow, 2020, p. 10.

in that region."[29] This statement was a cause for concern in New Delhi, but a senior U.S. diplomat quickly sought to reassure India, saying, "Of course, the United States is interested in perusing the best and healthiest possible partnership with China; but that does not come at the expense of other increasingly important partnership, particularly our relationship with India."[30] Under the Bush administration's U.S.-China Senior Dialogue and the Obama administration's U.S.-China Strategic and Economic Dialogue, there were several ongoing subregional meetings at the assistant secretary level, including on South Asia; these mostly focused on security and stability in Afghanistan and Pakistan, but at some points did cover the topic of India. Commenting on the state of the dialogue in 2011, Assistant Secretary of State for South and Central Asian Affairs Robert Blake said roughly a year later,

> In terms of how that reflects on China, we support growing relations between India and China and we have reassured our friends in China that growing relations between the United States and India will not come at China's expense, and that we want to see the growth of our relations with China, our relations with India, and India's relations with China.[31]

At the Track 1.5 and Track 2 levels of U.S.-China dialogue, India has been discussed in terms of fears of U.S.-led regional containment. At a September 2015 Track 1.5 meeting of the U.S.-China Strategic Dialogue, for example,

> The Chinese delegation specifically called out the shift from bilateral to trilateral alliances as worrisome, along with India's Act East policy and its convergence with the United States' rebalance. One delegate stated, "China is not trying to elbow the United States out of Asia, but the United States looks likely to check and contain China by utilizing the territorial disputes between China and its littoral neighbors."[32]

However, there is no evidence that Beijing is willing to negotiate or commit resources toward finding a mutually agreed role for India. Instead, as one recent analysis has argued, "Given its concerns about a nascent 'Asian NATO,' China will likely seek to weaken the alignment between the United States and its Quad partners."[33]

---

[29] Barack Obama and Hu Jintao, "U.S.-China Joint Statement," November 17, 2009.

[30] Lalit K. Jha, "Relationship with China Not at the Expense of India: US," Outlook India, November 18, 2009. For a broader review of U.S.-India relations in the early Obama years, see Jason A. Kirk, "India's Season of Discontent: U.S.-India Relations Through the Prism of Obama's "AfPak" Policy, Year One," *Asian Affairs: An American Review*, Vol. 37, No. 3, July-September 2010.

[31] U.S. Department of State, "Media Roundtable," March 18, 2011.

[32] Chris Twomey, "The U.S.-China Strategic Dialogue," Naval Postgraduate School, December 2016.

[33] Wuthnow, 2020, p. 11.

Russian Equities

Russia gives medium importance to deepening relations with India. Rhetorically, Moscow's position on its relations with New Delhi does not support U.S. objectives. Russia has not expressed any interest in negotiating with the United States over relations with India, nor have there been any indications of Moscow's willingness to commit substantial resources to achieve a common goal in India.

The 2016 Russian Foreign Policy Concept takes care to highlight Russia's historical ties to India, underscore the encompassing nature of Moscow–New Delhi relations, and emphasize convergent interests between the two countries to stress India's importance to Russia's strategic equities.[34] Notably, however, the document includes a reference to the "deep mutual distrust" between Moscow and New Delhi, which appears to be less a reflection of any residual negative Russian sentiments toward India than an acknowledgement of the past so that the two sides can move forward in their bilateral relations. Russia's top leadership also appears to acknowledge the importance of Russia-India relations and is careful to depict bilateral ties as mutually beneficial and gainful to their shared vision of a multipolar world.[35]

While Russia-India relations span bilateral and multilateral cooperation in the economic, energy, and defense fields, Moscow likely views its military-security ties to New Delhi as most critical to supporting its geopolitical objectives. In September 2019, Putin and Modi signed a joint statement that covered an expansive range of bilateral cooperation opportunities, including strong, multifaceted bilateral trade as the foundation for further expanding the range of Russia-India ties.[36] The two sides aimed to increase bilateral trade to $30 billion by 2025 and expand the participation of Russian businesses in the "Make in India" program. Despite these high-level efforts, however, Russia maintains a low trade volume with India, making up less than 2 percent of India's global annual trade since 2000. This marks a sharp contrast to India's trade volume with the United States, which ranges between 8 and 12 percent of India's global trade volume.[37] India's trade relations with China also surpass those with Russia, with China ranking as India's top import country and third-largest destination for exports.[38]

What merits greater attention in Russia-India trade relations, however, is Moscow's strategic partnership with New Delhi in energy and defense. In 2018, Russia and India signed a nuclear cooperation agreement to build six Russian-designed nuclear reactors in India, one of the largest deals in the nuclear industry in recent years between Russia and one of its larg-

---

[34] Ministry of Foreign Affairs of the Russian Federation, 2016b.

[35] Putin, 2012.

[36] Ministry of External Affairs of India, "India-Russia Joint Statement During Visit of Prime Minister to Vladivostok," September 5, 2019.

[37] Megan Maxwell, "Don't Blame Russia for the Problems in the U.S.-India Relationship," Carnegie Endowment for International Peace, September 16, 2019; Zakharov, 2017.

[38] World Integrated Trade Solution, "India Trade," undated-c.

est nuclear energy clients.[39] The two countries have also combined their nuclear technology know-how to construct Bangladesh's first-ever nuclear power plant in Rooppur.[40] In the oil industry, Russia's Rosneft has agreed to ship nearly 2 million tons of oil to India by the end of 2020.[41] Indian oil companies will also work with Russia's Vostok Oil on a development project in the Arctic to produce up to 100 million tons of oil by 2030 to lessen India's dependence on oil imports.[42]

Robust cooperation between Russia and India in the military and defense industrial sector serves Moscow's strategic objectives. The two countries hold regular military exchanges and joint exercises to strengthen bilateral military ties and enhance coordination and interoperability between their services. In 2017, Moscow and New Delhi signed a military cooperation roadmap to strengthen the foundations of their military planning and enhance joint combat readiness.[43] Most recently, in 2019, the two countries signed a military logistics agreement to facilitate reciprocal access to military facilities for fuel and services during their visits to their counterpart's military bases.[44] Russia has also inherited the critical role as one of India's key suppliers of military technology and hardware from the Soviet Union. More than 25 percent of Russia's military equipment and technology sales are delivered to India, which has consistently remained the top destination of Moscow's arms exports.[45] Between 2007 to 2017, India's defense imports from Russia totaled $24 billion out of a total of $34 billion.[46]

Russia has also been willing to transfer some of its more sensitive and capable military equipment to India. Since 2012, Moscow has leased its nuclear-powered B-class attack submarine (SSN), the INS *Chakra*, to India.[47] A second submarine of the same type will be deliv-

---

[39] Sanjeev Miglani and Geert de Clercq, "Russia Signs Pact for Six Nuclear Reactors on New Site in India," Reuters, October 5, 2018; "Russia Leads the World at Nuclear-Reactor Exports," *The Economist*, August 7, 2018.

[40] World Nuclear Association, "Nuclear Power in Bangladesh," updated May 2020; Laura Gil, "Construction Progresses on Bangladesh's First Nuclear Power Plant," *IAEA News,* International Atomic Energy Agency, January 31, 2019.

[41] Tomoyo Ogawa, "Russia Pulls India Closer with Oil and Weapons," *Nikkei Asian Review*, February 7, 2020; Nidhi Verma, "India's IOC Signs Annual Deal on Option to Buy Crude Oil from Russia's Rosneft," February 5, 2020.

[42] Yen Nee Lee, "Russia Can Help India to be Less Dependent on Oil, Says Indian Energy Minister," CNBC, October 4, 2019.

[43] "Russia and India Sign Military Cooperation Roadmap," Tass, June 23, 2017.

[44] Suhasini Haidar and Dinakar Peri, "India, Russia to Conclude Mutual Logistics Agreement," *The Hindu*, November 4, 2019.

[45] Pieter D. Wezeman, Aude Fleurant, Alexandra Kuimova, Nan Tian, and Siemon T. Wezeman, "Trends in International Arms Transfers, 2018," Stockholm International Peace Research Institute, March 2019.

[46] Alexey Kupriyanov, Amit Bhandari, Chaitanya Giri, and Kunal Kulkarni, "Russia-India Cooperation Against the Backdrop of Sanctions: Adverse Effects and New Opportunities," Russian International Affairs Council, November 15, 2018.

[47] "India Signs Pact with Russia on Chakra-3 Attack Submarine," *Economic Times*, March 8, 2019.

ered to the Indian Navy by 2025.[48] In 2019, India awarded a $1.2 billion contract to a Russian defense equipment manufacturer and arms export company for the technology transfer for local production of 464 Russian T-90S tanks.[49] In October 2018, the two countries concluded a deal for India to purchase five regiments of Russia's S-400 surface-to-air missiles.

The United States has warned India that it could face sanctions under CAATSA should it proceed with the $5.5 billion purchase. India, however, appears intent on acquiring the S-400s and maintaining relations with countries independently of the United States. With constraints related to the COVID-19 pandemic, Russia had deferred delivery of the S-400s to the end of 2020, but India has pressed the Russian government to expedite delivery in the aftermath of one of its worst border clashes with China in June 2020.[50] During his most recent visit to Russia, India's defense minister also sought Moscow's assurances that its delivery of spare parts for India's T-90S tanks, Kilo-class submarines, and fighter aircraft—all of Russian origins—would not be delayed during the crisis with China.[51] In July 2020, Russia and India agreed to fast-track Moscow's production of the S-400s. By contrast, Russia has reportedly suspended its delivery of the S-400 to China—Moscow's first foreign buyer of the missile defense system—citing shipment delays from COVID-19. Experts assess, however, that Moscow's concerns about Chinese expropriation of Russian military intelligence and defense trade secrets may have been the impetus for the withholding of missile deliveries to China.[52]

Ongoing tensions between New Delhi and Beijing may put Moscow in a bind, as it may be forced to choose between a lucrative arms export client and the most influential country in the region. Given Russia-India military cooperation efforts and their historical ties, India may have seen in Russia an ally willing to stand up for its partner against China. Russia, however, seems keen on presenting itself as a neutral party between the two countries, most likely because of its own need for a powerful diplomatic backer to help Moscow stand up to pressure from the United States and Europe.[53] Shortly after the India-China border clash, a Russian lawmaker was careful to lay out Moscow's position as an "honest broker" to prevent the use of military force between the two sides.[54] This position was subsequently echoed by Russian Foreign Minister Lavrov, who stated that he saw "no reason" for Russia or any other country to help India or China improve relations, and deferred the resolution of the Beijing–New

---

[48] "India Signs Pact with Russia on Chakra-3 Attack Submarine," 2019.

[49] Vivek Raghuvanshi, "India Pays Russia $1.2 Billion in Technology Transfer Fees for T-90S Tanks," *Defense News*, November 26, 2019.

[50] Sudhi Ranjan Sen and Henry Meyer, "India Urgently Seeks Russian Missile System After Military Clash with China," Bloomberg, June 23, 2020.

[51] Rajeswari Pillai Rajagopalan, "The Sino-Indian Clash: Russia in the Middle," *The Diplomat*, June 25, 2020.

[52] Frank Chen, "Russia May Be Withholding Missile Deliveries to China," *Asia Times*, July 29, 2020.

[53] Rajagopalan, 2020.

[54] Dipanjan Roy Chaudhury, "Russia Does Not Want to Interfere in India-China Standoff: Top Lawmaker," *Economic Times*, June 10, 2020.

Delhi conflict to bilateral talks and multilateral arrangements, including the BRICS nations (Russia, India, China Forum, and the SCO).[55] Russia's insistence on neutrality, while largely aimed toward preventing a backlash from China, may also underscore its policy of strategic ambiguity to maximize its benefits from ongoing, robust relations with China, budding cooperation with India, and participation in multilateral to ultimately reassert its geopolitical relevance in the region and beyond.[56]

Another apparent roadblock to more robust Russia-India defense cooperation is the United States' application of CAATSA sanctions against India's purchase of Russian weaponry and military equipment. These have been valuable to India's military for their affordability and compatibility as New Delhi seeks to upgrade its military hardware. Given the considerable size of the Indian market and demand for Russian weaponry, military vehicles, and other defense equipment, both New Delhi and Moscow may perceive CAATSA as constraining or suppressing the full potential for their bilateral military cooperation to expand and yield benefits. For Russia, securing relations with a lucrative arms client such as India is not only financially profitable; it also allows Russia to gradually reassert its relevance in the Indo-Pacific region and in so doing, may also help to reduce its own dependence on China's endorsement to be viewed as a legitimate stakeholder in the regional security, political, and economic architecture.

Space for Cooperation

As the foregoing analysis shows, the opportunities to cooperate on this goal are few and far between; instead, the United States is likely to have to compete with China and Russia on ties with India. Chinese and Russian relations with India have at points in time overlapped quite substantially, when China appeared weaker and more focused on coordinating a common position with other major powers seeking greater say in international society. Since the rise of a much more powerful and aggressive streak in Chinese foreign policy in the latter half of the 2000s, however, Beijing's ties with New Delhi have grown more conflictual. For its part, Russia may be reaching a point where it will have to choose between its interest in arms sales to India and its desires to cultivate broader geostrategic ties with China aimed at undermining the liberal international order. Table 9.1 lays out the three countries' views on the issue of cooperation on deepening ties with India.

Cooperating with China and Russia on improved ties with India is unlikely, though as with Indonesia, Malaysia, and Vietnam, the United States may wish to explore the possibil-

---

[55] Ministry of Foreign Affairs of the Russian Federation, "Foreign Minister Sergey Lavrov's Remarks and Answers to Media Questions During a News Conference Following the Video Conference of Foreign Ministers of Russia, India, and China, Moscow, June 23, 2020," June 23, 2020b.

[56] Aleksei Zakharov, "After Galwan Valley Standoff, Does the Russia-India-China Trilateral Still Matter?" *The Diplomat*, June 26, 2020.

TABLE 9.1

Interest in Cooperation on Deepening U.S. Relationship with India

Space for Cooperation	China	Russia
Stakes	Medium	Medium
Rhetorical alignment	Medium	Low
Demonstrated willingness to commit resources	Low	Low

ity of waiving CAATSA sanctions as a strategy to avoid damaging ties with India, strengthen Indian military capabilities, and potentially help maintain an issue that is a small but potentially significant wedge in Russia-China relations (albeit one they have consistently managed to overcome, to date). By contrast, successfully competing with China and Russia on India's strategic orientation requires a number of steps. These are explored below.

As noted above, China regards U.S. cooperation with India as aimed at containing its growing influence; it may also regard it as undercutting Beijing's ambitions to contain India in South Asia by surrounding New Delhi competitively through the PRC's relationships with Pakistan, Bangladesh, Myanmar, and Sri Lanka, as well as the small mountain states of Bhutan and Nepal. For Russia, the primary obstacles to cooperation with the United States are, as in the case of new partnerships in Southeast Asia (Chapter Five), the combination of Russia's overall goal of weakening the United States and its place in the world, as well as the direct competition between U.S. and Russian arms for market share and the role of CAATSA sanctions in possibly impeding foreign military sales that Russia would like to see go through to India.

The obstacles to cooperating with China and Russia over India's strategic role and orientation therefore include distrust, third-party problems, and issue linkages. Audience costs, definitional problems, immediacy, legal constraints, and capacity or capability concerns did not appear to pose challenges for cooperation with China and/or Russia on India's regional role and strategic orientation, and therefore we do not discuss them further here.

Trust. Beijing views Washington's engagement with New Delhi, especially on security issues, as part of a broader effort at containment. For Russia, underlying U.S.-Russian mutual distrust poses obstacles to successful cooperation over India. Historical ties between Russia and India and New Delhi's importance to Moscow in the cohesion and successful implementation of the Russia-India-China construct are likely to override U.S.-Russia cooperation over India.[57] Therefore, U.S.-Russia cooperation will likely be short-lived or based on a tenuous foundation of trust.

Third-party problems. China will likely react with displeasure to any attempts at U.S.-Russia cooperation over India, as it may diminish China's influence in the region by strengthening India and reducing Moscow's dependence on Beijing. Pakistan may also perceive closer

---

[57] Emily Tamkin, "Why India and Russia Are Going to Stay Friends," *Foreign Policy*, July 8, 2020.

U.S.-Russia coordination over India to be at odds with its own strategic interests and thus may seek to obstruct any efforts that place New Delhi in a strategic advantage over Islamabad, including closer relations with Washington and or Moscow. To discourage cooperation, Pakistan may, for instance, decide to no longer purchase military equipment from Russia or leverage the Taliban against cooperating with Russia over counterterrorism operations in Afghanistan.[58]

Issue linkage. For China, the issue of India's regional role directly affects its relationship with Pakistan, challenging Beijing's acceptance of a bigger role for India. Russian policy decisions on India are likely to affect its policies and interests in other domains—for instance, its relations with China or arms sales agreements with third-party countries, including Pakistan. More critically, any substantive U.S.-Russia cooperation over India would likely require Washington's lifting of CAATSA enforcement on New Delhi. This may not only be conducive to deepening Russia-India ties, but by allowing India to purchase critical missile systems and submarines to strengthen its air and naval defenses, it is likely to sensitize China's threat perceptions and insecurity vis-à-vis India and potentially compel China to expend greater resources to compensate for any perceived weaknesses in its defense capabilities against New Delhi. Indeed, in the wake of its recent border clash with China, India has already reached out to Russia to request accelerated transfer of defense articles and expanded access to new hardware.[59]

Should Russia assess that cooperation with the United States will impose costs or constrain mobility in other domains, it may not be willing to commit the resources and energy to cooperation with the United States over India.

Second-Order Effects of Cooperation

Competition with China and Russia over security ties with India is likely to result in substantial second-order effects on the two revisionist powers, as well as on the U.S. alliances with Japan and Australia.

Cooperation with China, as noted above, seems deeply improbable. Were it to occur, its impact on Russia would likely be greatest in the realm of arms sales, as it would likely lead India to conclude that it could no longer rely on or trust Washington, and needed to procure more advanced arms exclusively from Moscow. By contrast, cooperation with Russia in the form of a waiver of CAATSA sanctions on its arms sales to India would present China with a consequential problem if it resulted in a substantial improvement in Indian military capabilities, though as noted, to date Beijing and Moscow have managed to deepen their cooperation despite past Russian arms sales to India.

---

[58] Zakharov, 2017, 2019.

[59] Vivek Raghuvanshi, "India Accelerates Weapons Purchases in Wake of Border Clash with China," *Defense News*, July 6, 2020.

By contrast, if the United States moves into a much closer and deeper relationship with India in competition with China, the impact is likely to be an expansion of U.S. arms sales, and that could conceivably cut off both markets and opportunities for great power influence for Russia, perhaps with the consequence of making China more important to Russia's overall foreign policy.[60] Similarly, were the United States to move to effectively compete with Russia over India, such "success" would almost certainly entail a shift in the defense hardware, communications technology, and supporting command and control systems that New Delhi fields, again coming at the expense of Russia. In some sense then, any growth in U.S.-India security and defense cooperation is likely to redound to Russia's disadvantage.

U.S. allies Japan and Australia, the two other members of the Quadrilateral Dialogue group, stand to benefit substantially if U.S.-India defense and security cooperation deepens, enabling their own ties with India to advance and broadening the coalition of status quo–oriented countries that seek to resist Chinese revisionism.[61] So too might South Korea, which has extensive and growing ties with India and which some experts have suggested should be the next ally with whom the United States seeks to establish a trilateral partnership forum together with India.[62]

Conclusion

In light of the foregoing assessments, the room for cooperation with China and Russia on the goal of deepening U.S. security ties with India appears small and of uncertain value. Indeed, much of the geostrategic motivation for stronger U.S.-India defense cooperation is as a response to the rise of China, its more aggressive foreign policy push to reshape regional and global order, and its military expansion into the Indian Ocean region. For Russia, India is a key arms market, but one where its share is shrinking as U.S. efforts to cooperate with India eat into Russia's share of demand. Driven by concerns over China, the United States and India appear primed to continue deepening their security cooperation, and much of that is likely to come at Russia's expense.

---

[60] An alternative possibility would be that Russia would simply shift its competitive focus increasingly toward Southeast Asia or other regions. The authors thank Elizabeth Wishnick for suggesting this possibility.

[61] Harold, Madan, and Sambhi, 2020.

[62] Scott W. Harold, Derek Grossman, Brian Harding, Jeffrey W. Hornung, Gregory Poling, Jeffrey Smith, and Meagan L. Smith, *The Thickening Web of Asian Security Cooperation: Deepening Defense Ties Among U.S. Allies and Partners in the Indo-Pacific*, Santa Monica, Calif.: RAND Corporation, RR-3125-MCF, 2019; Skand R. Tayal, *India and the Republic of Korea: Engaged Democracies*, New Delhi, India: Routledge, 2014; Linda Butcher, "Building a U.S.-Korea-India Trilateral Dialogue," Korea Economic Institute, September 10, 2015.

CHAPTER TEN

Conclusions and Recommendations

Cooperation among great powers on issues of consequence is always valuable and certainly worth exploring and striving for—provided that doing so does not entail compromising core U.S. interests or values. Unfortunately, in the case of the Indo-Pacific, opportunities for genuine cooperation with China and Russia on shared interests are few and far between, and even those areas that are most promising, such as pursuing North Korean denuclearization or countering violent extremism in Afghanistan and Southeast Asia, are extremely difficult to achieve meaningful cooperation on, owing largely to the broader geopolitical competition between the United States, China, and Russia. Unsurprisingly, then, cooperation on even more core aspects of the U.S.-centric liberal international order, such as the goal of a free and open Indo-Pacific (Chapter Three), the defense of U.S. allies and partners (Chapter Four), the expansion of U.S. security ties with emerging Southeast Asian partner nations (Chapter Five), the resolution of disputes between China and Taiwan free from coercion (Chapter Six), and the expansion of U.S.-India strategic and defense cooperation (Chapter Nine), carries little appeal for Beijing or Moscow. Moreover, they tend to regard these steps, probably rightfully, as coming at their countries' expense, constraining their ability to revise the international order through coercion and intimidation, and cutting into their influence via arms sales or manipulation of regional crises. As the foregoing chapters throughout this study have demonstrated, core Chinese and Russian policy documents repeatedly invoke their opposition to the U.S.-led order as the primary lens through which they view questions of regional relations with the United States, and for that reason the opportunities to build trust through bottom-up engagement carry little appeal or prospect of success.

Nonetheless, as noted above, there may be opportunities along the margins to deepen U.S.-China military-to-military risk reduction and crisis communications agreements (Chapter Three); extend such agreements to include U.S. allies and partners (Chapter Four); avoid tensions with newer partners in India and Southeast Asia and complicate China-Russia relations by waiving the application of CAATSA (Chapters Five and Nine); cooperate with China on WMD-E in the wake of a North Korean collapse (Chapter Seven); and/or dialogue with Moscow and/or Beijing about how to stabilize Afghanistan if the United States decides to fully draw down its military presence in that country (Chapter Eight).

In this final chapter, we examine the takeaways from our study of opportunities for cooperation versus the need for competition in the Indo-Pacific.

Cooperation and Competition in the Indo-Pacific

To return now to a comment made in the introductory chapter, having surveyed at length U.S. policy positions, interests and values; examined Chinese ambitions, behaviors, and policy statements; and reviewed the actions, intentions, and implications of Russian activity in the Indo-Pacific, it is our unhappy conclusion that, in spite of the desirability of U.S.-China-Russia cooperation for the peace, stability, and development of the region, it is unavoidable that the prospects for such are dim and the demand for competition spans virtually the full gamut of issues examined herein. Table 10.1 maps the Chinese and Russian alignment with, stakes in, willingness to bargain over, and prospects of cooperating on the seven key goals that define U.S. aims and interests in the Indo-Pacific.

Table 10.2A lays out the obstacles to cooperation with China on the questions of regional order, alliance architecture, expanded strategic cooperation with Southeast Asian nations, managing cross-Strait differences, North Korean denuclearization, counterterrorism in key regional states, and India's future strategic orientation, assessing the extent to which these involve questions of trust, audience costs, definitional problems, third-party problems, immediacy, issue linkage, legal constraints, and capacity or capability. Table 10.2B tracks the same

TABLE 10.1

Interest in Cooperation in the Indo-Pacific

Issue area	China				Russia			
	Alignment	Stakes	Bargain	Cooperate	Alignment	Stakes	Bargain	Cooperate
Maintaining a peaceful and open regional order	Medium	High	Medium	Low	Medium	Medium	Low	Low
Promoting and preserving regional alliances	Low	High	Low	Low	Low	High	Low	Low
Expanding strategic cooperation with Indonesia, Malaysia, and Vietnam	Low	Medium	Low	Low	Low	Low	Low	Low
Managing cross-Strait differences between China and Taiwan	Low	High	Low	Low	Low	Low	Low	Low
Achieving the denuclearization of North Korea	High	Medium	High	Low	High	Medium	High	Low
Countering terrorism and violent Islamist Extremism in Afghanistan and Southeast Asia	Medium	Low	Medium	Low	Medium	Low	Medium	Low
India's regional role and strategic orientation	Medium	Medium	Medium	Low	Low	Medium	Low	Low

TABLE 10.2A

Obstacles to Cooperation in the Indo-Pacific: China

	Trust	Audience costs	Definitional Problems	Third-Party Problems	Immediacy Problem	Issue Linkage	Legal Constraints	Capacity/ Capability
Maintaining a peaceful and open regional order	✓	✓	✓			✓	✓	
Promoting and preserving regional alliances	✓	✓	✓			✓		
Expanding strategic cooperation with Indonesia, Malaysia, and Vietnam	✓						✓	
Managing cross-Strait differences between China and Taiwan	✓	✓	✓	✓	✓	✓	✓	
Achieving the denuclearization of North Korea	✓	✓	✓	✓	✓	✓		
Countering terrorism and violent Islamist extremism in Afghanistan and Southeast Asia	✓		✓		✓	✓		
India's regional role and strategic orientation	✓							

TABLE 10.2B

Obstacles to Cooperation in the Indo-Pacific: Russia

	Trust	Audience costs	Definitional Problems	Third-Party Problems	Immediacy Problem	Issue Linkage	Legal Constraints	Capacity/ Capability
Maintaining a peaceful and open regional order	✓		✓		✓	✓		
Promoting and preserving regional alliances	✓				✓	✓		
Expanding strategic cooperation with Indonesia, Malaysia, and Vietnam	✓			✓		✓		
Managing cross-Strait differences between China and Taiwan			✓	✓		✓		
Achieving the denuclearization of North Korea	✓		✓	✓				
Countering terrorism and Violent Islamist extremism in Afghanistan and Southeast Asia	✓							
India's regional role and strategic orientation	✓			✓		✓		

set of U.S. priority policy areas and explores how these fit with the positions and concerns that Russia has in the Indo-Pacific across that same list of potential obstacles to cooperation.

Finally, in Table 10.3, we capture the prospective second-order impacts on each party if the United States were to cooperate with the other power on one of these regional priorities.

As these tables demonstrate, the space for cooperation in the Indo-Pacific with China and Russia is quite limited, though there may perhaps still be some options for pursuing safer competition around the margins. Such cooperation, if it were to prove feasible, would potentially marginally complicate China-Russia relations and advantage the United States in its competition with China primarily via the mechanism of waiving CAATSA sanctions on Russian arms sales to India, Indonesia, Malaysia, and/or Vietnam. As noted in Chapters Five and Nine, such waivers involve many considerations (some of which lay outside the bounds of this study), and should be considered carefully before they are adopted, in no small part because, if adopted, they would probably prove more valuable for their avoidance of damage to U.S. relations with the countries in question than for driving a wedge in China-Russia relations, which have already dealt with these issues for many years (since Russia has long been the primary source of weapons for these countries).

The next section explores recommendations for the U.S. government, the Joint Force, and the U.S. Air Force stemming from our analysis.

Recommendations for the U.S. Government

As the foregoing analysis has argued, on issues ranging from the nature of the region's norms and accessibility, to key alliances and partnerships, and goals such as preserving the peace in the Taiwan Strait, denuclearizing North Korea, and countering violent extremism in South-Central and Southeast Asia, the space for cooperation with China and Russia is vanishingly small. Therefore, most of the recommendations below focus on competition, while noting that, should Beijing or Moscow undertake a fundamental shift in orientation, or should opportunities emerge that present genuine options to cooperate, the door to collaboration should, at least in theory, remain open.

Understanding that opportunities for genuine cooperation on pressing geopolitical issues are extremely limited by nearly diametrically opposed interests (at least as defined by the current U.S., PRC, and Russian governments), there may still be some limited space for U.S. cooperation with China or Russia aimed at managing peacetime competition with the goal of avoiding, or at least limiting, the risk of an accidental incident sparking a wider conflict.

Recommendation 1: Prepare for Long-Term Competition with China and Russia Across Most Issue Areas

As the analysis in Chapters One through Nine has demonstrated, despite hoped-for opportunities to transform mistrust, narrow divergent interests, and find common values through interactions and cooperation, the fundamental character of the U.S.-China and U.S.-Russia

TABLE 10.3

Second-Order Implications of Cooperation in the Indo-Pacific

	Impact of Cooperating with One Power on the Relations with the Other	Positive Externalities	Negative Externalities
Maintaining a peaceful and open regional order	Pursue expanded risk reduction and crisis communications mechanisms	Reduce risks of accidental conflict	Risk of undermining allied confidence by spurring image of great power condominium
Promoting and preserving regional alliances	Encourage China to extend risk reduction and crisis communication mechanisms; U.S. allies and partners could incentivize Russia to follow suit	Possible reduction in risk of accidental war/allied entrapment	N/A
Expanding strategic cooperation with Indonesia, Malaysia, and Vietnam	CAATSA waivers might introduce tensions in China-Russia relations by spurring sales of Russian arms to region that would most likely be used against China	Avoidance of tensions with Southeast Asian nations that would stem from sanctions; improvement to their ability to resist Chinese coercion; possible China-Russia tensions (though likely manageable)	Undercuts U.S. pressure on Russia, suggests U.S. sanctions not a matter of principles just politics; may simply lead to China buying more Russian arms to ensure Moscow remains closely aligned with Beijing
Managing cross-Strait differences between China and Taiwan	Meaningful opportunities to cooperate do not appear to exist	If cooperation with China was somehow achieved, it could free up resources for the defense of Europe from Russia; the reverse case is irrelevant	Would likely entail unacceptably high costs to reputation, values, national security interests, and allied trust
Achieving the denuclearization of North Korea	Pursue dialogue with China on WMD-E/"render safe" for DPRK nuclear weapons in event of a North Korean collapse	If cooperation with China was achieved, it would be hard for Russia to step in and provide the same level of support to North Korea; cooperation with Russia would have limited impact on China but might fuel North Korean resentment of increased dependence on PRC	Cooperation with China might make Russia even more obstinate and give it newfound leverage as a player on North Korean affairs once again
Countering terrorism and violent Islamist extremism in Afghanistan and Southeast Asia	Meaningful opportunities to cooperate do not appear to exist though a slim possibility that such may emerge should complete U.S. withdrawal prove imminent	Might marginally facilitate U.S. drawdown in Afghanistan (though highly unlikely)	Could taint U.S. policy by association with PRC genocide against Uyghurs, Russian human rights abuses in Caucasus
India's regional role and strategic orientation	CAATSA waivers might introduce tensions in China-Russia relations by spurring sales of Russian arms to region that would most likely be used against China	Possible China-Russia tensions (though likely manageable)	Undercuts U.S. pressure on Russia, suggests U.S. sanctions not a matter of principles just politics

relationships, at least under the CCP and Putin regimes, appears unlikely to reciprocate goodwill with genuine cooperation. Both the Chinese and Russian leadership fear their own countries' populations, as well as the values and power embodied in the United States and the international order that it has built and sustained. Consequently, neither China nor Russia is willing to support that order, and they instead regard even issues such as denuclearizing North Korea or countering violent extremism as arenas where competition predominates insofar as these issues are subordinate to the "principal contradiction" between democracy and authoritarian rule. U.S. policy, therefore, should not begin from a place of looking for cooperation with these adversarial nations, but instead should seek to define outcomes that can be achieved within the parameters of what the United States can do on its own or with its allies and partners. A corollary is that the United States should be prepared from very early on in any negotiation to treat Chinese and/or Russian cooperation as something that it can do without or else something it will have to compel Beijing or Moscow to render.

Recommendation 2: Consider Waiving CAATSA Sanctions in Order to Continue Expanding Partnerships with Key Regional Actors

U.S. allies and partners represent some of the most consequential actors in the Indo-Pacific to be sure, but they are not the totality of the region's important players, and new and emerging partners, including Indonesia, Malaysia, and Vietnam, represent potential additional sources of support for a free and open Indo-Pacific. Incremental steps and deeper cooperation with these partners are certainly possible, including through expanded arms sales, training and exercises, partner capacity building, and conceivably rotational access agreements (though these are unlikely in the near term, barring PRC aggression). Additionally, existing U.S. allies and partners are increasing their own engagement with each other, and in many cases reaching out to Indonesia and Vietnam as well (Malaysia has been less of a player in this space).[1]

With respect to the question of sowing division between Beijing and Moscow, Washington might study further the prospects of waiving CAATSA sanctions on Hanoi and Jakarta and how this would affect ties with those countries, as well as how it would resonate in Moscow, but that is not likely to be the most important reason to do so, if one exists. Instead, as other scholars have also argued, such a step might best be contemplated as a strategy for avoiding damaging the improving trajectory of U.S. ties with Indonesia, Malaysia, and Vietnam, especially if done over sales of armament types that the United States does not compete with Russia on.[2]

---

[1] Harold, et. al., 2019.

[2] Ely Ratner, *Rising to the China Challenge: Renewing American Competitiveness in the Indo-Pacific*, Washington, D.C.: Center for a New American Security, 2020.

Recommendation 3: Ensure Taiwan's Ability to Resist PRC Coercion

Taiwan's security and ability to resist PRC coercion is first and foremost the responsibility of the citizens of the Republic of China, but U.S. policy documents, U.S. law, and senior leaders' statements also make clear that this issue is of fundamental importance to U.S. national security, interests, and values in the region. As Taiwan has begun to adjust its defense strategy in the direction of asymmetry and force preservation, a number of thoughtful analyses have been put forward on how it might most effectively shift its force structure and concepts of operation.[3] Taipei can also benefit from assistance with the reform of its military reserves, which will play a key role in any defense of the island against a PLA assault.[4] Continued diplomatic support, arms sales, and expressions of commitment to the proposition that any differences between Beijing and Taipei must be resolved peacefully and in an environment free from coercion will be important. So too will be efforts to expand Taiwan's participation in international society via programs such as the Global Cooperation and Training Framework, which can enable the United States, Taiwan, Japan, Sweden, Australia, and others to engage collectively on good works and to good effect in ways that can raise the costs for China of threatening to or attempting to coerce Taiwan.

Wherever possible, it would also be valuable for the United States to hold discussions with Japan and other key regional actors (Australia, South Korea, and possibly a post-Duterte Philippines), as well as allies, partners, and like-minded nations farther afield, about what the United States might ask and how they might respond in a notional crisis with China over Taiwan so as to surface assumptions and improve planning and response. Although Russia is unlikely to discuss Taiwan in any official dialogue format with the United States, it may be worth exploring the possibility of leveraging Track 1.5 or Track 2.0 dialogues to probe the exact points at which Russian scholars and former officials expect their government's policy to overlap with or diverge from that of China in the event of a cross-Strait crisis, as well as the implications for U.S.-Russia relations of such a contingency.

Recommendation 4: Pursue Dialogue with China and Russia on DPRK Contingency Planning, but Do Not Rely on Them to Provide Any Substantial Assistance on Denuclearization

North Korea's accelerated advancement in its nuclear weapon technology and ballistic missile delivery systems will likely remain challenges for the United States and its allies and part-

---

[3] Drew Thompson, "Hope on the Horizon: Taiwan's Radical New Defense Concept," *War on the Rocks*, October 2, 2018; Jim Thomas, Iskander Rehman, and John Stillion, *Hard ROC 2.0: Taiwan and Deterrence Through Protraction*, Washington, D.C.: Center for Strategic and Budgetary Assessments, 2014; Michael J. Lostumbo, David R. Frelinger, James Williams, and Barry Wilson, *Air Defense Options for Taiwan: An Assessment of Relative Costs and Operational Benefits*, Santa Monica, Calif.: RAND Corporation, RR-1051-OSD, 2016.

[4] Ian Easton, Mark Stokes, Cortez A. Cooper, and Arthur Chan, *Transformation of Taiwan's Reserve Force*, Santa Monica, Calif.: RAND Corporation, RR-1757-OSD, 2017.

ners for years to come.[5] Furthermore, the steps the United States and its allies and partners are likely to take in responding to North Korea's growing capabilities are likely to introduce further frictions into the U.S.-China and U.S.-Russia relationships. At base, the policies and strategic objectives of China and Russia with respect to the North Korean nuclear issue are largely antithetical to U.S. interests and to realizing an enduring peace regime in the Korean Peninsula that is acceptable to the United States and its allies. Although Beijing and Moscow rhetorically underscore the goal of denuclearization, their visions of the process toward denuclearization and its end state differ from denuclearization as delineated by Washington. China and Russia have supported UN Security Council resolutions to sanction North Korea over its nuclear and missile activities, but the two countries have not fully enforced these measures themselves, as Chinese and Russian third-party entities and businesses have been complicit in North Korea's sanctions-violating activities, including illegal ship-to-ship transfers and other financial transactions.

It may well be that Beijing has once again retreated from engaging on the North Korean nuclear issue and is unlikely to do so unless the stakes rise for China's own geopolitical interests. Likewise, from Russia's perspective, the current state of relations with North Korea may not have attained the threshold for policy prioritization or justified the need for cooperation with the United States on the DPRK nuclear issue. Regardless, it may be to Washington's benefit to consider the prospects and pitfalls of cooperation with Beijing and Moscow over Pyongyang's denuclearization.

These differences notwithstanding, the United States, China, and Russia appear to agree on the security challenges and dangers posed by the North Korean nuclear weapon program to regional actors. The three parties are likely also in agreement over the imperative of monitoring North Korea's nuclear activities and securing its nuclear weapons program to prevent nuclear escalation or heightened tensions to the brink of regional conflict. Thus, it may be useful for the United States to pursue Tracks 1.5 and 2 dialogues with China and Russia as a means to indirectly glean insights into Beijing and Moscow's calculus on the North Korea issue. Washington should assume, however, that Beijing and Moscow—individually or in tandem with one another—are unlikely to be entirely forthcoming about their positions on North Korea, the information they are privy to about the Kim regime, or the extent to which they may be in contact with Pyongyang's senior officials. Thus, the information obtained would need to be vetted and thoroughly assessed for veracity and intent. These costs notwithstanding, Washington may still find some value in maintaining contact with counterparts in Beijing and Moscow in terms of contingency planning and gleaning insights into their decisionmaking.

In addition to engagement and dialogue, the United States could consider increased enforcement actions against Chinese and Russian firms involved in sanctions-breaking; seek to intercept at-sea bunkering rather than merely tracking it; and/or seek to publicize North

---

[5] Scott W. Harold and Soo Kim, "For the U.S., South Korea, and Japan, It's the North Korean Regime, Not Kim Jong Un Per Se, That Is the Threat," RealClearDefense, June 6, 2020.

Korean missile threat ranges by mapping them against PRC and/or Russian municipalities that could be targeted by such weapons, with an eye toward complicating the politics of supporting Pyongyang for Beijing or Moscow.[6] Increased sanctions levied against Chinese and Russian entities and more frequent enforcement and interception of illicit transfers of oil and other banned items could not only restrict North Korea's access to critical sources of fuel, goods, and other sources of revenue, but cutting Pyongyang's main pathways to bypass international sanctions could also weaken the Kim regime's dependence and diplomatic ties to Beijing and Moscow, as Pyongyang may derive less transactional value in maintaining these relations. By extension, China and Russia's ability to intervene or disrupt U.S. and allied efforts to reduce the North Korean nuclear threat may also face greater constraints, as the DPRK may find fewer incentives to engage with Beijing and Moscow.

Publicization of North Korean missile threat ranges—with emphasis on Chinese and Russian targets likely to be impacted by a DPRK ballistic missile launch—would lay bare the reality that neither Beijing nor Moscow will be spared from a DPRK missile or nuclear crisis. Both China and Russia are likely aware of this truth, but exposing this fact may create challenges for their decisionmakers in maintaining their defense of not only tolerating the North Korean nuclear threat, but also pursuing policies that are counterproductive to public interest and safety. This, by extension, may pose complications to China and Russia's long-standing stance on the North Korea issue and even push decisionmakers to either reassess or strive to find compelling justification for their positions to address their constituents' scrutiny.

Ultimately, however, any U.S. policy considering cooperation with China or Russia on the North Korean nuclear issue should be pursued in cognizance of the likelihood that Beijing and Moscow, by virtue of their strategic goals, long-standing positions on the DPRK issue, and previous record of policy and enforcement on North Korea, are unlikely to support Washington's objectives of achieving the complete, verifiable, and irreversible denuclearization of North Korea.

Some observers have suggested additional steps to pave the way for cooperation between the United States and China on North Korean denuclearization. For example, China expert Oriana Skylar Mastro maintains that the United States should accept Beijing taking a leading role on WMD-E inside North Korea during a contingency, mainly because the PLA is likely to reach DPRK sites first and it would free up U.S. and ROK forces for other competing missions. In support of this Chinese role, she argues that Washington should consider providing training for Chinese forces on nuclear weapon disarmament and disposal ("render safe") so that they can perform that mission more effectively. If North Korea were on the verge of or had already begun to collapse, Washington could consider sharing intelligence with Beijing on DPRK nuclear weapons to ensure that such weapons do not go missing or fall into the hands of smugglers and criminal networks that might seek to sell them on the black market—

---

[6]   Nathan Beauchamp-Mustafaga and Scott W. Harold, *Through the Looking Glass: Chinese Open Source Assessments of North Korea's Ballistic Missile Capabilities*, Washington, D.C.: Korea Economic Institute, 2020.

perhaps even sharing intelligence unilaterally, given the importance and urgency of such missions. Finally, Washington could encourage Beijing to provide Pyongyang with specific nuclear command and control technologies (such as the Chinese version of Permissive Action Links [PALS]) to enhance its nuclear security in the event Kim loses control.

Recommendation 5: Contrast U.S. Counterterrorism Efforts to Minimize Civilian Casualties with China's Genocide Against Uyghurs, and Do Not Premise U.S. Afghanistan Policy on Cooperation from China or Russia

U.S. CT/CVE efforts in South-Central and Southeast Asia are clearly essential to combating groups such as ISIS and al Qaeda and as their local affiliates or would-be partners. Still, for many countries in South-Central Asia and Southeast Asia, it is more appealing and politically sustainable to treat CT/CVE as an intelligence and policing problem than to pursue military solutions (the obvious exceptions being instances when groups such as the Taliban or Abu Sayyaf overrun a town or city such as Marawi). Insofar as is possible, U.S. officials and military personnel should operate in a supporting role, allowing local law enforcement, intelligence, or military forces to take the lead, as this will be politically advantageous to undercut the claims of China and Russia that the global Islamist terrorist problem is cause by U.S. policy.

On the other hand, China's policy of forcing the Uyghur population in Xinjiang into concentration camps and seeking to reduce their reproductive rates through forced sterilization and other measures has elicited strong global condemnation from some Western nations, as well as U.S. sanctions. U.S. policies to speak up for and highlight the stories of individual Uyghur families could have the dual effect of presenting the United States as a society that respects freedom of religion while at the same time imposing costs on China's global reputation for its crimes against humanity. A dedicated counter-genocide information operation targeting China over its treatment of the Uyghurs, if coordinated with allies and partners and presented as a principled approach to standing for human rights, could be particularly useful in U.S. outreach out to nations such as Indonesia and Malaysia and could also help complicate China's efforts to cultivate deeper ties with Pakistan and Iran. One possible stumbling block is that an emphasis on defending the human rights of Muslims could complicate U.S. ties with India, given New Delhi's recent moves to restrict access to immigration and naturalization for those arriving from majority Islamic countries.[7]

In light of the differences between the United States, China, and Russia on CT/CVE and Afghanistan, U.S. CT/CVE policies, including any decision to withdraw U.S. forces from

---

[7] Of course, many Islamic-majority countries are heavily dependent on economic interactions with China and are themselves led by authoritarian regimes that repress Muslims, so there may be limits to how much such a strategy can hope to achieve in terms of spurring such regimes to speak out against China over its treatment of the Uyghurs. Insofar as the approach is inherently righteous on its own terms irrespective of its effectiveness as an approach to competing with China in the Muslim world, it should be pursued regardless.

Afghanistan, should be considered on their own merits and should not be premised on hopes that such steps might elicit support or appreciation from Beijing or Moscow, both of which view Afghanistan through the lens of their strategic competition with the United States.

Recommendation 6: Minimize Impact of Any Cooperation with China or Competition with Russia on Efforts to Deepen Geostrategic Ties with India

Past administrations' efforts to pursue engagement with China have sometimes been seen by New Delhi as coming at India's expense; past U.S. efforts to sanction Russia have also put Indian equities at risk. Insofar as is possible, U.S. policy should strive to minimize the impacts of cooperation with China and/or competition with Russia on the prospects of deepening ties with India.

The Trump administration, building on the "pivot" or "rebalance" to the Asia-Pacific of the Obama administration, did well to revive the Quadrilateral Dialogue, a forum widely regarded as constraining China's geostrategic ambitions (though one that, to date, has yet to achieve its full potential). Routinizing the Quad, focusing on maritime exercises such as Malabar, expanding to include tri-service joint exercises, and developing a specific focus on antisubmarine warfare and air operations over water would all be extremely valuable as steps to counteract any PLAN attempts to operate out of the Indian Ocean. Such moves to expand defense ties could also include allies Japan and Australia but also conceivably South Korea, France, or the United Kingdom, as creating linkages between Europe and East Asia via India would be highly desirable.

At the same time, U.S. engagement with India may also benefit from a waiver on CAATSA sanctions in the short term, especially if combined with longer-range efforts to move New Delhi away from reliance on Russian hardware, especially for communications and command and control. It is beyond the scope of this paper to assess the costs and benefits, as well as the legal and procedural options, but waiving the application of CAATSA sanctions does appear to merit serious consideration. Open source reporting suggests that the Trump administration considered case-by-case waivers since at least mid-2018, and these may be helpful for avoiding tensions and continuing the smooth and rapid development of bilateral U.S.-India relations. As of mid-2021, no decision on the application to India of CAATSA sanctions has been made, but Indian officials are quite cognizant of the possibility that their decision to acquire the Russian S-400 air defense system may take purchases of the U.S. F-35 Joint Strike Fighter off the table and could even result in CAATSA sanctions. More importantly, policy experts assess that New Delhi may be willing to bear the cost of greater estrangement from U.S. relations as a consequence of engaging in military and arms cooperation with Russia. Some experts point out that imposing sanctions on India may drive New Delhi closer to Moscow as a reactive policy move to signal a foreign policy course independent of the United States. This may ultimately help invigorate a Russia-India-China bloc for opposing U.S. influence, or, at the least, sow greater suspicions toward the United States. For such reasons, the merits and drawbacks of waiving CAATSA sanctions on Indian arms purchases from Russia should be considered carefully.

Recommendation 7: Watch for Signs of, but Do Not Expect or Premise Any Substantial U.S. Policies on, Russia Breaking with China

As China's wealth and power grow, and especially as Chinese foreign and military policies become more aggressive, it is possible that Russia may come to reconsider its alignment with the PRC. U.S. policy, as well as that of allies such as Japan, should not overinvest in this prospect, as Putin has his own personal reasons for hewing closely to Beijing, even if this is increasingly deleterious to Russian national security. At a certain point, however, it is possible, even if not yet likely, that Russian leaders (perhaps in a post-Putin era) may conclude that China has surpassed Russia in defense technology, covets territories lost to Russian control in the 1860 Treaty of Beijing, is threatening Russian equities in Central Asia, will no longer tolerate Russian arms sales to India and Vietnam, and is moving into the Arctic in ways alarming to Moscow. Were such a series of events to come together in quick succession, it is conceivable—although again, not likely at present, despite long speculation about it from those who hope to see Russia as a strategic partner in constraining China's rise—that Russia might begin to reposition itself geostrategically, moving to partner with the United States. Unfortunately, at present and for the foreseeable future, the nature of the Russian Federation's leadership makes it extremely unlikely that it will reorient away from China and toward the United States. The United States should certainly not expect or premise its policies on such an eventuality. In the unlikely case that a genuine shift in Russian politics does take place, however, it could be important to perceive and adapt quickly to embrace such a move as it would signal a dramatic shift in the balance of power between the United States and China.

Recommendation 8: Take Steps to Reassure China and Russia That the United States Is Not Looking to Initiate Armed Conflict, Even as the United States Prepares for Intense Competition Across All Issue Areas

As officials in the Trump administration have stated, the United States is in a geostrategic competition with revisionist powers, but as former Deputy National Security Advisor Matthew Pottinger has stated, in the United States, "competition is not a four-letter word."[8] U.S. officials have striven to make clear, and should continue to do so, that the United States is not hostile to the people of China or Russia, but rather to the specific actions taken by, and ideals embodied in, their governments. Despite very, very strong differences with the CCP

---

[8]   Keegan Elmer, "U.S. Tells China: We Want Competition . . . but Also Cooperation," *South China Morning Post*, October 1, 2018.

and Putin regimes, the United States is not looking for conflict, though recent statements by former Secretary of State Pompeo led some to wonder whether the Trump administration was indeed seeking regime change in Beijing.[9] U.S. policy has been to criticize these regimes when they fall short of their obligations under global human rights norms, and to push back firmly when they take actions abroad that are threatening to U.S. interests, values, and national security, or those of U.S. allies and partners. This is the definition of intense geopolitical competition, and it behooves U.S. policy to strive to ensure that competition— even intense, across-the-board competition—remains bounded by a shared desire to avoid conflict and war. Doing so may require some signaling of the U.S. view about the bounds of competition and how intense it can get without slipping into outright conflict. One way to do so may be to continue high-level dialogue, senior leader meetings, and summitry with the leaders of China and Russia so as to clearly communicate U.S. intentions.

Recommendations for the Joint Force

To compete effectively, or to cooperate in the event of an opportunity to do so unexpectedly arising, the Joint Force will need to focus on preparedness, partnerships, and a networked region.[10]

Recommendation 1: Pursue Improved Military-to-Military Deconfliction with China for "Safe Competition"

The Joint Force should continue to pursue and engage in military-to-military deconfliction with the PLA as a way to support "safe competition," including regularly referencing, invoking, and employing preexisting mechanisms and points of contact. Broadly defined, this approach would seek to continue some level of military-to-military dialogue and would seek to develop any additional confidence-building measures, risk reduction and crisis communications mechanisms, and related communications channels, as well as agreed upon standards of behavior for unplanned encounters. However, understanding that all these items have been pursued with relative zeal by Washington over three decades only to be met with begrudging slow-rolling by Beijing, DoD should also conduct a critical and comprehensive assessment of military-to-military engagement, especially existing crisis management mechanisms, answering the question of whether these are sufficient or need to be otherwise optimized in some way to best serve for long-term heightened competition.

---

9   Michael R. Pompeo, "Communist China and the Free World's Fate," U.S. Department of State, July 23, 2020.

10   DoD, 2019.

Recommendation 2: Support Improved Allied and Partner Military-to-Military Deconfliction with China

In many cases, U.S. forces are not actually the frontline forces facing the Chinese military and subordinate Coast Guard and maritime militia in day-to-day competition. Rather, it is U.S. allies and partners that are defending their sovereignty in the land, maritime, and air domains that often encounter Chinese forces. For however much the United States feels China has been largely recalcitrant in supporting robust military-to-military deconfliction, China has been even more intractable in developing military-to-military deconfliction with its neighbors. In light of U.S. defense commitments to these countries and the acknowledged risk that any clash between allies and China could eventually involve the United States, the Joint Force has a direct interest in supporting allies (and partners) in moving toward "safe competition" as well. Additionally, by standing up for U.S. allies and partners in pressing China to extend its arrangements with the United States to these third countries, the United States will help guard against any perception of an emerging "great power condominium" or sense that the PLA is being used to drive wedges in the U.S. relationship with its allies and partners by respecting the United States but disrespecting America's less powerful partners.

In terms of specifics, DoD should lend its expertise, and even templates for agreements, as an additional component of security cooperation with allies and partners. DoD should also extend this to Taiwan, which has recently warned of these risks, though the PRC has likely even less interest in reassuring Taiwan through these steps.[11] This does not have to be confined to Indo-Pacific nations, and indeed, if the United States seeks to incorporate like-minded nations from Europe to operate their militaries in the region, they too should reach similar agreements with Beijing. This should be coordinated with the Department of State, potentially under a National Security Council–led process.

Recommendation 3: Pursue Dialogue over Possible DPRK Contingencies with China and Russia

As part of a whole-of-government outreach to Beijing on DPRK contingency planning, DoD should directly engage the Chinese military on operational and tactical level details. While the August 2017 visit by General Joseph Dunford to the PLA's Northern Theater Command, which reportedly included discussions of contingency planning, was a positive step, the public record stops here. The below items present varying amounts of strategic and operational costs and benefits, all of which must be weighed carefully and thoughtfully at the highest levels. Of course, DoD and the Department of State should also coordinate with U.S. allies in Tokyo, Seoul, Canberra, and Manila on this issue.

Several steps can be explored, if they do not already exist: direct communications channels between USINDOPACOM or even U.S. Forces Korea and China's Northern Theater

---

[11] Ben Blanchard, "Taiwan Warns of Accidental Conflict as Regional Tensions Rise," Reuters, August 27, 2020.

Command, between U.S. Special Operations Command and its Chinese counterpart, and between the National Nuclear Security Administration and China's Nuclear Emergency Response Center. All of these can be offered unilaterally by the United States with no operational cost and minimal political risk. However, because Beijing is highly likely to continue to view this issue as too sensitive to engage on through official channels, where possible, DoD should also seek to support Track 1.5 and Track 2 dialogues on this issue and emphasize the importance of including this issue on the agenda for broader dialogues.

Supporting potential contingency planning and tactical deconfliction, DoD should conduct a review of relevant planning documents and intelligence products that are necessary and suitable to share with Beijing. DoD should assume that, in the worst case, Beijing will share these documents with Pyongyang, but the importance of this deconfliction is such that the risk must be weighed against the strategic and operational benefit. Each service should also conduct a review of its communications equipment at the brigade level and below to ensure that it is physically capable of communicating with Chinese counterparts on the battlefield.

Because China is unlikely to consent to discuss how the United States and the PRC would handle a North Korean collapse scenario in advance of such a contingency actually coming to pass, DoD should consider conducting a classified assessment of which DPRK WMD sites (nuclear and nonnuclear) Chinese forces are likely to reach before U.S./ROK forces and develop a plan for de facto operational deconfliction by engagement with and/or avoidance of Chinese forces operating around those sites. This plan would benefit from coordination with South Korea.

Furthermore, in light of the possibility that Chinese forces may reach many or even most DPRK sites before U.S.-ROK forces do, and assuming that they would seek to execute the WMD-E mission on their own, DoD should conduct a review of U.S. WMD-E "render safe" practices to determine whether any of the operational guidance that U.S. forces would be following can be shared with China—unilaterally if necessary—to reduce the prospect of less experienced Chinese WMD-E forces precipitating a nuclear accident (or accidents) in North Korea.

Recommendation 4: Continually Encourage U.S. Allies and Partners to Cooperate in New Areas and Forums Despite, or in Some Cases Because of, Chinese Complaints That Doing So Constitutes "Containment"

As substantial research on regional order and architecture in the Indo-Pacific has shown, the U.S. hub-and-spokes alliance system and ASEAN collectively constitute the oldest and most enduring aspects of the regional architecture, yet new multilateral groupings are emerging and being layered onto these preexisting organizations.[12] At the same time, less institutional-

---

[12] Andrew Yeo, *Asia's Regional Architecture: Alliances and Institutions in the Pacific Century*, Stanford, Calif.: Stanford University Press, 2019.

ized patterns of security cooperation are emerging among U.S. allies, such as Japan, South Korea, Australia, and the Philippines, and burgeoning partners, such as India, Indonesia, and Vietnam, with some substantial consequences for regional security.[13] In almost all cases, such cooperation among U.S. allies and partners is in pursuit of policy goals that the United States seeks. U.S. policy should encourage and support such efforts to bolster the partner capacity of coastal states around the South China Sea, improve bilateral readiness and training, and develop ties that create incentives that may complicate the calculus of any revisionist power seeking to employ coercion to get its way. U.S. diplomats and defense officials should encourage regional actors to continue to pursue such engagement with their regional partners even in the face of Chinese complaints that such activities constitute destabilizing, anti-China steps that are aimed at containment or are increasing regional tensions. Where possible, U.S. policy should provide support for such efforts.

Recommendations for the U.S. Air Force

For the U.S. Air Force, operating in an increasingly competitive Indo-Pacific will require substantial transformation.

Recommendation 1: Continue to Leverage Existing Mechanisms and Consider Pursuing Improved Military-to-Military Deconfliction with Chinese Aerospace Forces and Russian Air and Naval Forces

This activity should also be coordinated with the U.S. Navy and U.S. Marine Corps, since the PLA Naval Aviation forces are under the PLAN, making them the natural counterparts. The U.S. Air Force might also explore developing deconfliction plans, crisis communications channels, and risk reduction mechanisms with the aviation wing of the Russian Pacific Fleet and the 11th Air Force and Air Defense Forces Army.

Recommendation 2: Pursue Improved DPRK WMD Monitoring and Preparations for WMD-E, Possibly in Close Proximity to Chinese Forces

The U.S. Air Force should consider, in consultation with the broader Joint Force and Department of State, whether to establish direct communications with the PLA Rocket Force, which will likely be involved with China's DPRK WMD-E mission. Should the United States pursue this policy option, the U.S. Air Force—perhaps in conjunction with U.S. intelligence organizations—will need to have ready-made plans for what it can share in a contingency with China from intelligence collection, vetting, and counterintelligence on North Korean

---

[13] Harold, Grossman, et al., 2019.

nuclear and missile programs, as well as how U.S. forces would liaise with, or at a minimum operate if in close proximity to, Chinese forces in such a contingency. The United States should also keep in mind that direct communications channels with the PLA Rocket Force may carry the risk of exposing U.S. vulnerabilities vis-à-vis the North Korean nuclear threat and, by extension, may create opportunities for China to exploit such areas for its own strategic interests.

Final Thoughts

The United States, in the goals it seeks in the Indo-Pacific region, starts from a position of enormous strength. It possesses the world's largest and most dynamic economy, its most capable and experienced military, the broadest set of allies and partners, and an attractive and generally well-regarded set of values and principles that appeal to publics and leaders in many of the region's most important and influential countries. By contrast, China and Russia are primarily mistrusted, resented, and feared where they are not outright hated. No country except North Korea calls China a treaty ally, and many, including India, Japan, Taiwan, and Vietnam, regard China as their number one national security threat. Russia fares better with some, such as India and Vietnam, but is seen as of only marginal importance by many and is recognized as a major challenge by Japan. Almost every country in the Indo-Pacific has had its intellectual property stolen, cybersecurity violated, maritime proteins poached, territorial integrity encroached upon, electoral democracy interfered with, and/or national security threatened by China, which in turn gives little in the way of financing or preferential market access to most of the region's more influential countries (though its use of investment and trade remain key sources of PRC sway).

In short, to achieve the goals it seeks, the United States must but play well the hand it has built for itself through seven decades of engagement in support of a liberal, democratic, rule-of-law, market-based economic order. China and Russia possess some substantial resources of their own, including geostrategic location, size, economic heft, technological sophistication, and unity of focus, as well as cunning in pursuit of disruptive policies that usually stay below the level of an outright and obvious assault on the international system. But such advantages, if countered smartly, should be possible to offset. Political strategy, skillful diplomacy, and a well-resourced, well-led, and well-postured military are some of the essential requirements for doing so. A key additional element is an understanding of when and where to compete, and the prospects for avoiding conflict, turning adversaries into partners, and achieving positive-sum outcomes through cooperation. But it is also true that assuming that opportunities for cooperation must exist in all times and places and that the challenge is simply to find them by perpetually seeking increasingly complicated formulas to describe a mythical "trade space" does little more than position one's country as an "ardent suitor" to a revisionist power, an approach almost guaranteed to encourage and empower aggression, drive away friends and allies, and leave a nation unprepared to compete successfully. This study is a down payment in support of the men and women of the U.S. Air Force in the hopes that it provides clarity of analysis empowering the service, the other components of the joint force, and DoD to understand how little hope there is for substantive cooperation with China or Russia on the key goals the United States seeks in the Indo-Pacific, and how best to prepare with our allies, friends, and partners for the long-term competition that will be necessary to keep the peace that has served the region and America so well for the past four decades.

Abbreviations

ASEAN	Association of Southeast Asian Nations
BRI	Belt and Road Initiative
BRICS	Brazil-Russia-India-China–South Africa
BUILD	Better Utilization of International Lending for Development Act
CAATSA	Countering America's Adversaries Through Sanctions Act
CCP	Chinese Communist Party
COVID-19	coronavirus disease 2019
CT/CVE	counterterrorism/countering violent extremism
CUES	Code for Unplanned Encounters at Sea
CVID	complete, verifiable, and irreversible denuclearization
DPRK	Democratic People's Republic of Korea
EAEU	Eurasian Economic Union
EEZ	exclusive economic zone
FOIP	free and open Indo-Pacific
HA/DR	humanitarian assistance/disaster relief
INDOPACOM	U.S. Indo-Pacific Command
ISIS	Islamic State of Syria and Iraq
ISR	intelligence, surveillance, and reconnaissance
MOU	memorandum of understanding
NATO	North Atlantic Treaty Organization
NDS	National Defense Strategy
PLA	People's Liberation Army
PLAN	PLA Navy
PRC	People's Republic of China (China)
RIC	Russia-India-China
ROK	Republic of Korea (South Korea)
SCO	Shanghai Cooperation Organization
THAAD	Terminal High-Altitude Area Defense
UN	United Nations
UNCLOS	United Nations Convention on the Law of the Sea
WMD	weapons of mass destruction
WMD-E	WMD elimination

References

"88th Joint Patrol on Mekong River Completed," *Global Times*, November 23, 2019. As of August 27, 2020:
http://www.globaltimes.cn/content/1170910.shtml

Afzal, Madiha, *"At All Costs": How Pakistan and China Control the Narrative on the China-Pakistan Economic Corridor*, Washington, D.C.: Brookings Institution, June 2020.

"Agreement Between the Department of Defense of the United States of America and the Ministry of National Defense of the People's Republic of China on Establishing a Consultation Mechanism to Strengthen Military Maritime Safety," January 19, 1998.

"Agreement on the Establishment of a Secure Defense Telephone Link Between the Department of Defense, the United States of America and the Ministry of National Defense, the People's Republic of China," February 2008. As of April 21, 2021:
https://www.state.gov/wp-content/uploads/2019/02/08-229-China-Telecommunication-Link.EnglishOCR.pdf

Allen, Kenneth, Phillip C. Saunders, and John Chen, *Chinese Military Diplomacy, 2003–2016: Trends and Implications*, Washington, D.C.: National Defense University, July 2017.

Allen-Ebrahimian, Bethany, "Documents Show China's Secret Extradition Request for Uighur in Turkey," *Axios*, May 20, 2020. As of June 14, 2020:
https://www.axios.com/documents-chinas-secret-extradition-request-uighur-turkey-6d5ba886-c22c-47e8-b970-804fae274e2d.html

Allison, Graham, *Destined for War: Can America and China Escape Thucydides' Trap?* New York: Houghton Mifflin Harcourt, 2017.

Antonopoulos, Paul, "The Kangaroo, the Bear, and the Dragon: Australia-Russia-China Relations in the 'Asian Century,'" *China Quarterly of International Strategic Studies*, Vol. 3, No. 3, 2017, pp. 411–428.

Armitage, Richard, and Joseph Nye, *More Important Than Ever: Renewing the U.S.-Japan Alliance for the 21st Century*, Washington, D.C.: Center for Strategic and International Studies, 2018.

Arms Control Association, "UN Security Council Resolutions on North Korea," April 2018. As of June 23, 2020:
https://www.armscontrol.org/factsheets/UN-Security-Council-Resolutions-on-North-Korea

Arms Control Association, "Chronology of U.S.–North Korea Nuclear and Missile Diplomacy," May 2020. As of June 23, 2020:
https://www.armscontrol.org/factsheets/dprkchron

Asian Development Bank, *Meeting Asia's Infrastructure Needs*, 2017. As of April 20, 2021:
https://www.adb.org/publications/asia-infrastructure-needs

Baculinao, Eric, and Jason Cumming, "China Spends Big in Tibet to Avert a Crisis When the Dalai Lama Dies," *NBC News*, August 30, 2018. As of June 14, 2020:
https://www.nbcnews.com/news/world/china-spends-big-tibet-avert-crisis-when-dalai-lama-dies-n904676

Beauchamp-Mustafaga, Nathan, and Scott W. Harold, *Through the Looking Glass: Chinese Open Source Assessments of North Korea's Ballistic Missile Capabilities*, Washington, D.C.: Korea Economic Institute, 2020. As of April 19, 2021:
http://www.keia.org/sites/default/files/publications/kei_sma_mustafagaharold_200827.pdf

Beech, Hannah, "U.S. Aircraft Carrier Arrives in Vietnam, with a Message for China," *New York Times*, March 4, 2018.

Beech, Hannah, and Mukita Suhartono, "China Chases Indonesia's Fishing Fleets, Staking Claim to Sea's Riches," *New York Times*, March 31, 2020.

Bernstein, Richard, "When China Convinced the U.S. That Uighurs Were Waging Jihad," *The Atlantic*, March 19, 2019. As of June 14, 2020:
https://www.theatlantic.com/international/archive/2019/03/us-uighurs-guantanamo-chin a-terror/584107/

Bitzinger, Richard A., *Russian Arms Transfers and Asian Military Modernisation*, Singapore: S. Rajaratnam School of International Studies (RSIS), RSIS Policy Report, 2015.

Blackwill, Robert, and Kurt Campbell, *Xi Jinping on the Global Stage: Chinese Foreign Policy under A More Powerful but Exposed Leader*, Washington, D.C.: Council on Foreign Relations, 2016.

Blanchard, Ben, "China Appoints Special Envoy for Afghanistan," Reuters, July 18, 2014. As of June 14, 2020:
https://www.reuters.com/article/us-china-afghanistan/idUSKBN0FN11Z20140718

Blanchard, Ben, "Taiwan Warns of Accidental Conflict as Regional Tensions Rise," Reuters, August 27, 2020. As of April 21, 2021:
https://www.reuters.com/article/us-taiwan-diplomacy/taiwan-warns-of-accidental-conflict-as-regional-tensions-rise-idUSKBN25N0QD

Blanchard, Ben, and Andrea Shalal, "Angry China Shadows U.S. Warship Near Man-Made Islands," Reuters, October 26, 2015.

Bolton, John, *The Room Where It Happened: A White House Memoir*, New York: Simon & Schuster, 2020.

Bonds, Timothy M., Eric V. Larson, Derek Eaton, and Richard E. Darilek, *Strategy-Policy Mismatch: How the U.S. Army Can Help Close Gaps in Countering Weapons of Mass Destruction*, Santa Monica, Calif.: RAND Corporation, RR-541-RC, 2014. As of August 25, 2020:
https://www.rand.org/pubs/research_reports/RR541.html

Borshchevskaya, Anna, "Russia's Questionable Counterterrorism Record: Why Moscow Is an Unreliable Partner for the West," *Foreign Affairs*, November 23, 2017. As of June 14, 2020:
https://www.foreignaffairs.com/articles/syria/2017-11-23/russias-questionabl e-counterterrorism-record

Bowie, Nile, "Is Malaysia's Position on MH17 Tragedy Shifting?" *Asia Times*, March 9, 2020. As of June 14, 2020:
https://asiatimes.com/2020/03/is-malaysias-position-on-mh-17-tragedy-shifting/

Bowman, Bradley and David Maxwell, *Maximum Pressure 2.0: A Plan for North Korea*, Washington, D.C.: Foundation for Defense of Democracies, 2019.

Bowman, Tom, "Defense Secretary Expresses Concern over Russian Support for Taliban," NPR, March 31, 2017. As of July 20, 2021:
https://www.npr.org/2017/03/31/522232584/defense-secretary-expresses-concern-over-r ussian-support-for-taliban

Brown, Daniel, "The Top 10 Countries That Bought Russia's Most Powerful Weapons in 2017," *Business Insider*, October 6, 2018. As of June 14, 2020:
https://www.businessinsider.com/russia-weapons-sales-top-countries-2018-4

Brown, Matthew, "U.S. Slams 'Unprofessional' Intercept by Chinese Fighter Jets," Associated Press, May 19, 2017. As of June 14, 2020:
https://www.usatoday.com/story/news/world/2017/05/19/china-united-states-fighter-je
t-surveillance-plane/101867224/

Browne, Andrew, "China Won't Help: It's Paralyzed by North Korea," *Wall Street Journal*, September 6, 2017.

Browne, Ryan, and Barbara Starr, "Chinese Fighter Jet Performed 'Unsafe' Intercept of U.S. Navy Plane," CNN, July 24, 2017.

Brunnstrom, David, and Patricia Zengerle, "Obama Administration Authorizes $1.83-Billion Arms Sale to Taiwan," Reuters, December 17, 2015. As of June 14, 2020:
https://www.reuters.com/article/us-usa-taiwan-arms-idUSKBN0TZ2C520151217

Brzezinski, Zbigniew, "The Group of Two That Could Change the World," *Financial Times*, January 13, 2009.

Buchanan, Elizabeth, "What a New Russian Ambassador Might Mean for Relations with Australia," *The Interpreter*, Lowy Institute, May 27, 2019a. As of June 14, 2020:
https://www.lowyinstitute.org/the-interpreter/what-new-russian-ambassado
r-might-mean-relations-australia

Buchanan, Elizabeth, "What Russia Wants in a Multipolar World," *The Interpreter*, Lowy Institute, October 31, 2019b. As of June 14, 2020:
https://www.lowyinstitute.org/the-interpreter/what-russia-wants-multipolar-world

Buckley, Chris, "As China's Woes Mount, Xi Jinping Faces Rare Rebuke at Home," *New York Times*, July 31, 2018.

Burns, John F., "India's New Defense Chief Sees Chinese Military Threat," *New York Times*, May 5, 1998.

Bush, George W., *Decision Points*, New York: Broadway Paperbacks, 2011.

Bush, Richard C., "China's Response to Collapse in North Korea," Brookings Institution, January 23, 2014. As of April 22, 2021:
https://www.brookings.edu/on-the-record/chinas-response-to-collapse-in-north-korea

Bush, Richard C., "8 Key Things to Notice from Xi Jinping's New Year's Speech on Taiwan," Washington, D.C.: Brookings Institution, January 7, 2019. As of June 14, 2020:
https://www.brookings.edu/blog/order-from-chaos/2019/01/07/8-key-things-to-notice-from-xi
-jinpings-new-year-speech-on-taiwan/

Bush, Richard C., Elizabeth Economy, David M. Finkelstein, Paul Gewirtz, Michael J. Green, John J. Hamre, Melanie Hart, Mira Rapp-Hooper, Scott Kennedy, Evan S. Medeiros, Phillip C. Saunders, and Randall G. Schriver, *Joint US-China Think Tank Project on the Future of US-China Relations: An American Perspective*, Washington, D.C.: Center for Strategic and International Studies, 2017. As of August 26, 2020:
https://www.csis.org/analysis/joint-us-china-think-tank-project-future-us-china-relations

Butcher, Linda, "Building a U.S.-Korea-India Trilateral Dialogue," Korea Economic Institute, September 10, 2015. As of July 6, 2020:
https://keia.org/the-peninsula/building-a-u-s-korea-india-trilateral-dialogue/

Cadell, Cate, "China Warns Outsiders Not to 'Sow Distrust' in South China Sea," Reuters, July 31, 2019. As of April 21, 2021:
https://www.reuters.com/article/us-asean-thailand/china-warns-outsiders-not-to-sow-distrust-in-south-china-sea-idUSKCN1UQ1HL

Campbell, Kurt, *The Pivot: The Future of American Statecraft in Asia*, New York: Twelve Books, 2016.

Campbell, Kurt M., and Ely Ratner, "The China Reckoning," *Foreign Affairs*, March/April 2018.

Carpenter, Michael, "Russia's Counterproductive Counter-Terrorism," testimony before the Commission on Security and Cooperation in Europe (Helsinki Commission), Commission on Security and Cooperation in Europe, June 12, 2019. As of June 14, 2020:
https://www.csce.gov/sites/helsinkicommission.house.gov/files/Carpenter%20Helsinki%20Testimony%20on%20Russia%20CT%206-12-19%20for%20web.pdf

Carter, Ash, "A Regional Security Architecture Where Everyone Rises," speech at Shangri-La Dialogue, International Institute for Strategic Studies, May 30, 2015. As of June 14, 2020:
https://www.defense.gov/Newsroom/Speeches/Speech/Article/606676/iiss-shangri-la-dialogue-a-regional-security-architecture-where-everyone-rises

Center for Strategic and International Studies, "What Does China Really Spend on Its Military?" undated. As of June 1, 2020:
https://chinapower.csis.org/military-spending/

Center for Strategic and International Studies, Asia Maritime Transparency Initiative, "Failing or Incomplete? Grading the South China Sea Arbitration," July 11, 2019. As of July 20, 2021:
https://amti.csis.org/failing-or-incomplete-grading-the-south-china-sea-arbitration/

Cha, Victor, *Powerplay: The Origins of the American Alliance System in Asia*, Princeton, N.J.: Princeton University Press, 2016.

Chan, Minnie, "Chinese Military Lashes Out at American Warship's 'Intrusion' in South China Sea," *South China Morning Post*, April 28, 2020. As of June 14, 2020:
https://www.scmp.com/news/china/diplomacy/article/3081970/chinese-military-lashes-out-american-warships-intrusion-south

Chaudhury, Dipanjan Roy, "Russia Does Not Want to Interfere in India-China Standoff: Top Lawmaker," *Economic Times*, June 10, 2020. As of June 14, 2020:
https://economictimes.indiatimes.com/news/defence/russia-does-not-want-to-interfere-in-india-china-stand-off-top-lawmaker/articleshow/76309365.cms?from=mdr

Chen Cheng-Hui, "TSMC Key to U.S. Supply Chains, Fitch Says," *Taipei Times*, May 25, 2020.

Chen, Frank, "Russia May Be Withholding Missile Deliveries to China," *Asia Times*, July 29, 2020. As of July 29, 2020:
https://asiatimes.com/2020/07/russia-may-be-withholding-missile-deliveries-to-china/

Cheng, Willard, "US Defense Official Warns PH on Buying Russian Military Equipment," *ABS-CBN News*, August 16, 2018. As of June 14, 2020:
https://news.abs-cbn.com/overseas/08/16/18/us-defense-official-warns-ph-on-buying-russian-military-equipment

China Military Online, "First Indonesia-Russia Joint Exercise Has Profound Implications," March 24, 2020. As of June 14, 2020:
http://english.chinamil.com.cn/view/2020-03/24/content_9776281.htm

"China, Russia Agree to Upgrade Relations for New Era," Xinhua, June 6, 2019. As of April 21, 2021:
http://www.xinhuanet.com/english/2019-06/06/c_138119879.htm

"China, Russia, U.S., Pakistan Hold Talks on Afghan Peace Process," Xinhua, October 26, 2019. As of June 14, 2020:
http://www.xinhuanet.com/english/2019-10/26/c_138504646.htm

"China Says 'Dual Suspension' Proposal Still Best for North Korea," Reuters, November 16, 2017.

"China, Southeast Asia to Set Up Hotline for South China Sea Issues," Reuters, July 31, 2015. As of April 21, 2021:
https://www.reuters.com/article/us-asean-malaysia-hotline/idUSKCN0Q51N220150731

"China Values Russia's Support on Taiwan—Foreign Ministry," Tass, May 20, 2016. As of June 14, 2020:
https://tass.com/world/877014

"China Will Not Allow War or Instability on Korean Peninsula." Xinhua, March 8, 2014. As of June 14, 2020:
http://news.xinhuanet.com/english/special/2014-03/08/c_133170724.htm

Chung, Jae Ho, and Jiyoon Kim, "Is South Korea in China's Orbit? Assessing Seoul's Perceptions and Policies," *Asia Policy*, No. 21, National Bureau of Asian Research, January 1, 2016. As of June 14, 2020:
https://www.nbr.org/publication/is-south-korea-in-chinas-orbit-assessing-seouls-perceptions-and-policies/

Clarke, Colin P., "Russia Is Not a Viable Counterterrorism Partner for the United States," *Russia Matters*, February 8, 2018. As of June 14, 2020:
https://www.russiamatters.org/analysis/russia-not-viable-counterterrorism-partner-united-states

Cliff, Roger, and David A. Shlapak, *U.S.-China Relations After Resolution of Taiwan's Status*, Santa Monica, Calif.: RAND Corporation, MG-567-AF, 2007. As of August 25, 2020:
https://www.rand.org/pubs/monographs/MG567.html

Clover, Charles, "Mystery Deepens over Chinese Forces in Afghanistan," *Financial Times*, February 26, 2017. As of June 14, 2020:
https://www.ft.com/content/0c8a5a2a-f9b7-11e6-9516-2d969e0d3b65

Cohen, David, "'A Clash of Security Concepts': China's Effort to Redefine Security," *China Brief*, Vol. 14, No. 11, June 4, 2014. As of April 21, 2021:
https://jamestown.org/program/a-clash-of-security-concepts-chinas-effort-to-redefine-security/

Cohen, Raphael S. , Elina Treyger, Nathan Beauchamp-Mustafaga, Asha Clark, Kit Conn, Scott W. Harold, Michelle Grisé, Marta Kepe, Soo Kim, Ashley L. Rhoades, Roby Valiaveedu, and Nathan Vest, *Vanishing Trade Space: Assessing the Prospects for Great Power Cooperation in an Era of Competition—A Project Overview*, Santa Monica, Calif.: RAND Corporation, RR-A597-1, 2023.

Colby, Elbridge, Abraham Denmark, and John Warden, *Nuclear Weapons and U.S.-China Relations: A Way Forward*, Washington, D.C.: Center for Strategic and International Studies, PONI Working Group on U.S.-China Nuclear Dynamics, March 2013. As of June 14, 2020:
https://www.csis.org/files/publication/130307_Colby_USChinaNuclear_Web.pdf

Cole, J. Michael, *Convergence or Conflict in the Taiwan Strait: The Illusion of Peace?* New York: Routledge, 2017.

Cole, J. Michael, *Cross-Strait Relations Since 2016: The End of the Illusion*, New York: Routledge, 2020.

Connolly, Richard, and Cecilie Sendstad, "Russia's Role as an Arms Exporter: The Strategic and Economic Importance of Arms Exports for Russia," Chatham House, March 2017. As of June 14, 2020:
https://www.chathamhouse.org/sites/default/files/publications/research/2017-03-20-russia-arms-exporter-connolly-sendstad.pdf

Council on Foreign Relations, "Managing Global Disorder: Prospects for U.S.-China Cooperation," April 18, 2018. As of August 28, 2020:
https://www.cfr.org/report/managing-global-disorder-prospects-us-china-cooperation

Cowell, Alan, "Putin 'Probably Approved' Litvinenko Poisoning, British Inquiry Says," *New York Times*, January 21, 2016.

Craft, Kelly, U.S. Representative to the United Nations, "Protesting China's Unlawful Maritime Claims at the UN," letter to António Guterres, Secretary-General of the United Nations, June 1, 2020. As of April 21, 2021:
https://usun.usmission.gov/protesting-chinas-unlawful-maritime-claims-at-the-un/

Cronin, Patrick, *The Cornerstone and the Linchpin: Securing America's Northeast Asian Alliances*, Washington, D.C.: The Hudson Institute, 2019.

Cronin, Patrick M., Abigail Grace, Daniel Kliman, and Kristine Lee, *Contested Spaces: A Renewed Approach to Southeast Asia*, Washington, D.C.: Center for a New American Security, 2019.

Cronk, Terri Moon, "Chinese Seize U.S. Navy Underwater Drone in South China Sea," *DoD News*, December 16, 2016.

Das, Krishna N., and Sunil Kataria, "Dalai Lama Contemplates Chinese Gambit After His Death," Reuters, March 18, 2019. As of June 14, 2020:
https://in.reuters.com/article/china-tibet-dalai-lama/exclusive-dalai-lama-contemplates-chinese-gambit-after-his-death-idINKCN1QZ1O1

Davis, Lynn E., Stacie L. Pettyjohn, Melanie W. Sisson, Stephen M. Worman, and Michael J. McNerney, *U.S. Overseas Military Presence: What Are the Strategic Choices?* Santa Monica, Calif.: RAND Corporation, MG-1211-AF, 2012. As of August 25, 2020:
https://www.rand.org/pubs/monographs/MG1211.html

DeAeth, Duncan, "Relations Between Taiwan and Russia Are Steadily Improving: VOA," *Taiwan News*, June 5, 2019. As of June 14, 2020:
https://www.taiwannews.com.tw/en/news/3717821

Defense Intelligence Agency, *China Military Power: Modernizing a Force to Fight and Win*, Washington, D.C., January 2019. As of June 14, 2020:
https://www.dia.mil/Portals/27/Documents/News/Military%20Power%20Publications/China_Military_Power_FINAL_5MB_20190103.pdf

DefenseWorld.net, "US to Exempt India, Indonesia, and Vietnam from CAATSA Sanctions," July 24, 2018. As of August 26, 2020:
https://www.defenseworld.net/news/23031/US_to_Exempt_India__Indonesia_and_Vietnam_from_CAATSA_Sanctions#.XyrVaS2ZO-x

DefenseWorld.net, "Indonesia, Russia Still Negotiating Su-35 Deal," March 16, 2020. As of August 26, 2020:
https://www.defenseworld.net/news/26522/Indonesia__Russia_Still_Negotiating_Su_35_Deal

Denmark, Abraham, and Lucas Myers, "Eternal Victory," *Wilson Quarterly*, Summer 2020. As of June 26, 2020:
https://www.wilsonquarterly.com/quarterly/korea-70-years-on/eternal-victory/

Department of Foreign Affairs and Trade, Australia, "Russian Sanctions Regime," undated. As of June 19, 2020:
https://www.dfat.gov.au/international-relations/security/sanctions/sanctions-regimes/Pages/russia

Department of Foreign Affairs of the Republic of the Philippines, "Key PH-Russia Security Agreement Enters into Force," January 16, 2018. As of August 26, 2018:
https://dfa.gov.ph/dfa-news/news-from-our-foreign-service-postsupdate/15277-key-ph-russia-security-agreement-enters-into-force

DeTrani, Joseph, "China Can Push North Korea for Complete and Verifiable Denuclearization," *Washington Times*, August 17, 2020.

Dingli, Shen, "North Korea's Strategic Significance to China," *China Security*, Autumn 2006, pp. 19–34.

Ditzler, Joseph, "Navy Sends Another Guided-Missile Destroyer Through Taiwan Strait," *Stars and Stripes*, June 8, 2020.

Dobbins, James, Howard J. Shatz, and Ali Wyne, *Russia Is a Rogue, Not a Peer; China Is a Peer, Not a Rogue: Different Challenges, Different Responses*, Santa Monica, Calif.: RAND Corporation, PE-310-A, 2019. As of August 18, 2020:
https://www.rand.org/pubs/perspectives/PE310.html

Donati, Jessica, and Ehsanullah Amiri, "China Offers Afghanistan Army Expanded Military Aid," *Wall Street Journal*, March 9, 2016.

Doshi, Rush, "Hu's to Blame for China's Foreign Assertiveness?" Brookings Institution, January 22, 2019. As of April 20, 2021:
https://www.brookings.edu/articles/hus-to-blame-for-chinas-foreign-assertiveness/

Doshi, Rush, "Beijing Believes Trump Is Accelerating American Decline," *Foreign Policy*, October 12, 2020.

Doshi, Rush, *The Long Game: China's Grand Strategy to Displace American Order*, Oxford, UK: Oxford University Press, 2021.

Duchâtel, Mathieu, "China's Foreign Fighters Problem," *War on the Rocks*, January 25, 2019. As of June 14, 2020:
https://warontherocks.com/2019/01/chinas-foreign-fighters-problem/

Dutton, Peter, ed., *Military Activities in the EEZ: A U.S.-China Dialogue on Security and International Law in the Maritime Commons*, Providence, R.I.: Naval War College China Maritime Studies Institute, Red Book Series No. 7, 2010. As of June 14, 2020:
https://digital-commons.usnwc.edu/cgi/viewcontent.cgi?article=1006&context=cmsi-red-books&httpsredir=1&referer=

Dyakina, Maya, and Lidia Kelly, "Russia Writes Off 90 Percent of North Korea's Debt," Reuters, September 18, 2012.

Easton, Ian, Mark Stokes, Cortez A. Cooper, and Arthur Chan, *Transformation of Taiwan's Reserve Force*, Santa Monica, Calif.: RAND Corporation, RR-1757-OSD, 2017. As of August 18, 2020:
https://www.rand.org/pubs/research_reports/RR1757.html

Elmer, Keegan, "U.S. Tells China: We Want Competition . . . but also Cooperation," *South China Morning Post*, October 1, 2018.

Embassy of India in Beijing, China, "India-China Trade and Economic Relations," undated. As of June 14, 2020:
https://www.eoibeijing.gov.in/economic-and-trade-relation.php

"Envoy Elaborates China's Position on Afghanistan," Xinhua, November 28, 2019. As of June 14, 2020:
http://www.xinhuanet.com/english/2019-11/28/c_138588110.htm

Erickson, Andrew, "U.S.-China Military-to-Military Relations: Policy Considerations in a Changing Environment," *Asia Policy*, Vol. 14, No. 3, July 2019, pp. 123–144.

Erickson, Andrew S., and Joel Wuthnow, "Barriers, Springboards and Benchmarks: China Conceptualizes the Pacific 'Island Chains,'" *China Quarterly*, Vol. 225, March 2016, pp. 1–22.

Everington, Keoni, "US Navy C-40 Reported Flying Directly over Taiwan," *Taiwan News*, June 9, 2020.

Feldman, Harvey, "President Reagan's Six Assurances to Taiwan and Their Meaning Today," Heritage Foundation, October 2, 2007. As of June 18, 2020:
https://www.heritage.org/asia/report/president-reagans-six-assurance
s-taiwan-and-their-meaning-today

Feng Liu, "The Recalibration of Chinese Assertiveness: China's Responses to the Indo-Pacific Challenge," *International Affairs*, Vol. 96, No. 1, January 2020, pp. 9–27.

Finkelstein, David M., *Washington's Taiwan Dilemma, 1949–1950: From Abandonment to Salvation*, Annapolis, Md.: Naval Institute Press, 1993.

Funabashi, Yoichi, *The Peninsula Question: A Chronicle of the Second North Korean Nuclear Crisis*, Washington, D.C.: Brookings Institution Press, 2007.

Fu Ying and Wang Jisi, eds., *China-US Relations: Exploring a New Pathway to a Win-Win Partnership*, Beijing: Collective Publication, July 2017. As of June 14, 2020:
https://csis-website-prod.s3.amazonaws.com/s3fs-public/
publication/170705_Chinese_Side_Report_Exploring_EN.pdf

Gabuev, Alexander, "Bad Cop, Mediator, or Spoiler: Russia's Role on the Korean Peninsula," Carnegie Moscow Center, April 24, 2019. As of June 14, 2020:
https://carnegie.ru/commentary/78976

Gady, Franz-Stefan, "2 Russian Nuclear-Capable Bombers Enter South Korea's Air Defense Identification Zone," *The Diplomat*, June 17, 2018. As of June 14, 2020:
https://thediplomat.com/2018/07/2-russian-nuclear-capable-bombers-enter-south-koreas-air
-defense-identification-zone/

Garamone, Jim, "U.S., Chinese Military Leaders Sign Agreement to Increase Communication," *DOD News*, August 15, 2017. As of June 14, 2020:
https://www.jcs.mil/Media/News/News-Display/Article/1278963/us-chinese-military-leaders-sig
n-agreement-to-increase-communication/

Garamone, Jim, "U.S.-India Defense Cooperation a 'Key Driver' of Overall Relationship," *DOD News*, September 6, 2018a. As of July 6, 2020:
https://www.defense.gov/Explore/News/Article/Article/1622396/us-india-defense-cooperation-
a-key-driver-of-overall-relationship/

Garamone, Jim, "U.S., India Strengthen Defense Cooperation," *DOD News*, December 3, 2018b. As of July 6, 2020:
https://www.defense.gov/Explore/News/Article/Article/1704150/us-india-strengthen-defens e-cooperation/

Garnaut, John, "We Value Your Call: US and China Test Hotline," *Sydney Morning Herald*, April 4, 2013. As of June 14, 2020:
https://www.smh.com.au/world/we-value-your-call-us-and-china-test-hotline-20130403-2h792. html

Garrett, Banning, and Jonathan Adams, U.S.-*China Cooperation on the Problem of Failing States and Transnational Threats*, Washington, D.C.: United States Institute of Peace, September 2004. As of June 14, 2020:
http://library.stmarytx.edu/acadlib/edocs/sr126.pdf

Gertz, Bill, "Inside the Ring: China in Kyrgyzstan," *Washington Times*, December 2, 2010.

Gil, Laura, "Construction Progresses on Bangladesh's First Nuclear Power Plant," *IAEA News*, International Atomic Energy Agency, January 31, 2019. As of June 14, 2020:
https://www.iaea.org/newscenter/news/construction-progresses-on-bangladeshs-first-nucle ar-power-plant

Glaser, Bonnie, "Understanding the Evolution of US-China-ASEAN Relations: A US Perspective," in C. J. Jenner, and Tran Truong Thu, eds., *The South China Sea: A Crucible of Regional Cooperation or Conflict-Making Sovereignty Claim?* Cambridge, UK: Cambridge University Press, 2016, pp. 97–117.

Glaser, Bonnie, and Brittany Billingsley, "Reordering Chinese Priorities on the Korean Peninsula," Center for Strategic International Studies, 2012.

Glaser, Bonnie, and Deep Pal, "China's Periphery Diplomacy Initiative: Implications for China Neighbors and the United States," China-US Focus, November 7, 2013. As of June 14, 2020:
https://www.chinausfocus.com/foreign-policy/chinas-periphery-diplomacy-initiative-im plications-for-china-neighbors-and-the-united-states

Glaser, Bonnie, Scott Snyder, and John Park, "Keeping an Eye on an Unruly Neighbor," Center for Strategic International Studies, January 3, 2008.

Glaser, Charles, "A U.S.-China Grand Bargain? The Hard Choice Between Military Competition and Accommodation," *International Security*, Vol. 39, No. 4, Spring 2015, pp. 49–90.

Goldstein, Avery, "First Things First: The Pressing Danger of Crisis Instability in U.S.-China Relations," *International Security*, Vol. 37, No. 4, Spring 2013, pp. 49–89.

Goldstein, Lyle J., *Meeting China Halfway: How to Defuse the Emerging U.S.-China Rivalry*, Washington, D.C.: Georgetown University Press, 2015.

Gomez, Jim, "Pompeo: US to Make Sure That China Can't Blockade South China Sea," Associated Press, March 1, 2019. As of June 14, 2020:
https://apnews.com/fd95922e6e334484b81941cf8fa4b566

Goncharov, Sergei, John Lewis, and Xue Litai, *Uncertain Partners: Stalin, Mao, and the Korean War*, Stanford, Calif.: Stanford University Press, 1995.

Gorenburg, Dmitry, and Paul Schwartz, *Russia's Relations with Southeast Asia*, Paris: Institut Français des Relations Internationales (IFRI), Russie.NEI.Reports No. 26, March 2019. As of June 14, 2020:
https://www.ifri.org/sites/default/files/atoms/files/gorenburg_schwartz_russia_relations_ southeast_asia_2019.pdf

Government of Russia, "O Strategii Nacionalnoy Bezopastnosti Rosiskli Federacii [National Security Strategy of the Russian Federation]," December 31, 2015. As of June 3, 2020, English translation at:
http://www.ieee.es/Galerias/fichero/OtrasPublicaciones/Internacional/2016/Russian-Nationa l-Security-Strategy-31Dec2015.pdf

Green, Michael, *By More Than Providence: Grand Strategy and American Power in the Asia-Pacific Since 1783*, New York: Columbia University Press, 2017.

Green, Michael J., "Trump and Asia: Continuity, Change and Disruption," Asan Forum, April 18, 2019. As of June 13, 2020:
http://www.theasanforum.org/trump-and-asia-continuity-change-and-disruption/

Green, Michael, Kathleen Hicks, Zack Cooper, John Schaus, and Jake Douglas, *Counter-Coercion Series: Scarborough Shoal Standoff*, Washington, D.C.: Center for Strategic and International Studies, 2017. As of August 5, 2020:
https://amti.csis.org/counter-co-scarborough-standoff/

Greenlees, Donald, "Russia Sanctions Putting Strains on US Relationship with Indonesia," Australian Strategic Policy Institute, June 17, 2019. As of June 14, 2020:
https://www.aspistrategist.org.au/russia-sanctions-putting-strain-on-us-relationship-with-indo nesia/

Greer, Tanner, "Taiwan Can Win a War with China," *Foreign Policy*, September 25, 2018. As of June 14, 2020:
https://foreignpolicy.com/2018/09/25/taiwan-can-win-a-war-with-china/

Greitens, Sheena Chestnut, Myunghee Lee, and Emir Yazici, "China's Changing Strategy in Xinjiang: Counterterrorism and Preventive Repression," *International Security*, Vol. 44, No. 3, 2020, pp. 9–47.

Grevatt, Jon, "Malaysia Considers 'Fighter Exchange' Offer from Russia," *Jane's*, November 28, 2019. As of June 13, 2020:
https://www.janes.com/defence-news/news-detail/malaysia-considers-fighte r-exchange-offer-from-russia

Gries, Peter, and Tao Wang, "Will China Seize Taiwan?" *Foreign Affairs*, February 15, 2019. As of June 13, 2020:
https://www.foreignaffairs.com/articles/china/2019-02-15/will-china-seize-taiwan

Griffiths, David, *U.S.-China Maritime Confidence Building: Paradigms, Precedents and Prospects*, Newport, R.I.: Naval War College, Maritime Studies Institute No. 6, 2010.

Groll, Elias, "Did China Just Re-Enact the Famous 'Birdie' Scene from 'Top Gun' with U.S. Plane?" *Foreign Policy*, August 22, 2014. As of June 14, 2020:
https://foreignpolicy.com/2014/08/22/did-china-just-re-enact-the-famous-birdie-scene-from -top-gun-with-u-s-plane/

Grossman, Derek, Michael S. Chase, Gerard Finin, Wallace Gregson, Jeffrey W. Hornung, Logan Ma, Jordan R. Reimer, and Alice Shih, *America's Pacific Island Allies: The Freely Associated States and Chinese Influence*, Santa Monica, Calif.: RAND Corporation, RR-2973-OSD, 2019. As of August 18, 2020:
https://www.rand.org/pubs/research_reports/RR2973.html

Gurganus, Julia, and Eugene Rumer, "Russia's Global Ambitions in Perspective," Carnegie Endowment for International Peace, February 20, 2019. As of June 14, 2020:
https://carnegieendowment.org/2019/02/20/russia-s-global-ambitions-in-perspective-pub-78067

Haidar, Suhasini, and Dinakar Peri, "India, Russia to Conclude Mutual Logistics Agreement," *The Hindu*, November 4, 2019. As of June 14, 2020:
https://www.thehindu.com/news/national/india-russia-to-conclude-mutual-logistics-agreement/article29881623.ece

Harold, Scott W., "Expanding Contacts to Enhance Durability: A Strategy for Improving US-China Military-to-Military Relations," *Asia Policy*, No. 16, July 2013, pp. 103–137.

Harold, Scott W., "Why Has Obama Lifted the Arms Embargo on Vietnam?" *Newsweek*, May 25, 2016.

Harold, Scott W., "The Future of China-U.S. Military Relations: A ChinaFile Conversation," ChinaFile, March 1, 2019a.

Harold, Scott W., "Making Sense of US Arms Sales to Taiwan," *Institut Montaigne Blog*, July 23, 2019b. As of June 13, 2020:
https://www.institutmontaigne.org/en/blog/making-sense-us-arms-sales-taiwan

Harold, Scott W., "Optimizing the U.S.-China Military-to-Military Relationship," *Asia Policy*, Vol. 14, No. 3, July 2019c, pp. 145–168.

Harold, Scott W., "Transformational Leaders in Asia: The Case of Donald Trump," Asan Forum, January 20, 2020. As of June 23, 2020:
http://www.theasanforum.org/the-case-of-donald-trump/

Harold, Scott W., Derek Grossman, Brian Harding, Jeffrey W. Hornung, Gregory Poling, Jeffrey Smith, and Meagan L. Smith, *The Thickening Web of Asian Security Cooperation: Deepening Defense Ties Among U.S. Allies and Partners in the Indo-Pacific*, Santa Monica, Calif.: RAND Corporation, RR-3125-MCF, 2019. As of August 18, 2020:
https://www.rand.org/pubs/research_reports/RR3125.html

Harold, Scott W., Koichiro Bansho, Jeffrey W. Hornung, Koichi Isobe, and Richard L. Simcock II, *U.S.-Japan Alliance Conference: Meeting the Challenge of Amphibious Operations*, Santa Monica, Calif.: RAND Corporation, CF-387-GOJ, 2018. As of August 18, 2020:
https://www.rand.org/pubs/conf_proceedings/CF387.html

Harold, Scott W., and Soo Kim, "For the U.S., South Korea, and Japan, It's the North Korean Regime, Not Kim Jong Un Per Se, That Is the Threat," RealClearDefense, June 6, 2020.

Harold, Scott W., Tanvi Madan, and Natalie Sambhi, *U.S.-Japan Alliance Conference: Regional Perspectives on the Quadrilateral Dialogue and the Free and Open Indo-Pacific*, Santa Monica, Calif.: RAND Corporation, CF-414-GOJ, 2020. As of August 18, 2020:
https://www.rand.org/pubs/conf_proceedings/CF414.html

Harris, Tobias, "'Quality Infrastructure': Japan's Robust Challenge to China's Belt and Road," *War on the Rocks*, April 9, 2019. As of April 20, 2021:
https://warontherocks.com/2019/04/quality-infrastructure-japans-robust-challenge-to-chinas-belt-and-road

Harvard University Belfer Center, "U.S.- China Track II Dialogue," undated. As of June 14, 2020:
https://www.belfercenter.org/publication/us-china-track-ii-dialogue

Hass, Ryan, "The Trajectory of Chinese Foreign Policy: From Reactive Assertiveness to Opportunistic Activism," Brookings Institution, November 4, 2017.

Hayton, Bill, *The South China Sea: The Struggle for Power in Asia*, New Haven, Conn.: Yale University Press, 2014.

Hayton, Bill, "The Modern Origins of China's South China Sea Claims: Maps, Misunderstandings, and the Maritime Geobody," *Modern China*, Vol. 45, No. 2, May 4, 2018.

Heath, Timothy, "Diplomacy Work Forum: Xi Steps Up Efforts to Shape a China-Centered Regional Order," *China Brief*, Vol. 13, No. 22, November 7, 2013. As of June 14, 2020: https://jamestown.org/program/diplomacy-work-forum-xi-steps-up-efforts-to-shape-a-china-centered-regional-order/

Heydarian, Richard Javad, "Duterte's Pivot to Russia," Center for Strategic and International Studies, Asia Maritime Transparency Initiative, October 17, 2019. As of June 14, 2020: https://amti.csis.org/dutertes-pivot-to-russia/

Hille, Kathrin, "Chinese Navy Accused of Using Laser on US Military Aircraft," *Financial Times*, February 28, 2020.

Hillman, Jonathan, "How Big Is China's Belt and Road?" Center for Strategic International Studies, April 3, 2018. As of April 20, 2021: https://www.csis.org/analysis/how-big-chinas-belt-and-road

Hillman, Jonathan, *The Emperor's New Road: China and the Project of the Century*, New Haven, Conn.: Yale University Press, 2020.

Hillman, Jonathan, and Maesea McCalpin, *The China-Pakistan Economic Corridor at Five*, Washington, D.C.: Center for Strategic and International Studies, April 2020. As of June 14, 2020: https://www.csis.org/analysis/china-pakistan-economic-corridor-five

Hirose, Yoko, "Japan-Russia Relations: Can the Northern Territories Issue Be Overcome?" *cogitAsia* (blog), Center for Strategic and International Studies, April 3, 2018. As of June 14, 2020: https://www.cogitasia.com/japan-russia-relations-can-the-northern-territories-issue-be-overcome/

Hope, Joseph, "Returning Uighur Fighters and China's National Security Dilemma," *China Brief*, Vol. 18, No. 13, July 25, 2018. As of June 14, 2020: https://jamestown.org/program/returning-uighur-fighters-and-chinas-national-security-dilemma/

Hornby, Lucy, "Mahathir Mohamad Warns Against 'New Colonialism' During China Visit," *Financial Times*, August 20, 2018. As of April 20, 2021: https://www.ft.com/content/7566599e-a443-11e8-8ecf-a7ae1beff35b

Houck, Caroline, "A Law Meant to Punish America's Foes Is Hurting Its Partners: Mattis," DefenseOne, April 26, 2018. As of June 14, 2020: https://www.defenseone.com/policy/2018/04/law-meant-punish-americas-foes-hurting-its-partners-mattis/147792/

"How Kim Jong-Un Gets His $500,000 Mercedes," *New York Times*, video, July 16, 2019. As of June 26, 2020: https://www.youtube.com/watch?v=BSe9JDVczUc

"How North Korea Evades Sanctions," *New York Times*, video, September 22, 2017. As of June 26, 2020: https://www.youtube.com/watch?v=ksyWnEVfUJk

Human Rights Watch, "Interpol: Address China's 'Red Notice' Abuses," September 25, 2017. As of June 29, 2020: https://www.hrw.org/news/2017/09/25/interpol-address-chinas-red-notice-abuses

霍丽杰 [Huo Lijie], 金贞顺 [Jin Zhenshun], 李莉 [Li Li], 何梅芳 [He Meifang], and 陈淑敏 [Chen Shumin], "边境地区未来核袭击后的护理特点及应解决的问题 [The Characteristics of Future Nursing and the Problems to Be Solved After Nuclear Attacks in Frontier Regions]," 护理管理杂志 [*Journal of Nursing Administration*], October 2005.

Hurst, Daniel, "South China Sea: Australian Warships Encounter Chinese Navy in Disputed Waters," *The Guardian*, July 23, 2020. As of July 23, 2020:
https://www.theguardian.com/world/2020/jul/23/south-china-sea-australian-warships-enc ounter-chinese-navy-in-disputed-waters

Huynh, Nicholas V., "U.S. Navy, Royal Australian Navy Team Up in South China Sea," U.S. Navy, April 29, 2020. As of June 14, 2020:
https://www.public.navy.mil/surfor/lha6/Pages/US-Navy-Royal-Australian-Nav y-team-up-in-the-South-China-Sea.aspx

Ibrahim, Azeem, "China Must Answer for Cultural Genocide in Court," *Foreign Policy*, December 3, 2019. As of June 29, 2020:
https://foreignpolicy.com/2019/12/03/uighurs-xinjiang-china-cultural-genocide-internatio nal-criminal-court/

"India Signs Pact with Russia on Chakra-3 Attack Submarine," *Economic Times*, March 8, 2019. As of August 26, 2020:
https://economictimes.indiatimes.com/news/defence/india-signs-pact-with-russia-o n-chakra-3-attack-submarine/articleshow/68307218.cms

Inkiriwang, Frega Wenas, "The Dynamic of US-Indonesia Defense Relations: The 'IMET Ban' Period," *Australian Journal of International Affairs*, Vol. 74, No. 4. January 12, 2020, pp. 377–393.

Jacobs, Andrew, and Chris Buckley, "China Blames Xinjiang Separatists for Stabbing Rampage at Train Station," *New York Times*, March 2, 2014.

Jha, Lalit K., "Relationship with China Not at the Expense of India: US," Outlook India, November 18, 2009. As of August 26, 2020:
https://www.outlookindia.com/newswire/story/relationship-with-china-not-at-the-expense-of -india-us/669694

Jian, Chen, *Mao's China and the Cold War*, Chapel Hill, N.C.: University of North Carolina Press, 2001.

Ji-Hye, Jun, "China Conducted Large-Scale Drill in Preparation for Sudden Change in NK," *Korea Times*, December 18, 2017. As of August 26, 2020:
http://www.koreatimes.co.kr/www/nation/2017/12/205_241095.html

"Joint Statement of the Fourth Round of the Six-Party Talks," September 19, 2005. As of June 21, 2020:
https://www.ncnk.org/resources/publications/September_19_2005_Joint_Statement.doc

Jones, Sam, "US and China Set Up 'Space Hotline,'" *Financial Times*, November 20, 2015. As of August 26, 2020:
https://www.ft.com/content/900870f4-8f9f-11e5-a549-b89a1dfede9b

Kamphausen, Roy D., and Jessica Drun, "What Are Mil-Mil Ties Between the U.S. And China Good for?" *War on the Rocks*, April 22, 2016. As of August 26, 2020:
https://warontherocks.com/2016/04/what-are-mil-mil-ties-between-the-u-s-and-china-good-for/

Kan, Shirley A., *U.S.-China Counterterrorism Cooperation: Issues for U.S. Policy*, Washington, D.C.: Congressional Research Service, July 15, 2010. As of June 14, 2020:
https://fas.org/sgp/crs/terror/RL33001.pdf

Kan, Shirley A., *Taiwan: Major U.S. Arms Sales Since 1990*, Washington, D.C.: Congressional Research Service, 2014.

Karve, Ameya, and Ann Koh, "Piracy Incidents Rise with Navies Stretched in South China Sea," Bloomberg, July 16, 2020. As of August 26, 2020:
https://www.bloomberg.com/news/articles/2020-07-17/piracy-in-asian-waters-rises-to-highes t-in-five-years-data-show

Kashin, Vassily, "Why Is China Buying Russian Fighter Jets?" Carnegie Moscow Center, September 2, 2016. As of August 26, 2020:
https://carnegie.ru/commentary/62701

Kendall-Taylor, Andrea and Jeffrey Edmonds, "Addressing Deepening Russia-China Relations," Center for a New American Security, August 31, 2020. As of April 20, 2021:
https://www.cnas.org/publications/commentary/addressing-deepening-russia-china-relations

Khalil, Ahmad Bilal, "Afghanistan's 'China Card' Approach to Pakistan, Part 1: 1991–2014," *The Diplomat*, April 11, 2019a. As of August 26, 2020:
https://thediplomat.com/2019/04/afghanistans-china-card-approac h-to-pakistan-part-1-1991-2014/

Khalil, Ahmad Bilal, "The Afghan National Unity Government's 'China Card' Approach to Pakistan: Part 2," *The Diplomat*, April 12, 2019b. As of April 21, 2021:
https://thediplomat.com/2019/04/the-afghan-national-unity-governments-china-card -approach-to-pakistan-part-2

Kirk, Jason A., "India's Season of Discontent: U.S.-India Relations Through the Prism of Obama's "AfPak" Policy, Year One," *Asian Affairs: An American Review*, Vol. 37, No. 3, July-September 2010, pp. 147–166.

Kleine-Ahlbrandt, Stephanie, "China's North Korea Policy: Backtracking from Sunnylands?" 38 North, July 2, 2013. As of August 26, 2020:
http://38north.org/2013/07/skahlbrandt070213/

Kleine-Ahlbrandt, Stephanie T., "China's Relations with North Korea," testimony presented before the U.S.-China Economic and Security Review Commission, Washington, D.C., June 5, 2014. As of August 26, 2020:
http://www.uscc.gov/sites/default/files/USCC%20Kleine-Ahlbrandt%20China-DPRK%20 3vi2014.pdf

Ko, Sangtu, "International Sanctions on North Korea: A Two-Level Solution," *Pacific Focus*, Vol. 34, No. 1, April 2019, pp. 55–71.

Koldunova, Ekaterina, "Russia's Ambivalence About an Indo-Pacific Strategy," *Asia-Pacific Bulletin*, No. 476, May 6, 2019. As of August 26, 2020:
https://www.eastwestcenter.org/publications/russia's-ambivalence-about-indo-pacific-strategy

Korolev, Alexander, "Russia's Reorientation to Asia: Causes and Strategic Implications," *Pacific Affairs*, Vol. 89, No. 1, March 2016, pp. 53–73.

Korolev, Alexander, "Australia's Approach to Cooperation with Russia," Russia in Global Affairs, December 17, 2019. As of August 26, 2020:
https://eng.globalaffairs.ru/articles/australias-approach-to-cooperation-with-russia/

Kotani, Tetsuo, "Crisis Management in the East China Sea," Stockholm International Peace research Institute, February 2015. As of April 21, 2021:
https://www.sipri.org/publications/2015/sipri-fact-sheets/crisis-management-east-china-sea

Kozyrev, Vitaly, "Demystifying Russo-Japanese Peace Treaty Talks Before the June 2019 G20 Osaka Summit," *Asia Pacific Bulletin*, No. 479, May 6, 2019. As of August 26, 2020: https://www.eastwestcenter.org/publications/demystifying-russo-japanese-peace-treaty-talks-the-june-2019-g20-osaka-summit

Kronstadt, K. Alan, and Shayerah Ilias Akhtar, *India-U.S. Relations: Issues for Congress*, Washington, D.C.: Congressional Research Service, R44876, June 19, 2017.

Kulacki, Gregory, and Jeffrey G. Lewis, "Understanding China's Antisatellite Test," *Nonproliferation Review*, Vol. 15, No. 2, June 12, 2008, pp. 335–347.

Kupriyanov, Alexey, Amit Bhandari, Chaitanya Giri, and Kunal Kulkarni, "Russia-India Cooperation Against the Background of Sanctions: Adverse Effects and New Opportunities," Russian International Affairs Council, November 15, 2018. As of August 26, 2020: https://russiancouncil.ru/en/activity/policybriefs/russia-india-cooperation-against-the-background-of-sanctions-adverse-effects-new-opportunities/

Lague, David, and Donald Greenlees, "Squeeze on Banco Delta Asia Hit North Korea Where It Hurt," *New York Times*, January 18, 2007.

Laird, Burgess, *War Control: Chinese Writings on the Control of Escalation in Crisis and Conflict*, Washington, D.C.: Center for a New American Security, March 2017. As of April 21, 2021: https://www.cnas.org/publications/reports/war-control

Lankov, Andrei, "North Korea, Nuclear Weapons, and the Search for a New Path Forward: A Russian Response," *Bulletin of the Atomic Scientists*, Vol. 72, No. 5, August 8, 2016, pp. 340–342.

Lee, Christy, "Experts: Russia Skirts Sanctions on N. Korean Workers to Defy US-Led Pressure," *Voice of America*, February 1, 2020. As of August 26, 2020: https://www.voanews.com/east-asia-pacific/experts-russia-skirts-sanctions-n-korean-workers-defy-us-led-pressure

Lee, Yen Nee, "Russia Can Help India to Be Less Dependent on Oil, Says Indian Energy Minister," CNBC, October 4, 2019. As of August 26, 2020: https://www.cnbc.com/2019/10/04/russia-can-help-india-be-less-dependent-on-oil-indian-energy-minister.html

Lendon, Brad, Ivan Watson, and Ben Westcott, "'Leave Immediately': U.S. Navy Plane Warned over South China Sea," CNN, August 23, 2018.

Lieberthal, Kenneth, and Michel Oksenberg, *Policy Making in China: Leaders, Structures, and Processes*, Princeton, N.J.: Princeton University Press, 1988.

Lieberthal, Kenneth N., and Wang Jisi, *Addressing U.S.-China Strategic Distrust*, Washington, D.C.: Brookings Institution, 2012.

Liff, Adam P., "China and the U.S. Alliance System," *China Quarterly*, Vol. 233, March 2018, pp. 137–165.

Liff, Adam P. and G. John Ikenberry, "Racing Toward Tragedy? China's Rise, Military Competition in the Asia Pacific, and the Security Dilemma," *International Security*, Vol. 39, No. 2, Fall 2014, pp. 52–91.

Liu Xiaoming, "China Will Not Tolerate US Military Muscle-Flexing off Our Shores," *Guardian*, June 27, 2018. As of August 26, 2020: https://www.fmprc.gov.cn/mfa_eng/wjb_663304/zwjg_665342/zwbd_665378/t1572651.shtml

Liu Xuanzun, "PLA Expels US Warship Illegally Trespassing into S. China Sea," *Global Times*, May 28, 2020. As of August 26, 2020: https://www.globaltimes.cn/content/1189799.shtml

Liu Xuanzun and Guo Yuandan, "PLA Expels Trespassing US Warship from Xisha Islands, Urges it to Fight COVID-19 at Home," *Global Times*, April 28, 2020. As of August 26, 2020: https://www.globaltimes.cn/content/1187053.shtml

Liu Xuefeng, Kong Xiangsong, and Hao Hongjun, "区域核辐射监测及安全风险评估系统研究 [Regional Nuclear Radiation Monitoring and Safety Risk Assessment System]," *2013 Proceedings of the China Command and Control Conference*, 2013, pp. 494–497.

Li Xiaodong, ed., 朝鲜半岛危机管理研究 [*A Study of Crisis Management on the Korean Peninsula*], Beijing: Military Science Publishing House, 2010.

Lo, Bobo, *Russia and the New World Disorder*, Washington, D.C.: Brookings Institution, 2015.

Lo, Bobo, "Going Legit? The Foreign Policy of Vladimir Putin," Lowy Institute, September 17, 2018. As of August 28, 2020: https://www.lowyinstitute.org/publications/going-legit-foreign-policy-vladimir-putin#sec35886

Lo, Bobo, and Fiona Hill, "Putin's Pivot: Why Russia Is Looking East," July 31, 2013. As of August 28, 2020: https://www.brookings.edu/opinions/putins-pivot-why-russia-is-looking-east/

Lostumbo, Michael J., David R. Frelinger, James Williams, and Barry Wilson, *Air Defense Options for Taiwan: An Assessment of Relative Costs and Operational Benefits*, Santa Monica, Calif.: RAND Corporation, RR-1051-OSD, 2016. As of August 18, 2020: https://www.rand.org/pubs/research_reports/RR1051.html

Lostumbo, Michael J., Michael J. McNerney, Eric Peltz, Derek Eaton, David R. Frelinger, Victoria A. Greenfield, John Halliday, Patrick Mills, Bruce R. Nardulli, Stacie L. Pettyjohn, Jerry M. Sollinger, and Stephen M. Worman, *Overseas Basing of U.S. Military Forces: An Assessment of Relative Costs and Strategic Benefits*, Santa Monica, Calif.: RAND Corporation, RR-201-OSD, 2013. As of August 26, 2020: https://www.rand.org/pubs/research_reports/RR201.html

Lukin, Artyom, "Russia and the United States in the Asia Pacific: A Perspective of the English School," *Asian Perspective*, Vol. 42, No. 3, 2018, pp. 307–331.

Lukin, Artyom, "Russia's Policy Toward North Korea: Following China's Lead," 38 North, December 23, 2019. As of August 28, 2020: https://www.38north.org/2019/12/alukin122319/

Luna, Franco, "Russia Willing to Help with Nuclear Energy, Counterterrorism Should Philippines Ask—Envoy," *PhilStar Global*, October 18, 2019. As of August 28, 2020: https://www.philstar.com/headlines/2019/10/18/1961275/russia-willing-help-nuclear-energy-counter-terrorism-should-philippines-ask-envoy

Mahadzir, Dzirhan, "Pentagon Asia Policy Chief Talks South East Asia Military Cooperation, U.S. South China Sea Operations," *USNI News*, August 15, 2018. As of June 18, 2020: https://news.usni.org/2018/08/15/pentagon-asia-policy-chief-talks-south-east-asia-military-cooperation-u-s-south-china-sea-operations

Mandhana, Niharika, and Aruna Viswanatha, "North Korea Built an Alternative Financial System Using a Shadowy Network of Traders," *Wall Street Journal*, December 28, 2018.

Mankoff, Jeffrey, "Russia's Asia Pivot: Confrontation or Cooperation?" *Asia Policy*, No. 19, January 2015, pp. 65–88.

Mastro, Oriana Skylar, "Why Chinese Assertiveness Is Here to Stay," *Washington Quarterly*, Vol. 37, No. 4, January 21, 2015, pp. 151–170.

Mastro, Oriana Skylar, "Conflict and Chaos on the Korean Peninsula: Can China's Military Help Secure North Korea's Nuclear Weapons?" *International Security*, Vol. 43, No. 2, 2018, pp. 84–116.

Mastro, Oriana Skylar, "The Future of China-U.S. Military Relations," ChinaFile, March 1, 2019. As of August 28, 2020:
https://www.chinafile.com/conversation/future-of-china-us-military-relations

Maxwell, Megan, "Don't Blame Russia for the Problems in the U.S.-India Relationship," Carnegie Endowment for International Peace, September 16, 2019. As of August 28, 2020:
https://carnegieendowment.org/2019/09/16/don-t-blame-russia-for-problem
s-in-u.s.-india-relationship-pub-79850

Mazarr, Michael J., *North Korea and the Bomb: A Case Study in Non-Proliferation*, New York: St. Martin's Press, 1995.

McGregor, Richard, *Xi Jinping: The Backlash*, Penguin Books, 2019.

Mearshimer, John J., *The Tragedy of Great Power Politics*, 2nd ed., New York: W.W. Norton & Co., 2014.

Mearsheimer, John J., and Stephen M. Walt, "The Case for Off-Shore Balancing," *Foreign Affairs*, July/August 2016.

"Memorandum of Understanding Between the Department of Defense of the United States of America and the Ministry of National Defense of the People's Republic of China Regarding the Rules of Behavior for Safety of Air and Maritime Encounters," November 10, 2014. As of August 28, 2020:
https://archive.defense.gov/pubs/141112_MemorandumOfUnderstandingRegardingRules.pdf

"Memorandum of Understanding Between the United States of America Department of Defense and the People's Republic of China Ministry Of National Defense on Notification of Major Military Activities Confidence-Building Measures Mechanism," November 4, 2014. As of April 21, 2021:
https://dod.defense.gov/Portals/1/Documents/pubs/141112_
MemorandumOfUnderstandingOnNotification.pdf

"Memorandum of Understanding Between the United States of America Department of Defense and the People's Republic of China Ministry Of National Defense on Notification of Major Military Activities Confidence-Building Measures Mechanism—Annex III: Military Crisis Notification Mechanism for Use of the Defense Telephone Link," September 2015. As of April 21, 2021:
https://china.usc.edu/sites/default/files/article/attachments/
US-CHINA_CRISIS_COMMUNICATIONS_ANNEX_SEP_2015.pdf

Meyer, Henry, "Russia Seeks 'Good Relations' with Taliban as US Troops Exit," Bloomberg, March 10, 2020.

Miglani, Sanjeev, and Geert de Clercq, "Russia Signs Pact for Six Nuclear Reactors on New Site in India," Reuters, October 5, 2018. As of August 28, 2020:
https://www.reuters.com/article/us-india-russia-nuclear/russia-signs-pact-for-six-nuclear-reacto
rs-on-new-site-in-india-idUSKCN1MF217

Ministry of Defense of the People's Republic of China, "南部战区新闻发言人就美舰非法闯我西沙领海发表谈话 [The Spokesperson of the Southern Theater Command Issued a Remarks on the Illegal Intrusion of US Ships into Our Territorial Waters in Xisha]," April 28, 2020. As of June 30, 2020:
http://www.mod.gov.cn/topnews/2020-04/28/content_4864295.htm

Ministry of Economic Affairs, Bureau of Foreign Trade, Republic of China, "Taiwan-Russia Economic Relations," revised December 5, 2018. As of July, 8, 2020:
https://www.trade.gov.tw/english/Pages/Detail.aspx?nodeID=2912&pid=655091&dl_DateRange=all&txt_SD=&txt_ED=&txt_Keyword=&Pageid=0

Ministry of Economic Affairs, Bureau of Foreign Trade, Republic of China, "Taiwan-U.S. Economic Relations," revised January 23, 2019. As of August 26, 2020:
https://www.trade.gov.tw/english/Pages/Detail.aspx?nodeID=2911&pid=655394&dl_DateRange=all&txt_SD=&txt_ED=&txt_Keyword=&Pageid=0

Ministry of Economic Affairs, Bureau of Foreign Trade, Republic of China, "Cross-Straits Economic Relations," revised May 12, 2020. As of June 14, 2020:
https://www.trade.gov.tw/english/Pages/Detail.aspx?nodeID=2910&pid=652155&dl_DateRange=all&txt_SD=&txt_ED=&txt_Keyword=&Pageid=1

Ministry of External Affairs of India, "India-Russia Joint Statement During Visit of Prime Minister to Vladivostok," September 5, 2019. As of August 26, 2020:
https://www.mea.gov.in/bilateral-documents.htm?dtl/31795/India__Russia_Joint_Statement_during_visit_of_Prime_Minister_to_Vladivostok

Ministry of Foreign Affairs of Japan, "Northern Territories Issue," March 1, 2011. As of August 28, 2020:
https://www.mofa.go.jp/region/europe/russia/territory/overview.html

Ministry of Foreign Affairs of Japan, "Japan-Australia-India Trilateral Dialogue Senior Officials Meeting," press release, December 8, 2017. As of June 12, 2020:
https://www.mofa.go.jp/press/release/press4e_001834.html

Ministry of Foreign Affairs of the People's Republic of China, "Treaty of Good Neighborliness and Friendly Cooperation Between the People's Republic of China and the Russian Federation," communiqué , July 24, 2001. As of June 14, 2020:
https://www.fmprc.gov.cn/mfa_eng/wjdt_665385/2649_665393/t15771.shtml

Ministry of Foreign Affairs of the People's Republic of China, "Anti-Secession Law," March 15, 2005. As of June 14, 2020:
http://www.china-embassy.org/eng/zt/999999999/t187406.htm

Ministry of Foreign Affairs of the People's Republic of China, "Xi Jinping: Let the Sense of Community of Common Destiny Take Deep Root in Neighbouring Countries," October 25, 2013. As of December 10, 2019:
https://www.fmprc.gov.cn/mfa_eng/wjb_663304/wjbz_663308/activities_663312/t1093870.shtml

Ministry of Foreign Affairs of the People's Republic of Republic of China, "Diplomatic Allies," 2014a. As of June 22, 2020:
https://www.mofa.gov.tw/en/AlliesIndex.aspx?n=DF6F8F246049F8D6&sms=A76B7230ADF29736

Ministry of Foreign Affairs of the People's Republic of China, "Foreign Minister Wang Yi Meets the Press," March 8, 2014b. As of August 28, 2020:
https://www.fmprc.gov.cn/mfa_eng/wjb_663304/wjbz_663308/2461_663310/t1135385.shtml

Ministry of Foreign Affairs of the People's Republic of China, "Position Paper of the Government of the People's Republic of China on the Matter of Jurisdiction in the South China Sea Arbitration Initiated by the Republic of the Philippines," December 7, 2014c. As of April 20, 2021:
https://www.fmprc.gov.cn/mfa_eng/zxxx_662805/t1217147.shtml

Ministry of Foreign Affairs of the People's Republic of China, "Wang Yi on the South China Sea Issue At the ASEAN Regional Forum," August 6, 2015. As of June 14, 2020:
https://www.fmprc.gov.cn/mfa_eng/zxxx_662805/t1287277.shtml

Ministry of Foreign Affairs of the People's Republic of China, "Wang Yi Talks About Principles China Upholds in Dealing with the Korean Peninsula Nuclear Issue," February 13, 2016a. As of June 14, 2020:
https://www.fmprc.gov.cn/mfa_eng/zxxx_662805/t1340527.shtml

Ministry of Foreign Affairs of the People's Republic of China, "Foreign Minister Wang Yi Meets the Press," March 9, 2016b. As of August 28, 2020:
https://www.fmprc.gov.cn/ce/cggb/eng/xwdt/t1346238.htm

Ministry of Foreign Affairs of the People's Republic of China, "Statement of the Ministry of Foreign Affairs of the People's Republic of China on the Award of 12 July 2016 of the Arbitral Tribunal in the South China Sea Arbitration Established at the Request of the Republic of the Philippines," July 12, 2016c. As of August 28, 2020:
https://www.fmprc.gov.cn/nanhai/eng/snhwtlcwj_1/t1379492.htm

Ministry of Foreign Affairs of the People's Republic of China, "Foreign Minister Wang Yi Meets the Press," March 8, 2017a. As of June 14, 2020:
https://www.fmprc.gov.cn/mfa_eng/zxxx_662805/t1444204.shtml

Ministry of Foreign Affairs of the People's Republic of China, "Foreign Ministry Spokesperson Hua Chunying's Regular Press Conference on August 17, 2017," August 17, 2017b. As of June 14, 2020:
https://www.fmprc.gov.cn/mfa_eng/xwfw_665399/s2510_665401/2511_665403/t1485511.shtml

Ministry of Foreign Affairs of the People's Republic of China, "Foreign Ministry Spokesperson Geng Shuang's Regular Press Conference on March 6, 2018," March 6, 2018a. As of June 14, 2020:
https://www.fmprc.gov.cn/mfa_eng/xwfw_665399/s2510_665401/2511_665403/t1539946.shtml

Ministry of Foreign Affairs of the People's Republic of China, "Foreign Minister Wang Yi Meets the Press," March 9, 2018b. As of June 14, 2020:
https://www.fmprc.gov.cn/mfa_eng/zxxx_662805/t1540928.shtml

Ministry of Foreign Affairs of the People's Republic of China, "Foreign Ministry Spokesperson Geng Shuang's Regular Press Conference on June 12, 2018," June 12, 2018c. As of June 14, 2020:
https://www.fmprc.gov.cn/mfa_eng/xwfw_665399/s2510_665401/2511_665403/t1568234.shtml

Ministry of Foreign Affairs of the People's Republic of China, "Foreign Ministry Spokesperson Lu Kang's Regular Press Conference on January 2, 2019," January 2, 2019a. As of June 14, 2020:
https://www.fmprc.gov.cn/mfa_eng/xwfw_665399/s2510_665401/2511_665403/t1626635.shtml

Ministry of Foreign Affairs of the People's Republic of China, "Wang Yi on Neighborhood Diplomacy: Making Friends with Heart, and Resolving Differences with Sincerity and Promoting Cooperation with Persistence," July 18, 2019b. As of December 9, 2019:
https://www.fmprc.gov.cn/mfa_eng/wjb_663304/wjbz_663308/activities_663312/t1682452.shtml

Ministry of Foreign Affairs of the People's Republic of China, "The Second Informal Meeting Between Chinese and Indian Leaders Has Yielded Fruitful Results," October 13, 2019c. As of June 19, 2020:
https://www.fmprc.gov.cn/mfa_eng/wjbxw/t1707881.shtml

Ministry of Foreign Affairs of the Russian Federation, "Statement by Mikhail Kamynin, the Spokesman of Russia's Ministry of Foreign Affairs, Regarding Taiwan Preparations for Referendum on UN Entry," December 17, 2007. As of June 30, 2020:
https://www.mid.ru/en/press_service/spokesman/official_statement/-/asset_publisher/t2GCdmD8RNIr/content/id/354038

Ministry of Foreign Affairs of the Russian Federation, "Briefing by Foreign Ministry Spokesperson Maria Zakharova, Sochi, May 19, 2016," May 19, 2016a. As of August 28, 2020:
https://www.mid.ru/en/brifingi/-/asset_publisher/MCZ7HQuMdqBY/content/id/2287934#18

Ministry of Foreign Affairs of the Russian Federation, "Foreign Policy Concept of the Russian Federation: Approved by President of the Russian Federation Vladimir Putin on November 30, 2016," December 1, 2016b. As of June 14, 2020:
https://www.mid.ru/en/foreign_policy/official_documents/-/asset_publisher/CptICkB6BZ29/content/id/2542248

Ministry of Foreign Affairs of the Russian Federation, "Выступление и ответы на вопросы СМИ Министра иностранных дел России С.В.Лаврова в ходе пресс-конференции по итогам переговоров с Министром иностранных дел Японии Т.Коно, Москва, 14 января 2019 года [Foreign Minister Sergey Lavrov's Remarks and Answers to Media Questions at a News Conference Following Talks with Japanese Foreign Minister T. Kono, Moscow, January 14, 2019]," January 14, 2019a. As of June 14, 2020:
https://www.mid.ru/en/vistupleniya_ministra/-/asset_publisher/MCZ7HQuMdqBY/content/id/3472147?p_p_id=101_INSTANCE_MCZ7HQuMdqBY&_101_INSTANCE_MCZ7HQuMdqBY_languageId=ru_RU

Ministry of Foreign Affairs of the Russian Federation, "Foreign Minister Sergey Lavrov's Remarks and Answers to Media Questions at a News Conference Following His Visit to the U.S., Washington, December 10, 2019," December 11, 2019b. As of June 23, 2020:
https://www.mid.ru/en/press_service/minister_speeches/-/asset_publisher/7OvQR5KJWVmR/content/id/3945562

Ministry of Foreign Affairs of the Russian Federation, "Acting Foreign Minister Sergey Lavrov's Remarks and Answers to Media Questions at a News Conference on Russia's Diplomatic Performance in 2019 Moscow, January 17, 2020," January 17, 2020a. As of August 28, 2020:
https://www.mid.ru/en/vistupleniya_ministra/-/asset_publisher/MCZ7HQuMdqBY/content/id/4001740

Ministry of Foreign Affairs of the Russian Federation, "Foreign Minister Sergey Lavrov's Remarks and Answers to Media Questions During a News Conference Following the Video Conference of Foreign Ministers of Russia, India, and China, Moscow, June 23, 2020," June 23, 2020b. As of June 23, 2020:
https://www.mid.ru/en/press_service/minister_speeches/-/asset_publisher/7OvQR5KJWVmR/content/id/4171520

Mogato, Manuel, "Duterte Says China's Xi Threatened War if Philippines Drills for Oil," Reuters, May 19, 2017. As of August 28, 2020:
https://www.reuters.com/article/us-southchinasea-philippines-china/duterte-says-chinas-xi-threatened-war-if-philippines-drills-for-oil-idUSKCN18F1DJ

Mogato, Manuel, Michael Martina, and Ben Blanchard, "ASEAN Deadlocked on South China Sea, Cambodia Blocks Statement," Reuters, July 25, 2016. As of August 28, 2020:
https://www.reuters.com/article/us-southchinasea-ruling-asean/asean-deadlocked-on-south-china-sea-cambodia-blocks-statement-idUSKCN1050F6

Mohan, Geeta, "Modi-Xi Meet: India, China to Issue Separate Statements Today," *India Today*, October 12, 2019. As of August 28, 2020:
https://www.indiatoday.in/mail-today/story/modi-xi-meet-india-china-to-issue-separate-statem
ents-today-1608513-2019-10-12

Mollman, Steve, "It's Time to Start Considering What a North Korean Refugee Crisis Would Look Like," *Quartz*, May 17, 2017. As of April 21, 2021:
https://qz.com/976659/its-time-to-start-considering-what-a-north-korean-refugee-cri
sis-would-look-like/

Morris, Lyle J., and Giacomo Persi Paoli, *A Preliminary Assessment of Indonesia's Maritime Security Threats and Capabilities*, Santa Monica, Calif.: RAND Corporation, RR-2469-RC, 2018. As of August 26, 2020:
https://www.rand.org/pubs/research_reports/RR2469.html

"Moscow, Jakarta Embark on Strategic Partnership in Their Relations, Lavrov Says," Tass, March 13, 2018. As of August 28, 2020:
https://tass.com/politics/993702

Mulvenon, James, "Civil-Military Relations and the EP-3 Crisis: A Content Analysis," *China Leadership Monitor*, January 30, 2002.

Mulvenon, James, "Rogue Warriors? A Puzzled Look at the Chinese ASAT Test," *China Leadership Monitor*, February 28, 2007.

Muraviev, Alexey, "Understanding Russia's Strategic Engagement with the Indo-Asia-Pacific," *Asia-Pacific Bulletin*, No. 475, May 6, 2019. As of August 28, 2020:
https://www.eastwestcenter.org/publications/understanding-russia%E2%80%99s-strategic-
engagement-the-indo-asia-pacific

Murray, Bennett, *Russia's Awkward Dance with Vietnam*, Philadelphia, Pa.: Foreign Policy Research Institute, 2019a. As of August 28, 2020:
https://www.fpri.org/wp-content/uploads/2019/10/rfp2murray.pdf

Murray, Bennett, "Vietnam's Strange Ally in its Fight with China," *Foreign Policy*, August 1, 2019b. As of August 28, 2020:
https://foreignpolicy.com/2019/08/01/vietnams-strange-ally-in-its-fight-with-china/

Nakazawa, Katsuji, "Pyongyang Missile Footage is a Dagger to Xi's Throat," *Nikkei Asian Review*, August 21, 2017. As of August 28, 2020:
https://asia.nikkei.com/Features/China-up-close/Pyongyang-missile-footage-is-
a-dagger-to-Xi-s-throat

Nathan, Andrew J., and Andrew Scobell, *China's Search for Security*, New York: Columbia University Press, 2012.

National Committee on U.S.-China Relations, "2018 U.S.-China Track II Dialogue on Maritime Issues & International Law (United States)," undated. As of June 23, 2020:
https://www.ncuscr.org/program/us-china-track-ii-dialogue-maritime-issues-interna
tional-law/2018/us

Nebehay, Stephanie, "1.5 Million Muslims Could Be Detained in China's Xinjiang," Reuters, March 13, 2019.

Nelson, Craig, and Thomas Grove, "Russia, China Vie for Influence in Central Asia as U.S. Plans Afghan Exit," *Wall Street Journal*, June 18, 2019.

"New Northern Policy Seeks to Contribute to Peace on Korean Peninsula," *Yonhap News*, March 19, 2018. As of August 28, 2020:
https://en.yna.co.kr/view/AEN20180319006600320

Nichols, Michelle, "Russia, China to Hold More U.N. Talks on Lifting North Korea Sanctions: Diplomats," Reuters, December 29, 2019. As of August 28, 2020:
https://www.reuters.com/article/us-northkorea-usa-un/russia-china-to-hold-more-u-n-tal ks-on-lifting-north-korea-sanctions-diplomats-idUSKBN1YX0LD

Ning, Lu, *Dynamics of Foreign-Policy Decisionmaking in China*, New York: Routledge, 1997.

"North Korea 'Dual Freeze' Plan Working, Russia's UN Envoy Says," Tass, February 9, 2018. As of August 28, 2020:
https://tass.com/politics/989330

Obama, Barack, and Abe Shinzo, "Joint Press Conference with President Obama and Prime Minister Abe of Japan," April 24, 2014. As of April 19, 2021:
https://obamawhitehouse.archives.gov/the-press-office/2014/04/24/joint-press-conferenc e-president-obama-and-prime-minister-abe-japan

Obama, Barack, and Hu Jintao, "U.S.-China Joint Statement," November 17, 2009. As of June 14, 2020:
https://obamawhitehouse.archives.gov/realitycheck/the-press-office/us-china-joint-statement

Obama, Barack, and Joko Widodo, "Joint Statement by the United States of America and the Republic of Indonesia," October 26, 2015. As of April 19, 2021:
https://obamawhitehouse.archives.gov/the-press-office/2015/10/26/joint-statement-united-state s-america-and-republic-indonesia

Office of the Secretary of Defense, *Military and Security Developments Involving the People's Republic of China 2018: Annual Report to Congress*, Washington, D.C.: U.S. Department of Defense, May 2018. As of August 26, 2020:
https://media.defense.gov/2018/Aug/16/2001955282/-1/-1/1/ 2018-CHINA-MILITARY-POWER-REPORT.PDF

Office of the Secretary of Defense, *Military and Security Developments Involving the People's Republic of China 2019: Annual Report to Congress*, Washington, D.C.: U.S. Department of Defense, May 2019. As of August 26, 2020:
https://media.defense.gov/2019/May/02/2002127082/-1/-1/1/2019_CHINA_MILITARY_ POWER_REPORT.pdf

Ogawa, Tomoyo, "Russia Pulls India Closer with Oil and Weapons," *Nikkei Asian Review*, February 7, 2020. As of August 28, 2020:
https://asia.nikkei.com/Politics/International-relations/Russia-pulls-India-closer-wit h-oil-and-weapons

O'Hanlon, Michael E., *The Senkaku Paradox: Risking Great Power War over Small Stakes*, Washington, D.C.: Brookings Institution, 2019.

Olson, Wyatt, "U.S. to Give Vietnam Another Coast Guard Cutter Amid Rising Tensions in the South China Sea," *Stars and Stripes*, November 20, 2019.

Omelicheva, Mariya Y., "Russia's Counterproductive Counter-Terrorism: An Overview and Assessment of Trends in Russia's Counterterrorism Policy and Moscow's Efforts to Promote It Internationally," testimony before the U.S. Helsinki Commission, Washington, D.C., June 12, 2019. As of August 28, 2020:
https://www.csce.gov/sites/helsinkicommission.house.gov/files/III.%20a.%20Omelicheva%20 Testimony.pdf

Opall-Rome, Barbara, "U.S. Wants a Space Debris Hotline with China Patterned on the One with Russia," *Space News*, February 13, 2012. As of August 28, 2020:
https://spacenews.com/us-wants-space-debris-hotline-china-patterned-one-russia-0/

Ortagus, Morgan, "Chinese Coercion on Oil and Gas Activity in the South China Sea," U.S. Department of State, July 20, 2019. As of April 20, 2021, archived at:
https://web.archive.org/web/20201223154329/https://www.state.gov/chinese-coercion-on-oil-an d-gas-activity-in-the-south-china-sea/

Panda, Ankit, "China, South Korea Establish Military Hotline," *The Diplomat*, July 25, 2014. As of April 21, 2021:
https://thediplomat.com/2014/07/china-south-korea-establish-military-hotline/

Panda, Ankit, and Vipin Narang, "The Hanoi Summit Was Doomed from the Start," *Foreign Affairs*, March 5, 2019. As of June 23, 2020:
https://www.foreignaffairs.com/articles/north-korea/2019-03-05/
hanoi-summit-was-doomed-start

"Panmunjom Declaration on Peace, Prosperity and Reunification of the Korean Peninsula, issued by the Republic of Korea and the Democratic People's Republic of Korea," April 27, 2018.

Pape, Robert, "A Hotline to Cool Asian Crises," *Washington Post*, April 29, 2014.

"Paradise Lost: Chinese Maoists in North Korea," *The Economist*, November 24, 2012.

Parameswaran, Prashanth, "What's in the New China Military Aid to the Philippines?" *The Diplomat*, October 5, 2017. As of April 21, 2021:
https://thediplomat.com/2017/10/whats-in-the-new-china-military-aid-to-the-philippines/

Parameswaran, Prashanth, "Fighter Jet Challenge Spotlights Russia-Malaysia Defense Relations," *The Diplomat*, August 2, 2018. As of June 21, 2020:
https://thediplomat.com/2018/08/fighter-jet-challenge-spotlights-russia-malaysia-defense-relat ions/

Parameswaran, Prashanth, "New Arms Deals Highlight Indonesia-Russia Military Cooperation," *The Diplomat*, May 1, 2019a. As of June 20, 2020:
https://thediplomat.com/2019/05/new-arms-deals-highlight-indonesia-russia-military-coope ration/

Parameswaran, Prashanth, "US Southeast Asia Maritime Security Assistance in the Headlines with New Drones," *The Diplomat*, June 4, 2019b. As of June 20, 2020:
https://thediplomat.com/2019/06/us-southeast-asia-maritime-security-assistance-in-the-headl ines-with-new-drones/

Park, John, and Jim Walsh, *Stopping North Korea, Inc.: Sanctions Effectiveness and Unintended Consequences*, Cambridge, Mass.: Massachusetts Institute of Technology, August 2016. As of June 26, 2020:
https://www.belfercenter.org/sites/default/files/legacy/files/Stopping%20North%20Korea%20 Inc%20Park%20and%20Walsh%20.pdf

Park, Jong Chul, "How to Promote Peace on the Korean Peninsula After PyeongChang Winter Olympics," Korea Institute for National Unification, February 8, 2018. As of June 19, 2020:
http://repo.kinu.or.kr/bitstream/2015.oak/8626/1/CO%2018-05%28E%29.pdf

Pearson, James, "U.S. Delivers More Patrol Boats to Vietnam amid Deepening Security Ties," Reuters, March 29, 2018. As of April 21, 2021:
https://www.reuters.com/article/us-usa-vietnam-security-boats/u-s-delivers-more-patrol-boats -to-vietnam-amid-deepening-security-ties-idUSKBN1H51DQ

Pearson, James, and Jeff Mason, "Trump Pitches U.S. Arms Exports in Meeting with Vietnam," *Reuters*, February 27, 2019. As of June 19, 2020:
https://www.reuters.com/article/us-northkorea-usa-vietnam/trump-pitches-u-s-arms-export
s-in-meeting-with-vietnam-idUSKCN1QG1HU

Perlez, Jane, "North Korean Leader, Young and Defiant, Strains Ties with Chinese," *New York Times*, April 13, 2013.

Perlez, Jane, "Tribunal Rejects Beijing's Claims in South China Sea," *New York Times*, July 12, 2016.

Perlez, Jane, and Peter Baker, "Trump Eyes China Sanctions While Seeking Its Help on North Korea," *New York Times*, August 12, 2017.

Perlez, Jane, and Yufan Huang, "Behind China's $1 Trillion Plan to Shake Up the Economic Order," *New York Times*, May 13, 2017.

Permanent Court of Arbitration, "The South China Sea Arbitration: The Republic of the Philippines vs The People's Republic of China," The Hague, Netherlands, July 12, 2016. As of July 7, 2020:
https://pca-cpa.org/en/cases/7/

Pettyjohn, Stacie L., *U.S. Global Defense Posture, 1783–2011*, Santa Monica, Calif.: RAND Corporation, MG-1244-AF, 2012. As of August 18, 2020:
https://www.rand.org/pubs/monographs/MG1244.html

Pirnazarov, Nazarali, and Olzhas Auyezov, "China to Build Outposts for Tajik Guards on Tajikistan-Afghanistan Border," *Reuters*, September 26, 2016. As of June 14, 2020:
https://www.reuters.com/article/us-tajikistan-china-border-idUSKCN11W0T1

"Россия не ведет переговоров с Японией о принадлежности Курил [Russia Does Not Negotiate with Japan About the Kuril Islands]," *RIA Novosti*, June 30, 2020. As of August 28, 2020:
https://ria.ru/20200630/1573690794.html

"Россия и Китай согласовали новый проект плана по корейскому урегулированию [Russia and China Agreed on a New Draft Plan for a Korean Settlement]," *Tass*, November 19, 2019. As of June 14, 2020:
https://tass.ru/politika/7156745

Pollack, Jonathan D., *No Exit: North Korea, Nuclear Weapons, and International Security*, New York: Routledge, 2011.

Pomfret, John, "U.S. Takes a Tougher Tone with China," *Washington Post*, July 30, 2010.

Pomfret, James, and Ben Blanchard, "China's Xi Says Political Solution for Taiwan Can't Wait Forever," *Reuters*, October 6, 2013. As of June 10, 2020:
https://www.reuters.com/article/us-asia-apec-china-taiwan/chinas-xi-says-political-solution-fo
r-taiwan-cant-wait-forever-idUSBRE99503Q20131006

Pompeo, Michael R., "Communist China and the Free World's Fate," U.S. Department of State, July 23, 2020. As of July 29, 2021:
https://2017-2021.state.gov/communist-china-and-the-free-worlds-future-2/index.html

Ponomareva, Elena, and Georgij Rudov, "Russia-North Korea: State of Affairs and Trends," *Journal of Asian Public Policy*, Vol. 9, No. 1, December 18, 2015.

Pritchard, Charles L., *Failed Diplomacy: The Tragic Story of How North Korea Got the Bomb*, Washington, D.C.: Brookings Institution Press, 2007.

Public Law 96-8, Taiwan Relations Act, January 1, 1979. As of June 18, 2020:
https://www.ait.org.tw/our-relationship/policy-history/key-u-s-foreign-policy-document
s-region/taiwan-relations-act/

Public Law 115-44, Countering America's Adversaries Through Sanctions Act (CAATSA),
August 2, 2017. As of June 14, 2020:
https://home.treasury.gov/policy-issues/financial-sanctions/sanctions-programs-and-countr
y-information/countering-americas-adversaries-through-sanctions-act

Public Law 115-135, Taiwan Travel Act, March 16, 2018. As of June 18, 2020:
https://www.congress.gov/115/plaws/publ135/PLAW-115publ135.pdf

Public Law 116-135, Taiwan Allies International Protection and Enhancement Initiative
(TAIPEI) Act, March 26, 2020. As of June 18, 2020:
https://www.congress.gov/116/plaws/publ135/PLAW-116publ135.pdf

Purushothaman, Uma, "India-Russia Relations Are Evolving and Strengthening," London
School of Economics, January 18, 2018. As of June 20, 2020:
http://blogs.lse.ac.uk/southasia/2018/01/18/india-russia-relations-ar
e-evolving-and-strengthening/

"Putin Signs Deal with Malaysia to Provide Jet Fighters—2003-08-05," *Voice of America*,
October 26, 2009. As of June 13, 2020:
https://www.voanews.com/archive/putin-signs-deal-malaysia-provide-jet-fighters-2003-08-05

Putin, Vladimir, "Vladimir Putin on Foreign Policy: Russia and the Changing World," Valdai
Club, February 27, 2012. As of August 26, 2020:
https://valdaiclub.com/a/highlights/vladimir_putin_on_foreign_policy_russia_and_the_
changing_world/?sphrase_id=251286/

Putin, Vladimir, "Valdai Discussion Club Session," October 3, 2019. As of June 14, 2020:
http://en.kremlin.ru/events/president/news/61719

Qiao Zhongwei, Wang Jiasheng, and Zou Hao, eds., 边境危机应急控制 [*Border Crises
Emergency Response and Control*], Beijing: Academy of Military Science, 2013.

Radin, Andrew, and Clint Reach, *Russian Views of the International Order*, Santa Monica, Calif.:
RAND Corporation, RR-1826-OSD, 2017. As of August 26, 2020:
https://www.rand.org/pubs/research_reports/RR1826.html

Raghuvanshi, Vivek, "India Pays Russia $1.2 Billion in Technology Transfer Fees for T-90S
Tanks," *Defense News*, November 26, 2019. As of June 20, 2020:
https://www.defensenews.com/land/2019/11/26/india-pays-russia-12-billion-in-technology-tra
nsfer-fees-for-t-90s-tanks/

Raghuvanshi, Vivek, "India Accelerates Weapons Purchases in Wake of Border Clash with
China," *Defense News*, July 6, 2020. As of April 21, 2021:
https://www.defensenews.com/global/asia-pacific/2020/07/06/india-accelerates-weapons-pu
rchases-in-wake-of-border-clash-with-china/

Raisina Dialogue, "Sergey Lavrov, Foreign Minister of Russia, at Raisina Dialogue 2020,'" video,
January 15, 2020. As of June 3, 2020:
https://www.youtube.com/watch?v=O6F2cTmDIQo

Rajagopalan, Rajeswari Pillai "The Sino-Indian Clash: Russia in the Middle," *The Diplomat*,
June 25, 2020. As of June 21, 2020:
https://thediplomat.com/2020/06/the-sino-indian-clash-russia-in-the-middle/

Ramachandran, Sudha, "Rivalries and Relics: Examining China's Buddhist Public Diplomacy," *China Brief*, Vol. 19, No. 5, March 5, 2019. As of June 20, 2020:
https://jamestown.org/program/rivalries-and-relics-examining-chinas-buddhist-public-dipl omacy/

Ramzy, Austin, and Chris Buckley, "'Absolutely No Mercy': Leaked Files Expose How China Organized Mass Detentions of Muslims," *New York Times*, November 16, 2019.

Rank, David, *Leveraging US-China Cooperation to Build a Regional Consensus on Afghanistan*, Washington, D.C.: United States Institute of Peace, March 2018. As of June 14, 2020:
https://www.usip.org/sites/default/files/2018-03/sr420-leveraging-us-china-cooperation-to-b uild-a-regional-consensus-on-afghanistan.pdf

Ratner, Ely, *Rising to the China Challenge: Renewing American Competitiveness in the Indo-Pacific*, Washington, D.C.: Center for a New American Security, 2020.

Robertson, Matthew, "Counterterrorism or Cultural Genocide? Theory and Normativity in Knowledge Production About China's 'Xinjiang Strategy,'" *Made in China Journal*, June 12, 2020. As of June 23, 2020:
https://madeinchinajournal.com/2020/06/12/counterterrorism-or-cultural-genocide/

Robles, Raissa, "Russia Offers Arms Technology to the Philippines with 'No Conditions' as US Ties Falter," *South China Morning Post*, October 24, 2019. As of June 19, 2020:
https://www.scmp.com/week-asia/politics/article/3034460/russia-offers-arms-technology-phi lippines-no-conditions-us-ties

Rolland, Nadège, *China's Eurasian Century? Political and Strategic Implications of the Belt and Road Initiative*, Seattle, Wash.: National Bureau of Asian Research, May 23, 2017.

Rolland, Nadège, "Beijing's Vision for a Reshaped International Order," *China Brief*, Vol. 18, No. 3, February 26, 2018. As of June 19, 2020:
https://jamestown.org/program/beijings-vision-reshaped-international-order/

Rozman, Gilbert, "Russia in Northeast Asia: In Search of a Strategy," in Robert Levgold, ed., *Russian Foreign Policy in the Twenty-First Century and the Shadow of the Past*, New York: Columbia University Press, 2007.

Rozman, Gilbert, ed., *Japan-Russia Relations: Implications for the U.S.-Japan Alliance*, Sasakawa Peace Foundation, May 6, 2016. As of June 19, 2020:
https://spfusa.org/wp-content/uploads/2016/05/Sasakawa_Japan-Russia.pdf

Runde, Daniel, and Romina Bandura, "The BUILD Act Has Passed: What's Next?" Center for Strategic and International Studies, October 12, 2018. As of June 13, 2020:
https://www.csis.org/analysis/build-act-has-passed-whats-next

"Russia Against Taiwan's Membership in Int'l Civil Aviation Organization," Tass, October 3, 2019. As of June 7, 2020:
https://tass.com/world/1081315

"Russia and India Sign Military Cooperation Roadmap," Tass, June 23, 2017. As of June 6, 2020:
https://tass.com/defense/953030

"Russia and South Korea Spar over Airspace 'Intrusion,'" BBC, July 24, 2019. As of June 4, 2020:
https://www.bbc.com/news/world-asia-49091523

"Russia Leads the World at Nuclear-Reactor Exports," *The Economist*, August 7, 2018. As of June 6, 2020:
https://www.economist.com/graphic-detail/2018/08/07/russia-leads-the-world-a t-nuclear-reactor-exports

"Russian Firm Provides New Internet Connection to North Korea," Reuters, October 2, 2017. As of June 3, 2020:
https://www.reuters.com/article/us-nkorea-internet/russian-firm-provides-new-internet-connection-to-north-korea-idUSKCN1C70D2

"Russia Offers Most Advanced Types of Military Hardware to Vietnam," Tass, October 4, 2019. As of June 3, 2020:
https://tass.com/defense/1081480

"Russia Ready to Help Philippines Fight Against Terrorism, Says Putin," Tass, October 3, 2019. As of June 6, 2020:
https://tass.com/politics/1081292

"Russia Resumes Coals Supplies Via North Korea: Ifax Citing Official," Reuters, September 5, 2018. As of June 7, 2020:
https://www.reuters.com/article/us-russia-north-korea-coal-sanctions/russia-resumes-coal-supplies-via-north-korea-ifax-citing-official-idUSKCN1LL0YM

"Russia's Arms Exports to Indonesia Top $2.5 Bln over 25 Years," Tass, February 21, 2018. As of June 2, 2020:
https://tass.com/defense/991061

"Russia, Thailand Sign Military Cooperation Agreement," Tass, September 14, 2017. As of June 6, 2020:
https://tass.com/defense/965543

"Russia to Share Intelligence with Philippines, Train Duterte Guards," Reuters, February 16, 2017. As of June 7, 2020:
https://www.reuters.com/article/us-philippines-russia-defence/russia-to-share-intelligence-with-philippines-train-duterte-guards-idUSKBN15V1I9

"Russia, Vietnam Ink Military Cooperation Roadmap Until 2020," Tass, April 4, 2018. As of June 4, 2020:
https://tass.com/defense/997801

Saberon, Anna Patricia L., "Philippine Defense Cooperation with Russia: A Wake-Up Call for the United States?" *Asia-Pacific Bulletin*, East-West Center, No. 444, October 24, 2018. As of June 13, 2020:
https://scholarspace.manoa.hawaii.edu/bitstream/10125/59176/apb%20no.444.pdf

Sales, Nathan A., "Keeping the Pressure on al-Qaida," U.S. Department of State, Office of the Coordinator for Counter-Terrorism, September 12, 2019. As of June 29, 2020, archived at:
https://2017-2021.state.gov/keeping-the-pressure-on-al-qaida/index.html

Savage, Charlie, Eric Schmitt, and Michael Schwirtz, "Russia Secretly Offered Afghan Militants Bounties to Kill U.S. Troops, Intelligence Says," *New York Times*, June 26, 2020.

Schlein, Lisa, "US Warns China's Detention of Uighurs to Counter Terrorism Will Backfire," *Voice of America*, March 14, 2019. As of June 20, 2020:
https://www.voanews.com/east-asia-pacific/us-warns-chinas-detention-uighurs-counter-terrorism-will-backfire

Scobell, Andrew, "The J-20 Episode and Civil-Military Relations in China," written testimony submitted to the U.S. China Economic and Security Review Commission, March 10, 2011. As of June 20, 2020:
https://www.uscc.gov/sites/default/files/3.10.11Scobell.pdf

Scobell, Andrew, and Scott W. Harold, "An 'Assertive' China? Insights from Interviews," *Asian Security*, Vol. 9, No. 2, July 3, 2013, pp. 111–131.

Sen, Sudhi Ranjan, and Henry Meyer, "India Urgently Seeks Russian Missile System After Military Clash with China," Bloomberg, June 23, 2020. As of June 18, 2020:
https://www.bloomberg.com/news/articles/2020-06-23/china-india-border-tensions-simmer-in-lead-up-to-moscow-meeting

Shambaugh, David, "Coping with a Conflicted China," *Washington Quarterly*, Vol. 34, No. 1, December 16, 2010, pp. 7–27.

Shanghai Cooperation Organization, "General Information," undated. As of June 14, 2020:
http://eng.sectsco.org/cooperation/

Sharma, Ashok, "Russia Says US Indo-Pacific Strategy Is to Contain China," *The Diplomat*, January 15, 2020. As of June 22, 2020:
https://thediplomat.com/2020/01/russia-says-us-indo-pacific-strategy-is-to-contain-china/

沈同强 [Shen Tongqiang] and 张文宇 [Zhang Wenyu], "认清当前核安全威胁形势, 提升军队核应急处置能力 [Recognize the Current Nuclear Security Threat Situation and Enhance the Military's Nuclear Emergency Response Capability]," 核安全 [*Nuclear Safety*], June 2018.

Shih, Gerry, "In Central Asia's Forbidding Highlands, a Quiet Newcomer: Chinese Troops," *Washington Post*, February 18, 2019.

Shim, Elizabeth, "Report: Russia Delivers S-400 Missile System to China," *UPI*, January 27, 2020. As of June 13, 2020:
https://www.upi.com/Top_News/World-News/2020/01/27/Report-Russia-delivers-S-400-missile-system-to-China/2001580136451/

Sipalan, Joseph, "As Beijing Flexes Muscles in South China Sea, Malaysia Eyes Harder Response," Reuters, May 31, 2016. As of June 27, 2020:
https://uk.reuters.com/article/us-southchinasea-malaysia/as-beijing-flexes-muscles-in-south-china-sea-malaysia-eyes-harder-response-idUKKCN0YM2SV

Sipalan, Joseph, "Exclusive: Malaysia Shelves Plan to Buy New Fighter Jets—Defense Source," Reuters, July 13, 2017. As of July 1, 2020:
https://www.reuters.com/article/us-malaysia-defence-exclusive/exclusive-malaysia-shelves-plan-to-buy-new-fighter-jets-defense-source-idUSKBN19Y17X

Siregar, Kiki, "Indonesia Deploys 4 Additional Warships to Natuna Amid Standoff with Chinese Vessels," *Channel News Asia*, January 6, 2020. As of June 18, 2020:
https://www.channelnewsasia.com/news/asia/indonesia-china-natuna-islands-dispute-south-china-sea-12237456

"Six Russian Military Aircraft Break into South Korea's Air Defense Zone," *Korea Times*, October 22, 2019. As of July 1, 2020:
http://www.koreatimes.co.kr/www/nation/2020/04/205_277500.html

Small, Andrew, *The China-Pakistan Axis: Asia's New Geopolitics*, Oxford, UK: Oxford University Press, 2015.

Smith, Josh, "U.S.-Led Pressure Fractures as China, Russia Push for North Korea Sanctions Relief," Reuters, December 17, 2019. As of December 9, 2019:
https://www.reuters.com/article/us-northkorea-usa-un-china-analysis/u-s-led-pressure-fractures-as-china-russia-push-for-north-korea-sanctions-relief-idUSKBN1YL0OX

Smith, Stephen N., "Harmonizing the Periphery: China's Neighborhood Strategy Under Xi Jinping," *Pacific Review*, August 15, 2019, pp. 1–29.

Snyder, Scott A., "Where Does the Russia–North Korea Relationship Stand?" Council on Foreign Relations, April 29, 2019. As of June 29, 2020:
https://www.cfr.org/in-brief/where-does-russia-north-korea-relationship-stand

Sokolsky, Richard, and Eugene Rumer, "U.S.-Russia Relations in 2030," Carnegie Endowment for International Peace, June 15, 2020. As of June 15, 2020:
https://carnegieendowment.org/2020/06/15/u.s.-russian-relations-in-2030-pub-82056

Son Daekwon, "What Does North Korea Think of China's 'Dual Freeze' Proposal?" *The Diplomat*, July 25, 2017. As of July 7, 2020:
https://thediplomat.com/2017/07/what-does-north-korea-think-of-chinas-dual-freeze-proposal/

Soto, Alonso, "BRICS Bank to Defy Western Clout in Global Finances," Reuters, July 11, 2014. As of July 7, 2020:
https://www.reuters.com/article/brics-summit/brics-bank-to-defy-western-clout-in-global-finan ces-idUSL2N0PJ1U120140711

"South Korea Scrambled Jets to Warn Russian Warplanes in Air Defense Zone," Reuters, October 22, 2019. As of June, 30, 2020:
https://www.reuters.com/article/us-southkorea-russia-airspace/south-korea-says-scrambled-fi ghters-after-russian-warplanes-violated-air-defense-zone-idUSKBN1X10QQ

State Council Information Office of the People's Republic of China, "China's Policies on Asia-Pacific Security Cooperation," January 11, 2017. As of June 14, 2020:
http://english.gov.cn/archive/white_paper/2017/01/11/content_281475539078636.htm

State Council Information Office of the People's Republic of China, "China's National Defense in the New Era," July 24, 2019a.

State Council Information Office of the People's Republic of China, "China and the World in the New Era," September 28, 2019b. As of April 20, 2021:
http://english.scio.gov.cn/2019-09/28/content_75252746.htm

State Information Center of China, "已同中国签订共建"一带一路"合作文件的国家一览 [List of Countries That Have Signed Cooperation Documents with China to Jointly Build the 'Belt and Road']," Belt and Road Portal, updated January 2020. As of April 21, 2021:
https://www.yidaiyilu.gov.cn/xwzx/roll/77298.htm

Stewart, Phil, "China Calls on U.S. to 'Stop Flexing Muscles' in South China Sea," Reuters, November 17, 2019. As of July 7, 2020:
https://www.reuters.com/article/us-china-usa-military/china-calls-on-u-s-to-stop-flexing-muscl es-in-south-china-sea-idUSKBN1XS09W

Stewart, Phil, "China Putting Minority Muslims in 'Concentration Camps,' U.S. Says," Reuters, May 3, 2019. As of July 7, 2020:
https://www.reuters.com/article/us-usa-china-concentrationcamps/china-putting-minorit y-muslims-in-concentration-camps-u-s-says-idUSKCN1S925K

Stilwell, David R., "Advancing U.S. Engagement and Countering China in the Indo-Pacific and Beyond," testimony before the Senate Committee on Foreign Affairs, September 17, 2020. As of April 21, 2021, archived at:
https://web.archive.org/web/20201030015803/https://www.state.gov/advancing-u.s.-engagemen t-and-countering-china-in-the-indo-pacific-and-beyond/

Stokes, Jacob, *China's Periphery Diplomacy: Implications for Peace and Security in Asia*, Washington, D.C.: United States Institute of Peace, May 2020. As of July, 7, 2020:
https://www.usip.org/publications/2020/05/chinas-periphery-diplomacy-implications- peace-and-security-asia

Stratfor, "With CAATSA, the U.S. Is Trying to Make Russia Hurt," May 28, 2018. As of August 26, 2020:
https://worldview.stratfor.com/article/caatsa-us-trying-make-russia-hurt

Suliman, Adela, "China Says It 'Expelled' U.S. Navy Vessel from South China Sea," *NBC News*, April 30, 2020. As of April 30, 2020:
https://www.nbcnews.com/news/world/china-says-it-expelled-u-s-nav
y-vessel-south-china-n1196261

Sun, Yun, *Myanmar in US-China Relations*, Washington, D.C.: Stimson Center, Issue Brief No. 3, June 2014. As of July 6, 2020:
https://www.stimson.org/wp-content/files/file-attachments/Myanmar_Issue_Brief_3.pdf

Sun, Yun, "The Real Agenda of Xi Jinping's First Trip to North Korea," 38 North, June 25, 2019. As of July 7, 2020:
https://www.38north.org/2019/06/ysun062519/

Sun, Yun, "China's Strategic Assessment of Afghanistan," *War on the Rocks*, April 8, 2020. As of April 8, 2020:
https://warontherocks.com/2020/04/chinas-strategic-assessment-of-afghanistan/

"Supplement to the Memorandum of Understanding on the Rules of Behavior for Safety of Air and Maritime Encounters Between the Department of Defense of the United States of America and the Ministry of National Defense of the People's Republic of China," September 15, 2015. As of July 9, 2020:
https://archive.defense.gov/pubs/141112_MemorandumOfUnderstandingRegardingRules.pdf

Sutter, Robert, *Taiwan's Future: Narrowing Straits*, Seattle, Wash.: National Bureau of Asian Research, 2011.

Swaine, Michael D., "Chinese Views and Commentary on Periphery Diplomacy," *China Leadership Monitor*, July 28, 2014. As of July 7, 2020:
https://carnegieendowment.org/files/clm44ms.pdf

Swaine, Michael, "Chinese Views on the South China Sea Arbitration Case Between the People's Republic of China and the Philippines," *China Leadership Monitor*, August 24, 2016. As of July 7, 2020:
https://www.hoover.org/sites/default/files/research/docs/clm51ms.pdf

Swaine, Michael D., *Time to Accept Reality and Manage a Nuclear-Armed North Korea*, Washington, D.C.: Carnegie Endowment for International Peace, 2017.

Swaine, Michael, Zhang Tuosheng, and Danielle Cohen, *Managing Sino-American Crises: Case Studies and Analysis*, Washington, D.C.: Carnegie Endowment for International Peace, 2006.

Tamkin, Emily, "Why India and Russia Are Going to Stay Friends," *Foreign Policy*, July 8, 2020. As of April 21, 2021:
https://foreignpolicy.com/2020/07/08/russia-india-relations/

Tang, Anton, "Are Closer Taiwan-Russia Relations Possible? How?" *The Commonwealth*, February 5, 2018. As of June 18, 2020:
https://english.cw.com.tw/article/article.action?id=1838

Tanner, Murray Scot, and James Bellacqua, *China's Response to Terrorism*, Washington, D.C.: U.S.-China Economic and Security Review Commission, June 2016. As of June 14, 2020:
https://www.uscc.gov/sites/default/files/Research/Chinas%20Response%20to%20Terrorism_CNA061616.pdf

Tarabay, Jamie, "Russia's Foreign Minister Is Headed to North Korea," CNN, May 31, 2018. As of August 26, 2020:
https://www.cnn.com/2018/05/30/asia/russia-foreign-minister-north-korea-intl/index.html

Tayal, Skand R., *India and the Republic of Korea: Engaged Democracies*, New Delhi, India: Routledge, 2014.

Tellis, Ashley J., Abraham M. Denmark, and Greg Chaffin, eds., *Strategic Asia 2014–15: U.S. Alliances and Partnerships at the Center of Global Power*, Seattle, Wash.: National Bureau of Asian Research, 2014.

Thayer, Carl, "Vietnam's Cam Ranh Bay Caught in US-Russia Crossfire," *The Diplomat*, March 13, 2015. As of April 21, 2021:
https://thediplomat.com/2015/03/vietnams-cam-ranh-bay-caught-in-us-russia-crossfire/

Thomas, Jim, Iskander Rehman, and John Stillion, *Hard ROC 2.0: Taiwan and Deterrence Through Protraction*, Washington, D.C.: Center for Strategic and Budgetary Assessments, 2014.

Thompson, Drew, "Hope on the Horizon: Taiwan's Radical New Defense Concept," *War on the Rocks*, October 2, 2018.

Thompson, Drew, "China Is Still Wary of Invading Taiwan," *Foreign Policy*, May 11, 2020. As of July 9, 2020:
https://foreignpolicy.com/2020/05/11/china-taiwan-reunification-invasion-coronavirus-pandemic/

Thompson, Drew, and Carla Freeman, *Flood Across the Border: China's Disaster Relief Operations and Potential Response to a North Korean Refugee Crisis*, US-Korea Institute at the Johns Hopkins School of Advanced International Studies (SAIS), April 2009.

Tobin, Daniel, *How Xi Jinping's 'New Era' Should Have Ended U.S. Debate on Beijing's Ambitions*, Center for Strategic International Studies, May 2020. As of June 17, 2020:
https://www.csis.org/analysis/how-xi-jinpings-new-era-should-have-ended-us-debate-beijings-ambitions

Tobin, Liza, "Xi's Vision for Transforming Global Governance: A Strategic Challenge for Washington and Its Allies," *Texas National Security Review*, Vol. 2, No. 1, November 2018. As of April 21, 2021:
https://tnsr.org/2018/11/xis-vision-for-transforming-global-governance-a-strategic-challenge-for-washington-and-its-allies/

Torode, Greg, and Thomas Escritt, "Factbox: Why the Philippines' South China Sea Legal Case Matters," Reuters, July 11, 2016. As of April 20, 2021:
https://www.reuters.com/article/us-southchinasea-ruling-factbox/factbox-why-the-philippines-south-china-sea-legal-case-matters-idUSKCN0ZR283

Torode, Greg, and Mai Nguyen, "Vietnam Seeks to Pacify China as Landmark U.S. Carrier Visit Signals Warming Ties," Reuters, March 3, 2018. As of August 26, 2020:
https://www.reuters.com/article/us-usa-vietnam-carrier/vietnam-seeks-to-pacify-china-as-landmark-u-s-carrier-visit-signals-warming-ties-idUSKCN1GG03W

Trenin, Dmitri, "US Obsession with Containment Driving China and Russia Closer Together," Carnegie Endowment for International Peace, July 31, 2019. As of June 4, 2020:
https://carnegie.ru/2019/07/31/us-obsession-with-containment-driving-china-and-russia-closer-pub-79609

Trenin, Dmitri, "What Does Russia Want from the United States?" Carnegie Moscow Center, April 15, 2020. As of April 15, 2020:
https://carnegie.ru/commentary/81562

Trickett, Nicholas, "Working with Vietnam, Russia's Rosneft Draws China's Ire," *The Diplomat*, March 19, 2018. As of June 4, 2020:
https://thediplomat.com/2018/05/working-with-vietnam-russias-rosneft-draws-chinas-ire/

Trump, Donald J., "Remarks by President Trump at APEC CEO Summit, Da Nang, Vietnam," speech delivered at the Ariyana Da Nang Exhibition Center, Da Nang, Vietnam, November 10, 2017a. As of June 23, 2020:
https://www.whitehouse.gov/briefings-statements/remarks-president-trump-apec-ce
o-summit-da-nang-vietnam/

Trump, Donald J., "Remarks by President Trump Before Bilateral Meeting with Prime Minister Phuc of Vietnam, Hanoi, Vietnam," Washington, D.C.: November 12, 2017b. As of April 19, 2021, archives at:
https://web.archive.org/web/20171221060028/https://www.whitehouse.gov/briefings-statements/
remarks-president-trump-bilateral-meeting-prime-minister-phuc-vietnam-hanoi-vietnam/

Trump, Donald J., and Kim Jong Un, "Joint Statement of President Donald J. Trump of the United States of America and Chairman Kim Jong Un of the Democratic People's Republic of Korea at the Singapore Summit," June 12, 2018. As of June 23, 2021:
https://trumpwhitehouse.archives.gov/briefings-statements/joint-statement-president-donald-j-
trump-united-states-america-chairman-kim-jong-un-democratic-peoples-republic-korea-sin
gapore-summit/

Trump, Donald J., and Narendra Modi, "Joint Statement: Vision and Principles for the United States–India Comprehensive Global Strategic Partnership," February 25, 2020.

Trump, Donald J., and Xi Jinping, "Remarks by President Trump and President Xi of China in Joint Press Statement," November 9, 2017. As of April 21, 2021:
https://www.whitehouse.gov/briefings-statements/remarks-president-trump-president-xi-c
hina-joint-press-statement-beijing-china

Tsvetov, Anton, "Can US-Vietnam Reconciliation Hurt Russia's Ties with Hanoi?" Russian International Affairs Council, May 27, 2016. As of July 8, 2020:
https://russiancouncil.ru/en/analytics-and-comments/analytics/can-us-vietnam-reconciliatio
n-hurt-russia-s-ties-with-hanoi/

Tsvetov, Anton, "What Does Trump's Indo-Pacific Strategy Mean for Russia?" *The Diplomat*, April 17, 2018a. As of August 26, 2020:
https://thediplomat.com/2018/04/what-does-trumps-indo-pacific-strategy-mean-for-russia/

Tsvetov, Anton, "What Stands Between Russia and Close Ties with Indonesia?" East Asia Forum, June 3, 2018b. As of August 26, 2020:
https://www.eastasiaforum.org/2018/06/03/what-stands-between-russia-an
d-close-ties-with-indonesia/

Tucker, Nancy Bernkopf, "If Taiwan Chooses Unification, Should the United States Care?" *Washington Quarterly*, Vol. 25, No. 3, 2002, pp. 15–28.

Tucker, Nancy Bernkopf, and Bonnie Glaser, "Should the United States Abandon Taiwan?" *Washington Quarterly*, Vol. 34, No. 4, 2011, pp. 23–37.

Twomey, Chris, "The U.S.-China Strategic Dialogue," Naval Postgraduate School, December 2016.

"UK Says Nerve Agent Used to Poison Ex-Russian Spy Was in Liquid Form: BBC," Reuters, April 17, 2018.

64

United Nations, *2019 Midterm Report of the Panel of Experts Submitted Pursuant to Resolution 2464 (2019)*, S/2019/691, August 30, 2019. As of June 14, 2020:
https://undocs.org/S/2019/691

"U.S. Asks Vietnam to Stop Russian Use of Cam Ranh Bay," *Voice of America*, March 13, 2015.

U.S. Department of Defense, *Asia-Pacific Maritime Security Strategy*, Washington, D.C., 2015a. As of April 20, 2021:
https://dod.defense.gov/Portals/1/Documents/pubs/NDAA%20A-P_Maritime_SecuritY_Strategy-08142015-1300-FINALFORMAT.PDF

U.S. Department of Defense, "The Guidelines for U.S.-Japan Defense Cooperation," April 27, 2015b. As of April 19, 2021:
https://archive.defense.gov/pubs/20150427_--_GUIDELINES_FOR_US-JAPAN_DEFENSE_COOPERATION.pdf

U.S. Department of Defense, *Annual Report to Congress: Military and Security Developments: Involving the People's Republic of China 2017*, Washington, D.C., May 2017a. As of April 16, 2021:
https://dod.defense.gov/Portals/1/Documents/pubs/2017_China_Military_Power_Report.PDF

U.S. Department of Defense, "Readout of Secretary of Defense Mattis' Meeting with Japanese Minister of Defense Onodera," October 23, 2017b.

U.S. Department of Defense, *Report to Congress—Annual Freedom of Navigation Report, Fiscal Year 2018*, Washington, D.C., 2018a.

U.S. Department of Defense, *Summary of the 2018 National Defense Strategy of the United States: Sharpening the American Military's Competitive Edge*, Washington, D.C., 2018b. As of December 6, 2019:
https://dod.defense.gov/Portals/1/Documents/pubs/2018-National-Defense-Strategy-Summary.pdf

U.S. Department of Defense, *Assessment on U.S. Defense Implications of China's Expanding Global Access*, Washington, D.C., December 2018c.

U.S. Department of Defense, *Indo-Pacific Strategy Report: Preparedness, Partnerships, and Promotion of a Networked Region*, Washington, D.C., 2019. As of April 19, 2021:
https://media.defense.gov/2019/Jul/01/2002152311/-1/-1/1/DEPARTMENT-OF-DEFENSE-INDO-PACIFIC-STRATEGY-REPORT-2019.PDF

U.S. Department of Defense and the Ministry of National Defense of the People's Republic of China, "Notification of Major Military Activities Confidence-Building Measures Mechanism," Annex III, "Military Crisis Notification Mechanism for Use of the Defense Telephone Link," memorandum of understanding, 2015. As of August 28, 2020:
https://www.hsdl.org/?abstract&did=787567

U.S. Department of State, "U.S.-India: Civil Nuclear Cooperation," undated. As of July 2, 2020:
https://2001-2009.state.gov/p/sca/c17361.htm

U.S. Department of State, "Agreement Between the Department of Defense of the United States of America and the Ministry of National Defense of the People's Republic of China on Establishing a Consultation Mechanism to Strengthen Military Maritime Safety," January 19, 1998. As of June 13, 2020:
https://2009-2017.state.gov/documents/organization/107599.pdf

U.S. Department of State, "U.S.-India Relations: A Vision for the 21st Century," March 21, 2000. As of July 2, 2020:
https://1997-2001.state.gov/global/human_rights/democracy/fs_000321_us_india.html

U.S. Department of State, "Media Roundtable," March 18, 2011. As of August 27, 2020:
https://2009-2017.state.gov/p/sca/rls/rmks/2011/158583.htm

U.S. Department of State, "Joint Press Release of the Quadrilateral Coordination Group on Afghan Peace and Reconciliation," January 11, 2016a. As of June 29, 2020:
https://2009-2017.state.gov/r/pa/prs/ps/2016/01/251105.htm

U.S. Department of State, "U.S.-China Strategic & Economic Dialogue Outcomes of the Strategic Track," June 7, 2016b. As of June 29, 2020:
https://2009-2017.state.gov/r/pa/prs/ps/2016/06/258146.htm

U.S. Department of State, "Joint Statement on the U.S.-India-Japan Trilateral Meeting," April 5, 2018a. As of April 21, 2021, archived at:
https://web.archive.org/web/20180406032932/https://www.state.gov/r/pa/prs/ps/2018/04/280254.htm

U.S. Department of State, "U.S.-China Diplomatic and Security Dialogue," November 9, 2018b. As of April 20, 2021, archived at:
https://web.archive.org/web/20200716011936/https://www.state.gov/u-s-china-diplomatic-and-security-dialogue-3/

U.S. Department of State, *A Free and Open Indo-Pacific: Advancing a Shared Vision*, Washington, D.C., November 4, 2019. As of June 13, 2020:
https://www.state.gov/wp-content/uploads/2019/11/Free-and-Open-Indo-Pacific-4Nov2019.pdf

U.S. Department of State, "Briefing with Assistant Secretary for East Asian and Pacific Affairs David Stilwell on Readout of Secretary Pompeo's Meeting with Politburo Member Yang Jiechi," June 18, 2020. As of April 21, 2021, archived at:
https://web.archive.org/web/20201204125222/https://www.state.gov/briefing-with-assistant-secretary-for-east-asian-and-pacific-affairs-david-stilwell-on-readout-of-secretary-pompeos-meeting-with-poliburo-member-yang-jiechi/

U.S. Department of State, Bureau of Counter-Terrorism, "State Sponsors of Terrorism," undated. As of June 26, 2020:
https://www.state.gov/state-sponsors-of-terrorism/

U.S. Department of State, Bureau of East Asian and Pacific Affairs, "Bilateral Relations Fact Sheet: U.S. Relations with Indonesia," January 21, 2020a. As of April 21, 2021, archived at:
https://web.archive.org/web/20200714040225/https://www.state.gov/u-s-relations-with-indonesia/

U.S. Department of State, Bureau of East Asian and Pacific Affairs, "Bilateral Relations Fact Sheet: U.S. Relations with Malaysia," January 21, 2020b. As of April 21, 2021:
https://web.archive.org/web/20200701205804/https://www.state.gov/u-s-relations-with-malaysia/

U.S. Department of State, Bureau of East Asian and Pacific Affairs, "Bilateral Relations Fact Sheet: U.S. Relations with Vietnam," January 21, 2020c. As of April 21, 2021, archived at:
https://web.archive.org/web/20200701190632/https://www.state.gov/u-s-relations-with-vietnam/

U.S. Department of State, Bureau of European and Eurasian Affairs, "Bilateral Relations Fact Sheet: U.S. Relations with Russia," June 25, 2019. As of June 14, 2020, archived at:
https://web.archive.org/web/20190715074518/https://www.state.gov/u-s-relations-with-russia/

U.S. Department of State, Bureau of Political-Military Affairs, "Fact Sheet: U.S. Security Cooperation with India," June 4, 2019. As of April 21, 2021, archived at:
https://web.archive.org/web/20200103164955/https://www.state.gov/u-s-security-cooperation-with-india/

U.S. Department of State, Bureau of South and Central Asian Affairs, "Bilateral Relations Fact Sheet: U.S. Relations with India," June 21, 2019a. As of April 21, 2021, archived at: https://web.archive.org/web/20190720212714/https://www.state.gov/u-s-relations-with-india/

U.S. Department of State, Bureau of South and Central Asian Affairs, "Bilateral Relations Fact Sheet: U.S. Relations with Pakistan," June 21, 2019b. As of April 21, 2021: https://web.archive.org/web/20190626033736/https://www.state.gov/u-s-relations-with-pakistan/

U.S. Department of State, Bureau of South and Central Asian Affairs, "Bilateral Relations Fact Sheet: U.S. Relations with Afghanistan," July 8, 2019c. As of April 21, 2021, archived at: https://web.archive.org/web/20190720101147/https://www.state.gov/u-s-relations-wit h-afghanistan/

U.S. Department of State, Office of the Spokesperson, "Media Note: Ambassador Sales Signs MOU to Strengthen Counterterrorism Cooperation with Indonesia," September 14, 2018. As of June 29, 2021: https://2017-2021.state.gov/ambassador-sales-signs-mou-to-strengthen-counterterroris m-cooperation-with-indonesia/index.html

U.S. Department of State, Office of the Spokesperson, "Media Note: Joint Statement on Trilateral Meeting of Afghan Peace Process," April 26, 2019. As of June 29, 2021: https://2017-2021.state.gov/joint-statement-on-trilateral-meeting-on-afghan-peace-process/ index.html

U.S. Department of the Treasury, "Treasury Acts to Increase Economic Pressure on North Korea and Protect the U.S. Financial System," press release, June 29, 2017. As of June 14, 2020: https://www.treasury.gov/press-center/press-releases/Pages/sm0118.aspx

U.S. Department of the Treasury, "Treasury Targets Russian Shipping Companies for Violations of North Korea–Related United Nations Security Council Resolutions," press release, August 21, 2018. As of June 14, 2020: https://home.treasury.gov/news/press-releases/sm463

U.S. Embassy Indonesia, "Fact Sheet: U.S. Building Maritime Capacity in Southeast Asia," undated. As of June 18, 2019: https://id.usembassy.gov/our-relationship/policy-history/embassy-fact-sheets/fact-sheet-u s-building-maritime-capacity-in-southeast-asia/

"US, Japan, India and Philippines Challenge Beijing with Naval Drills in South China Sea," Reuters, May 9, 2019.

"U.S., Japan, South Korea, Australia Hold First Naval Drills in Western Pacific," Reuters, May 23, 2019. As of June 14, 2020: https://www.reuters.com/article/us-usa-japan-australia-southkorea/u-s-japan-south-kor ea-australia-hold-first-naval-drills-in-western-pacific-idUSKCN1ST0MA

"US Should Come Clean if It's Looking for Pretext to Destroy N. Korea–Russian FM Lavrov," RT, November 30, 2017. As of June 14, 2020: https://www.rt.com/news/411394-us-provoked-nkorea-lavrov/

Van Oudenaren, John S., "Why Are Russian Military Planes Flying Around Taiwan?" The Diplomat, January 16, 2020. As of June 14, 2020: https://thediplomat.com/2020/01/why-are-russian-military-planes-flying-around-taiwan/

Varagur, Krithika, "The Coming Fight for the Dalai Lama's Soul," Foreign Policy, January 22, 2019. As of June 14, 2020: https://foreignpolicy.com/2019/01/22/dalai-lama-reincarnation-beijing-politics-tibet/

Verma, Nidhi, "India's IOC Signs Annual Deal on Option to Buy Crude Oil from Russia's Rosneft," Reuters, February 5, 2020. As of June 14, 2020:
https://www.reuters.com/article/us-india-oil-russia/indias-ioc-signs-annual-deal-on-option-to-buy-crude-from-russias-rosneft-idUSKBN1ZZ1CD

Voloshchak, Valentin, "A Closer Look at South Korea's Plan for Cooperation with Russia," *The Diplomat*, January 9, 2019. As of June 14, 2020:
https://thediplomat.com/2019/01/a-closer-look-at-south-koreas-plan-for-cooperation-with-russia/

Walia, Simran, "Japan-Russia Dilemma over the Territorial Dispute," Observer Research Foundation, May 20, 2019. As of June 14, 2020:
https://www.orfonline.org/research/japan-russia-dilemma-over-territorial-dispute-50973/

王海燕 [Wang Haiyan], 周慧贞 [Zhou Huizhen], 姜晓峰 [Jiang Xiaofeng], and 王秀华 [Wang Xiuhua], "参与处置周边国家核事故行动装备保障初探 [Preliminary Study on Emergency Disposal Equipment Support for Neighboring Countries' Nuclear Accidents]," 装备学院学报 [*Journal of Equipment Academy*], February 2016.

王缉思 [Wang Jisi], "西进, 中国地缘战略的再平衡 [Marching West: China's Geo-Strategic Re-Balancing]," 环球时报 [*Huanqiu Times*], October 17, 2012.

Wang, Sue-Lin, "United States Says IT Supports China's Infrastructure Connectivity Plan," Reuters, May 14, 2017. As of April 21, 2021:
https://www.reuters.com/article/us-china-silkroad-usa/united-states-says-it-supports-chinas-infrastructure-connectivity-plan-idUSKCN18A0D2

"王毅: 中国在朝鲜半岛问题上有"红线" 绝不允许生战生乱 [Wang Yi: China Has a "Red Line" on the Korean Peninsula Issue and Will Never Allow War and Chaos]," People.cn, March 8, 2014. As of June 14, 2020:
http://lianghui.people.com.cn/2014npc/n/2014/0308/c382333-24573067.html

Webster, Graham, "How China Maintains Strategic Ambiguity in the South China Sea," *The Diplomat*, October 29, 2015. As of April 20, 2021:
https://thediplomat.com/2015/10/how-china-maintains-strategic-ambiguity-in-the-south-china-sea

Wezeman, Pieter D., Aude Fleurant, Alexandra Kuimova, Nan Tian, and Siemon T. Wezeman, "Trends in International Arms Transfers, 2018," Stockholm International Peace Research Institute, March 2019. As of June 14, 2020:
https://www.sipri.org/sites/default/files/2019-03/fs_1903_at_2018_0.pdf

The White House, "Joint Vision for the Alliance of the United States of America and the Republic of Korea," June 16, 2009. As of April 21, 2021:
https://obamawhitehouse.archives.gov/the-press-office/joint-vision-alliance-united-states-america-and-republic-korea

The White House, *The National Security Strategy of the United States*, Washington, D.C., 2017. As of July 14, 2021:
https://trumpwhitehouse.archives.gov/wp-content/uploads/2017/12/NSS-Final-12-18-2017-0905.pdf

The White House, *National Strategy for Counterterrorism of the United States of America*, Washington, D.C.: 2018. As of April 19, 2021:
https://www.odni.gov/files/NCTC/documents/news_documents/NSCT.pdf

The White House, *United States' Strategic Approach to the People's Republic of China*, Washington, D.C.: May 26, 2020. As of July 14, 2021:
https://trumpwhitehouse.archives.gov/articles/united-states-strategic-approach-to-the-peoples-republic-of-china/

The White House, Office of the Press Secretary, "The U.S.-Indonesia Comprehensive Partnership," June 27, 2010. As of April 19, 2021:
https://obamawhitehouse.archives.gov/the-press-office/us-indonesia-comprehensive-partnership

Williams, Robert D., "Tribunal Issues Landmark Ruling in South China Sea Arbitration," *Lawfare*, July 12, 2016. As of April 20, 2021:
https://www.lawfareblog.com/tribunal-issues-landmark-ruling-south-china-sea-arbitration

Wishnick, Elizabeth, "In Search of the 'Other' in Asia: Russia-China Relations Revisited," *Pacific Review*, Vol. 30, No. 1, 2017, pp. 114–132.

Wit, Joel S., Daniel B. Poneman, and Robert L. Gallucci, *Going Critical: The First North Korean Nuclear Crisis*, Washington, D.C.: Brookings Institution Press, 2005.

Wong, Chun Han, "China Breaks with Taiwan Precedent, Omitting Call for 'Peaceful' Policy," *Wall Street Journal*, May 22, 2020.

Wong, Edward, and Christoph Koettl, "How North Korea's Leader Gets His Luxury Cars," *New York Times,* July 16, 2019.

World Integrated Trade Solution, database, undated-a. As of April 20, 2021:
https://wits.worldbank.org

World Integrated Trade Solution, "Russia Trade," undated-b. As of June 4, 2020:
https://wits.worldbank.org/countrysnapshot/en/RUSSIA

World Integrated Trade Solution, "India Trade," undated-c. As of June 24, 2020:
https://wits.worldbank.org/countrysnapshot/en/IND

World Integrated Trade Solution "Trade Summary for Malaysia, 2018," 2018. As of April 19, 2021:
https://wits.worldbank.org/countrysnapshot/en/MYS

World Nuclear Association, "Nuclear Power in Bangladesh," updated May 2020. As of August 28, 2020:
https://www.world-nuclear.org/information-library/country-profiles/countries-a-f/bangladesh.aspx

Wortzel, Larry M., "PLA Contingency Planning and the Case of India," in Andrew Scobell, Arthur S. Ding, Phillip C. Saunders, and Scott W. Harold, eds., *The People's Liberation Army and Contingency Planning in China*, Washington, D.C.: National Defense University Press, 2015, pp. 225–250.

Wuthnow, Joel, *Just Another Paper Tiger? Chinese Perspectives on the U.S. Indo-Pacific Strategy*, Washington, D.C.: National Defense University, June 2020. As of June 14, 2020:
https://inss.ndu.edu/Media/News/Article/2206704/just-another-paper-tiger-chinese-perspectives-on-the-us-indo-pacific-strategy/

Wuthnow, Joel, Oriana Skylar Mastro, Scott W. Harold, and Li Chen, "The Future of China-U.S. Military Relations," ChinaFile, March 1, 2019. As of July 20, 2021:
https://www.chinafile.com/conversation/future-of-china-us-military-relations

Wuthnow, Joel, Satu Limaye, and Nilanthi Samaranayake, "Doklam, One Year Later: China's Long Game in the Himalayas," *War on the Rocks*, June 7, 2018. As of April 19, 2021: https://warontherocks.com/2018/06/doklam-one-year-later-chinas-long-game-in-the-himalayas/

Xi Jinping, "New Asian Security Concept for New Progress in Security Cooperation," speech at the Fourth Summit of the Conference on Interaction and Confidence-Building Measures in Asia, May 21, 2014. As of June 14, 2020: https://www.fmprc.gov.cn/mfa_eng/zxxx_662805/t1159951.shtml

Xi Jinping, "Secure a Decisive Victory in Building a Moderately Prosperous Society in All Respects and Strive for the Great Success of Socialism with Chinese Characteristics for a New Era," speech delivered at the 19th Party Congress, October 18, 2017. As of June 14, 2020: http://www.chinadaily.com.cn/china/19thcpcnationalcongress/2017-11/04/content_34115212.htm

Xi Jinping, "Working Together to Realize Rejuvenation of the Chinese Nation and Advance China's Peaceful Reunification," speech delivered at the Meeting Marking the 40th Anniversary of the Issuance of the Message to Compatriots in Taiwan, January 2, 2019. As of June 14, 2020: http://www.gwytb.gov.cn/m/news/201904/t20190412_12155846.htm

"Xi Jinping Speaks with South Korean President Park Geun-hye," Xinhua, February 5, 2016. As of August 27, 2020: http://news.xinhuanet.com/world/2016-02/05/c_1118005545.htm

"Xi Urges Breaking New Ground in Major Country Diplomacy with Chinese Characteristics," Xinhua, June 23, 2018. As of August 27, 2020: http://www.xinhuanet.com/english/2018-06/24/c_137276269.htm

Xie, Heng, and Megha Rajagopalan, "Bank of China Closes Account of Key North Korean Bank," Reuters, May 7, 2013. As of August 27, 2020: https://www.reuters.com/article/us-korea-north-china-bank-idUSBRE9460CX20130507

Yan Xuetong "From 'Keeping a Low Profile' to 'Striving for Achievement,'" *Chinese Journal of International Politics*, Vol. 7, No. 2, 2014, pp. 153–184.

Yeo, Andrew, *Asia's Regional Architecture: Alliances and Institutions in the Pacific Century*, Stanford, Calif.: Stanford University Press, 2019.

Yeo, Mike, "Indonesia Eyes American F-16 Jets as It Moves to Secure Russian Su-35 Deal," *Defense News*, November 4, 2019. As of August 27, 2020: https://www.defensenews.com/global/asia-pacific/2019/11/04/indonesia-eyes-american-f-16-jets-as-it-moves-to-secure-russian-su-35-deal/

Yeo, Mike, "China Announces $178.2 Billion Military Budget," *Defense News*, May 22, 2020. As of August 27, 2020: https://www.defensenews.com/global/asia-pacific/2020/05/22/china-announces-1782-billion-military-budget/

Zakharov, Aleksei, *Exploring New Drivers in India-Russia Cooperation*, Observer Research Foundation, ORF Occasional Paper No. 124, October 2017.

Zakharov, Aleksei, "The Geopolitics of the US-India-Russia Strategic Triangle," *Strategic Analysis*, Vol. 43, No. 5, 2019, pp. 357–371.

Zakharov, Aleksei, "After Galwan Valley Standoff, Does the Russia-India-China Trilateral Still Matter?" *The Diplomat*, June 26, 2020. As of August 27, 2020: https://thediplomat.com/2020/06/after-galwan-valley-standoff-does-the-russia-india-china-trilateral-still-matter/

Zakharova, Liudmila, "Economic Relations Between Russia and South Korea in the New Northern Policy," Korea Economic Institute of America, December 10, 2019.

Zarate, Juan, *Treasury's War: The Unleashing of a New Era of Financial Warfare*, New York: Public Affairs, 2013.

Zenn, Jacob, "An Overview of Chinese Fighters and Anti-Chinese Militant Groups in Syria and Iraq," *China Brief*, Vol. 14, No. 19, October 10, 2014. As of August 27, 2020:
https://jamestown.org/program/an-overview-of-chinese-fighters-and-anti-chinese-militant-groups-in-syria-and-iraq/

Zheng, Sarah, "China Arms Philippine Police for Counterterrorism Mission," *South China Morning Post*, October 5, 2017. As of August 27, 2020:
https://www.scmp.com/news/china/diplomacy-defence/article/2114152/china-arms-philippine-police-counterterrorism-mission

Zoellick, Robert, "Whither China? From Membership to Responsibility," speech delivered to the National Committee on U.S.-China Relations, September 21, 2005. As of August 27, 2020:
https://www.ncuscr.org/sites/default/files/migration/Zoellick_remarks_notes06_winter_spring.pdf

Ingram Content Group UK Ltd.
Milton Keynes UK
UKHW030635170523
421890UK00008B/257